Contents

How to Use This Book

ABOUT THE MAPS

This book is divided into chapters based on regions that are within close reach of the city; an overview map of these regions precedes the table of contents. Each chapter begins with a region map that shows the locations and numbers of the trails listed in that chapter.

Each trail profile is also accompanied by a detailed trail map that shows the hike route.

Map Symbols

– – – – – ·	Featured Trail	(80)	Interstate Freeway	○	City/Town
– – – – – – ·	Other Trail	(101)	U.S. Highway	✗ ✗	Airfield/Airport
░░░░░░░░	Expressway	(21)	State Highway	♁	Golf Course
▒▒▒▒▒▒	Primary Road	(66)	County Highway	✎	Waterfall
▬▬▬▬	Secondary Road	★	Point of Interest	▭	Swamp
▪ ▪ ▪ ▪ ▪ ▪	Unpaved Road	🅿	Parking Area	▲	Mountain
··············	Ferry	🛈	Trailhead	♣	Park
▬▬ · ▬▬ ·	National Border	⚑	Campground	)(	Pass
▬▬ · · ▬▬	State Border	▪	Other Location	✦	Unique Natural Feature

ABOUT THE TRAIL PROFILES

Each profile includes a narrative description of the trail's setting and terrain. This description also typically includes mile-by-mile hiking directions, as well as information about the trail's highlights and unique attributes.

The trails marked by the **BEST** 🅲 symbol are highlighted in the author's Best Hikes list.

Options

If alternative routes are available, this section is used to provide information on side trips or note how to shorten or lengthen the hike.

Directions

This section provides detailed driving directions to the trailhead from the city center or from the intersection of major highways. When public transportation is available, instructions will be noted here.

Information and Contact

This section provides information on fees, facilities, and access restrictions for the trail. It also includes the name of the land management agency or organization that oversees the trail, as well as an address, phone number, and website if available.

ABOUT THE ICONS

The icons in this book are designed to provide at-a-glance information on special features for each trail.

- ⬚ The trail climbs to a high overlook with wide views.
- ⬚ The trail offers an opportunity for wildlife-watching.
- ⬚ The trail offers an opportunity for bird-watching.
- ⬚ The trail features wildflower displays in spring.
- ⬚ The trail visits a beach.

- ⬚ The trail travels to a waterfall.
- ⬚ The trail visits a historic site.
- ⬚ The trail is open to snowshoers in winter.
- ⬚ Dogs are allowed.
- ⬚ The trail is appropriate for children.
- ⬚ The trail is wheelchair accessible.
- ⬚ The trailhead can be accessed via public transportation.

ABOUT THE DIFFICULTY RATING

Each profile includes a difficulty rating. The ratings are defined as follows:

Easy: Easy hikes are 5 miles or less round-trip and have less than 700 feet of elevation gain (nearly level). They are generally suitable for families with small children and hikers seeking a mellow stroll.

Easy/Moderate: Easy/Moderate hikes are between 4 and 8 miles round-trip and have 500-1,200 feet of elevation gain. They are generally suitable for families with active children above the age of six and hikers who are reasonably fit.

Moderate: Moderate hikes are between 5 and 9 miles round-trip and have 1,000-2,000 feet of elevation gain. They are generally suitable for adults and children who are fit.

Strenuous: Strenuous hikes are between 5 and 10 miles round-trip and have 1,800-2,800 feet or more of elevation gain. They are suitable for very fit hikers who are seeking a workout.

Butt-Kicker: Butt-Kicker hikes are between 7 and 14 miles round-trip and have 3,000 feet or more of elevation gain. These hikes are suitbable only for advanced hikers who are very physically fit.

INTRODUCTION

Author's Note

When it comes to easy access to the great outdoors, there are few major metropolitan areas in the United States that compare to Salt Lake City. Even in the mountain West, where open spaces and outdoor adventures are never far away, Salt Lake is known for its uniquely accessible mountain playground. From the hill above the State Capitol building downtown, a trail leads up Ensign Peak in the foothills; with a 30-minute car ride, hikers can surround themselves with wild, inspiring mountains. The Wasatch Mountain Range, climbing abruptly above the Salt Lake Valley, contains an extensive network of trails accessing sparkling mountain lakes, wildflower-painted meadows, and sweeping summit vistas. For the many who call Salt Lake City home, the mountains are a backyard paradise for hikers.

Only minutes from a population of more than one million people, the Wasatch Mountains offer an intriguing patchwork of wild nature and human development. Well-maintained, paved roads curl into the heart of the range—in part to reach world-renowned ski resorts, but also to access the adjoining wilderness. Twenty-five miles south of downtown Salt Lake, one of these access roads twists up Little Cottonwood Canyon.

At the top of Little Cottonwood Canyon sits the destination town of Alta. What started out as an avalanche-battered silver-mining hamlet in the 1870s became home to the second chairlift in the United States in 1937. It has since developed into one of the most beloved ski areas and mountain villages in North America. The same beautiful alpine terrain that has inspired the passion of countless skiers over the years offers summer hikers a serene environment in which to stretch their legs and recharge their nature-loving souls. Above town in Albion Basin, hikers will discover a lush meadow landscape. Purple lupine and red Indian paintbrush flowers complement the green valley floor with clusters of bright color. Hemmed in by a fortress of craggy peaks, Albion Basin can be a destination in itself, or the starting point for hikes leading across ridge tops or to the summits themselves. These upper reaches of Little Cottonwood Canyon can accurately be described as the heart of the Wasatch.

But like the human body, the heart of these mountains is not complete on its own. The trail network weaves a complex web through the Central Wasatch, extending out like arteries in every direction to equally deserving parts of the range. In the south, the highest and broadest peaks in the range rise above the valley floor. Famous peaks like Mount Timpanogos and Mount Nebo reach nearly 12,000 feet in elevation. These peaks are some of the most popular hikes in the entire state, thanks to a combination of challenging nature and undeniable beauty. To the north, Willard and Ben Lomond Peaks stand like scouts over the Great Salt Lake, lifting hikers to high-country vantage points.

Beyond the Wasatch Mountains, other mountain ranges await. The high Uinta Range holds the state's highest peaks and retains its wildest character. Alpine lakes are so plentiful in the Uintas that they don't all have names. Westward there are great hikes as well, hidden in places like the Deseret Peak Wilderness and on islands in the Great Salt Lake.

Best Hikes

◖ Best Butt-Kickers

Twin Peaks of Broads Fork, Salt Lake City and Central Wasatch, page 72.

Red Pine Lake to the Pfeifferhorn, Salt Lake City and Central Wasatch, page 115.

Ben Lomond via the North Skyline Trail, Northern Wasatch, page 150.

Lone Peak on the Jacob's Ladder Trail, Southern Wasatch, page 180.

Aspen Grove Trail, Southern Wasatch, page 205.

◖ Best for Dogs

Neff's Canyon, Salt Lake City and Central Wasatch, page 47.

Big Water Trail to Dog Lake, Salt Lake City and Central Wasatch, page 63.

Ferguson Canyon, Salt Lake City and Central Wasatch, page 66.

Waterfall Canyon, Northern Wasatch, page 162.

Battle Creek Falls, Southern Wasatch, page 214.

◖ Best for Families

Doughnut Falls, Salt Lake City and Central Wasatch, page 86.

Cecret Lake, Salt Lake City and Central Wasatch, page 133.

Y Mountain, Southern Wasatch, page 221.

Fehr Lake, Uinta Mountains, page 274.

Ruth Lake, Uinta Mountains, page 283.

◖ Best for Historic Sites

Ensign Peak, Salt Lake City and Central Wasatch, page 31.

Little Emigration Canyon, Salt Lake City and Central Wasatch, page 40.

Temple Quarry, Salt Lake City and Central Wasatch, page 110.

Kenny Creek Trail, Northern Wasatch, page 168.

Sentry Trail, Western Mountains, page 240.

◖ Best for Mountain Lakes

Lake Blanche, Salt Lake City and Central Wasatch, page 76.

Brighton Lakes Trail, Salt Lake City and Central Wasatch, page 93.

Red Pine Lake to the Pfeifferhorn, Salt Lake City and Central Wasatch, page 115.

Divide Lakes, Uinta Mountains, page 262.

Lofty Lake Loop, Uinta Mountains, page 280.

◖ Best Quick Escapes

Living Room, Salt Lake City and Central Wasatch, page 34.

Emigration Canyon, Salt Lake City and Central Wasatch, page 37.

Grandeur Peak, Salt Lake City and Central Wasatch, page 50.

Alexander Basin to Gobbler's Knob, Salt Lake City and Central Wasatch, page 59.

Bells Canyon, Salt Lake City and Central Wasatch, page 106.

◖ Best Vistas

Mount Olympus, Salt Lake City and Central Wasatch, page 44.

Red Pine Lake to the Pfeifferhorn, Salt Lake City and Central Wasatch, page 115.

Malans Peak via Taylor Canyon, Northern Wasatch, page 159.

Squaw Mountain, Southern Wasatch, page 218.

Bald Mountain, Uinta Mountains, page 268.

◖ Best for Wildlife-Viewing

Desolation Lake via Mill D North Fork, Salt Lake City and Central Wasatch, page 83.

Brighton Lakes Trail, Salt Lake City and Central Wasatch, page 93.

Ben Lomond from Inspiration Point, Northern Wasatch, page 147.

Timpooneke Trail, Southern Wasatch, page 202.

Frary Peak, Western Mountains, page 236.

Hiking Tips

ESSENTIALS
Clothing

The best way to assure you'll be comfortable on any hike is to dress in layers. Body temperatures will be all over the map on most hiking days. Strenuous exercise, inclement weather, or hot, sunny days can challenge the body's ability to effectively regulate its temperature. The best way to keep your core temperature near its ideal is to think of hiking clothing as a layering system. The number and thickness of layers you'll need depends on the range of temperatures you'll encounter on your adventure. The wider the possible temperature range, the more layers required. On sunny summer days, a simple T-shirt and light jacket will suffice. But on a cold outing, you'll want as many as four layers. This might include merino wool long underwear, a mid-weight fleece insulating layer, a goose-down coat, and a water-resistant nylon shell. Add a warm hat and wool socks, and you'll be comfortable even on the coldest days. Of course, all those layers add considerable weight to your pack, so finding the right mix is at least as important as having enough.

When it comes to choosing the best layers for the job, not all fabrics are created equal. Cotton is notoriously dangerous as a base layer, because it doesn't insulate the body well when it's wet. On strenuous hikes, perspiration makes it hard to keep your base layer dry. A wet cotton base layer can quickly cool the body's core temperature, even in relatively warm weather, leading to the first stages of hypothermia. To avoid the possibility of hypothermia, remember this tidbit of backcountry wisdom: Cotton kills in the high country. Leave the jeans in the drawer and choose base layers made from polyester or wool that do a better job of keeping the body warm even once they've become saturated. Modern polyester fabrics are designed to wick moisture away from the skin and help release it into the air. Merino wool offers a natural alternative that rivals these petroleum-based products in its ability to insulate when wet.

It's a good idea to carry an insulation layer to go on top of the base layer. A thin fleece vest works great as a mid-layer and will add only a few ounces to your rucksack. On colder days, consider supplementing your layering system with a nylon wind shirt or mid-weight wool sweater. Some fleece jackets have a wind-stopping membrane sewn in, allowing them to double as either an insulation layer or an outer layer when the weather is cold but dry.

If rain or snow is in the forecast, a water-resistant jacket is an essential component of an effective layering system. Nylon fabrics laminated with polyurethane that repel water, but also allow moisture to move away from the body, do the best job of keeping under-layers dry.

Socks are an important detail in your hiking wardrobe. The right pair of socks can make the difference between comfortable, happy feet and a sweaty, blistered nightmare. Similar to base-layer clothing, cotton socks are a poor choice for hiking. Cotton socks tend to absorb a lot of water; if your feet get wet on a hike, cotton socks will leave your feet soggy for the rest of the trip. Wet socks are less durable, while wet feet are more susceptible to friction and blisters than dry feet. Socks made of wool, polyester, or a blend of the two are a better choice on the trail than cotton. Different manufacturers weave together wool, polyester, acrylic, and elastic to produce the most effective hiking socks.

Food

Eating smart on the trail will make your adventures more enjoyable and will let you hike farther and faster to reach your hiking destination and goals. Think of your body as a hiking machine: It needs fuel for its engine to run smoothly. On a strenuous hike, your body will burn up to twice as many calories as it does in daily life. Good trail food should be nutritious, lightweight, and ready to eat. It's also a good idea to take some extra food along on any trip into the backcountry, just in case you are out longer than expected. If you're concerned about keeping your pack weight to a minimum, removing any unnecessary packaging can help shave off a few ounces.

Water

Nothing is more important for your body's performance on a hike than staying hydrated. Water is one of the essential supplies for any hike. Drinking water consistently on the trail will keep your body running smoothly so you can concentrate on enjoying the hike. Although many of the hikes in this guide have access to fresh water along the trail, the safest plan is to pack enough for the entire outing. Plan to take at least half a liter of water per mile hiked.

Water bottles and hydration bladders are the two most popular methods of carrying water on hikes. Water bottles are simple and effective and come in a variety of shapes, sizes, and materials. If

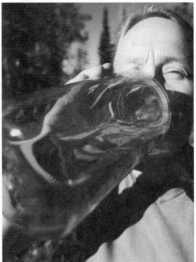

© MIKE MATSON

It's important to stay hydrated.

you have older plastic water bottles in your collection, it's a good idea to upgrade to new Bisphenol A (BPA)–free bottles or metal bottles. BPA is a reactive compound found in plastic water bottles made before 2008. (BPA mimics the estrogen hormone in the body and can lead to a long list of health concerns.)

Hydration bladders help hikers stay hydrated because they are so convenient. The bladder reservoir tucks neatly away inside a backpack, and the hose is clipped to the pack's shoulder strap. This helps you drink frequent, small quantities of water, rather than waiting until your body is thirsty to pull out the water bottle. Another advantage to hydration bladders is size. Large bladders can hold up to three liters of water compared with one liter in a standard water bottle.

With all that in mind, there are times when it makes sense to drink water found along the trail. For example, on long hikes with multiple stream crossings, it may reduce the weight of your pack considerably to carry only a single water bottle and refill it along the way. If you decide to rely on available water sources, be sure to treat or filter the water before drinking it. You never know what animals have affected that water upstream. Untreated surface water could contain bacteria, viruses, and protozoa that can make you sick—including giardia and cryptosporidium.

There are several effective ways to make water potable on the trail. Iodine tablets—sold in tiny, three-ounce glass jars of 50 tablets—are a cheap, easy way to treat water in the backcountry. Iodine effectively kills giardia, bacteria, and viruses, but doesn't eliminate cryptosporidium. Iodine tablets can also be purchased with neutralizing tablets that reduce iodine's undesirable flavor and color. Chlorine drops offer a similar solution to iodine but don't color the water or leave as strong a taste. Unfortunately, chlorine also doesn't kill cryptosporidium.

Small, lightweight water filters are another viable option for water treatment. One big advantage to filters is that they require no chemical additives. As a result the treated water comes out of the filter cold, clean, and without taste—just as you would expect from a mountain stream. There are many different models of water purification filters made by several manufacturers. The best units for day hikes are those built into the cap of the water bottle, combining the bottle and filter into a single unit. These bottle-filter combos are particularly well suited for day hikes with frequent stream crossings because they don't hold large volumes of water. Ultraviolet (UV) light offers another effective, lightweight method of water sterilization. UV sterilizers come built into the caps of water bottles, or as a sterilization pen that is inserted into a water bottle before drinking. UV sterilization is fast, light, tasteless, and effective against cryptosporidium—but is also the most expensive option for backcountry water purification.

Navigational Tools

Accurate map reading is one of the most essential tools for traveling safely in the outdoors. Nothing will build your confidence more than knowing exactly where you are on the trail at all times. The only way to get good at reading maps is to practice. Keep a map handy and pull it out often. Check it regularly while hiking and compare the landscape with what is drawn on the map; this is the best way to keep track of where you are.

The United States Geological Survey (USGS) makes the most detailed and useful maps for hiking. The scale of 1:24,000 is very detailed and provides hikers with lots of information about the geography surrounding them. Other topographic maps that are less detailed, but cover a broader area, are available for the Wasatch and Uinta mountain ranges. Both the USGS maps and other topographic maps represent a three-dimensional world on a flat piece of paper and use contour lines to show elevation changes and a grid system for distance.

A compass can make your map reading a lot easier by telling you exactly which way you are oriented. Good maps will have a key at the top to orient your compass and help adjust it from magnetic north to true north. If you don't have a compass, the sun can provide you with an approximation of directions if you pay close attention.

Handheld GPS units take most of the guesswork out of map reading and tell you precisely where you are at all times. It does take some work to get good at reading a GPS as well, so don't assume that buying one will automatically keep you found. In addition, GPS maps do not provide the same level of detail as the USGS Topographic maps. In some cases you might need both. To make things easier, I've included the GPS coordinates in the description of each trail in this guide.

First Aid and Emergencies

The prudent hiker carries a first-aid kit. Prepackaged first-aid kits come in all shapes and sizes and can provide anything you might need for an injury short of stitches or a plaster cast. A small but useful first-aid kit should always be included in your pack.

What do I include in my minimalist backcountry kit? There are a few items you shouldn't leave the trailhead without. The most versatile piece of any first-aid kit is a small roll of one-inch cotton medical tape. Other must-haves include ibuprofen or other painkillers, and antihistamine in the event of an allergic reaction. If you or someone in your group is prone to strong allergic reactions, an epinephrine pin can save a life. Make sure someone who isn't allergic knows how to use it. If you feel more comfortable with a larger kit, by all means bring it. In my experience, larger, heavier kits tend to get left behind, whereas smaller, less cumbersome kits are there when you need them.

In addition, a small emergency kit can be worth its weight in gold—in fact, it might even save your life. Although it's unlikely you'll get lost while day hiking, you never know when something unexpected might happen. After all, part of the reason we seek out adventure is that we cannot always predict the outcome. An emergency kit containing a space blanket for warmth, a lighter or waterproof matches for starting a fire, and a small pocketknife weighs almost nothing. And it will make an unexpected night spent outdoors much more tolerable. These items also complement a lightweight first-aid kit in the case of injury on the trail.

Even more important in the case of a backcountry injury, however, is a cool head and resourceful, creative approach. Using what you have with you, rather than pounds of first-aid supplies, will get you through most injuries. For example, the metal stays in your backpack's frame, combined with an Ace bandage, make a perfectly functional splint for a broken arm. A cut-up cotton T-shirt doubles as a bandage or gauze, and a cold mountain stream will reduce the swelling in a sprained ankle as well as any ice pack. If you plan to spend a lot of time in the backcountry, consider taking a Wilderness First Responder (WFR) course. This one-week first-aid training course will boost your confidence in an emergency and fill your mind with creative solutions for any trauma you encounter on your hikes.

ON THE TRAIL
Trail Etiquette

Although the backcountry may be a place to seek solitude, you won't always find yourself alone. It's important to share the trail with other users and to show them respect. From horseback riders to mountain bikers, to dogs and wildlife, you'll have to share Salt Lake City trails with a varied cast of characters. Trail etiquette is simple: Treat those you encounter with respect and kindness.

RIGHT-OF-WAY

When it comes to the right-of-way on the trail, hikers should yield to other users. Horses should be given the right-of-way when they pass. Horses spook easily, and they're unpredictable. It's also easier for a hiker to move safely off the trail than it is for a horse, so give them a wide berth and remain quiet and calm when they pass.

Mountain bikers should yield to hikers on the trail, but don't assume they will. On trails where mountain biking is allowed, be prepared to move out of the way of bikers. Although most are considerate of hikers, it takes only one who is going

WHAT'S KILLING THE FORESTS OF NORTHERN UTAH?

Look around on the trail and you'll see dying forests – stands of evergreen trees that have lost their green. The lodgepole pine trees found in the Uinta Mountains have been the hardest hit, but other prolific conifer species, like spruce and fir trees, have also been affected. First the trees turn orange as they start to die, and then brown once their needles fall to the ground, leaving only barren, lifeless trunks behind. An epidemic is sweeping the coniferous forests of the American West – from New Mexico to British Columbia – and Utah's woodlands are right in the thick of it.

The killer is a tiny pest known as the bark beetle. The **mountain pine beetle** (*Dendroctonus ponderosae)*, which attacks these lodgepole pines, has done the most damage, but similar species from the same weevil family also decimate other evergreens. The beetles lay their larvae in the tree's bark while at the same time introducing a blue stain fungus to the tree's wood. The fungus blocks water and nutrient transport within the tree. The combined affects of the fungus and the beetle larvae eating the bark kills the infested trees.

Under normal circumstances, healthy trees produce sap or resin as a defense to kill or immobilize the bark beetles. In this scenario only the weak or older trees die, in turn leaving a healthier forest. But during the outbreak conditions found since about 2005, the beetles are simply too numerous; even healthy trees can't adequately defend themselves.

Forest ecologists believe this may be the worst, most widespread beetle infestation to date. Intensely cold winters have historically kept beetle populations in check. It is thought that a long pattern of warmer winters over the last decade is to blame for the dying forests.

Aside from the general concern for the forest's health, large swaths of dead or dying trees are worrisome because they represent potential fuel for forest fires. All this unspent fuel, coupled with record summer heat, makes for a troubling future for the forests of the mountain west. Only time will tell if the forests will adapt and recover, or be at the mercy of this tiny, yet powerful killer.

---

too fast to ruin your hike. Again, it's easier for a hiker to move off the trail than a biker, so bikers will appreciate it if you step off the single track for them.

If you're hiking downhill, yield to hikers coming uphill. Large groups should also be considerate of smaller parties if they want to pass on the trail.

When you encounter wildlife on the trail, remember you're visiting their home and treat them with respect. It's always wise to give wildlife lots of space, but for your safety it's particularly important with large animals. Consider yourself lucky if you spot moose, bears, cougars, mountain goats, or bighorn sheep on a Salt Lake City trail—and remember that these animals are wild and potentially dangerous. Moose are common in the Wasatch and Uinta Mountains and can be quite aggressive if threatened. Pull out the camera and the long zoom lens, but don't crowd wildlife. If they're on the trail, let them leave on their own or walk around them.

Leave No Trace

Leave No Trace is a simple, all-encompassing philosophy hikers should take with them on every hike. The trails around Salt Lake City get a lot of traffic. Dubbed the "Wasangeles," the mountains in our backyard are in danger of being loved to death. Take care on your hikes to minimize any negative effect you'll have on these wild places. Stay on the trail and avoid cutting switchbacks, especially in alpine areas where natural vegetation can be quite delicate. Remember that these stunted, high-altitude species can take years to reestablish. Pack out anything you bring in, including banana peels and apple cores—just because it's biodegradable doesn't mean it's not litter. Pick up any trash you find on your outings, and bring a bag or container to clean up after your dog.

Hiking with Dogs

There are many great trails near Salt Lake City where dogs are permitted. In fact, I can't think of a better city to live in for a dog that loves to romp in the woods. Hikes are great exercise for dogs, and dogs are wonderful companions for their humans. But hitting the trail with your hound demands added responsibility. First and foremost, know the rules of each specific trail.

In the Wasatch Mountains, some of the canyons allow dogs on the trails, and others do not. Little Cottonwood, Big Cottonwood, City Creek, and Parley's Canyons are watersheds for Salt Lake City's municipal water supply. To protect the water supply, no dogs are allowed in these canyons or their tributaries. Dogs are allowed in Mill Creek (odd days off-leash, even days leashed), Neff's, Ferguson, American Fork, and East Canyons.

On dog-friendly trails it is the dog owners' responsibility to monitor their dogs' behavior and pick up their waste. Even on off-leash trails, dogs should be kept on a leash at the trailhead and not let off until they are safely on the trail. Along the trail, owners should watch their dogs and keep them from harassing wildlife or digging. These common dog behaviors negatively affect the wild character of the trail by disrupting wildlife and plant communities.

Hiking with Kids

Hiking can be a wonderful way to spend time in the outdoors with your children. It's a great opportunity to teach them about nature, see new places, and get exercise as a family. Hiking with kids, especially young ones, does take a little extra planning. It's important to choose appropriate hikes for kids, so that it's an enjoyable experience for everybody involved. Start with short hikes that don't gain much elevation, and slowly build up to more challenging trails as your children's experience and endurance develops. Remember to bring lots of food and water,

© MIKE MATSON

Dogs are allowed on the Stansbury Island Trail.

including high-energy snacks to keep your young hikers happy. With young children in particular, choose hikes that lead to interesting destinations, like waterfalls. Interpretive trails with educational signs about the area's natural history also make great choices. As the kids get older, teaching them skills like reading topographic maps or using a GPS unit can make the hike more exciting.

Wildlife

If you spend enough time on the trails in this guide, you'll inevitably see your share of wildlife. Wildlife encounters are one of the things that make the trails around Salt Lake City so enticing. Encountering wild animals in their environment can be thrilling and add greatly to the hiking experience. It can also occasionally be dangerous, depending upon the situation. It's a good idea to know what to do in case of an encounter. Mountain goats, moose, elk, and deer are among the "charismatic mega-fauna" you're likely to see along the trails in Northern Utah. Mountain lions and a small black bear population live in these environments too, but the likelihood of seeing one on the trail during daylight hours is minimal. Regardless, it's good to know they're out there and how to act when you see them.

Mountain Goats

Several mountain goat herds are thriving in the Wasatch Mountains. The goats were first transplanted to the Wasatch Range from Olympic National Park in

a herd of mountain goats on Willard Peak

Washington State in 1967, and then again in larger numbers in 1981. Herds can now be found in the Northern Wasatch on Willard Peak; in the Central Wasatch on Mount Superior, the south side of Little Cottonwood Canyon, and Lone Peak; and finally in the Southern Wasatch on Box Elder Peak and Mount Timpanogos. There's also a herd in the Uinta Mountains near Bald Mountain.

Many of these goats are docile and will let hikers get quite close. This doesn't mean the goats are not dangerous. They are wild animals with sharp horns and can easily maul or even kill a hiker. So treat these animals with respect and maintain a safe distance.

MOOSE

The first recorded moose sightings in Utah were in 1906 and 1907. But it wasn't until 1947 that a year-round population was believed to live in the state. As the beaver populations slowly rebounded from heavy fur trapping in the Uinta Mountains, creating better wetlands and therefore food supplies for moose, the moose population in the Uinta Mountains increased considerably. That population has continued to expand and has spilled over into the Wasatch Mountains.

Moose can be extremely aggressive, unpredictable, and dangerous. In fact, many wildlife professionals consider them to be far more of a threat to hikers than bears. Bull moose have huge, sharp racks, and cows can attack with their long legs. Give them a wide berth and don't approach them on the trail.

ELK AND DEER

Elk may be seen in the northern Wasatch Mountains east of Ogden, or in the southern Wasatch part of the range from Mount Timpanogos to Mount Nebo. Deer can be found throughout Northern Utah's mountains. Deer and elk are not considered dangerous, but they shouldn't be approached or harassed.

MOUNTAIN LIONS

The Utah Division of Wildlife Resources estimates that about 3,000 mountain lions live on approximately 35,000 square miles of suitable habitat in the state of Utah. This habitat includes all the mountain ranges covered in this guide, including the Wasatch Mountains, Uinta Mountains, and western ranges. Although seeing a mountain lion in the wild is extremely rare, sightings do occur. Cougars are most active in the evening, at night, and in the early mornings. Mountain lions rarely attack hikers. If you're worried about the possibility of encountering a cougar, then hike with other people and avoid hiking around sunrise or sunset, when these cats are most active.

BLACK BEARS

Black bears can be encountered in all the mountain ranges covered in this guide. Black bears are generally wary of people and stay away from heavily traveled trails. But the possibility of an encounter does exist. If you see a bear on the trail, slowly back away, but do not turn and run. If you're with other hikers, bunch together to appear larger, and make lots of noise so the bear knows you are human. Bears have poor eyesight and may smell or hear you before they see you. If the bear moves toward you, yell and wave your arms in an effort to appear more threatening.

Backpackers should always hang their food or use bear canisters when traveling in bear country. Bear canisters are the easiest and most foolproof method of keeping bears out of your food supply, but they will add about two pounds of weight to your pack. If you're hanging food, it should be 15 feet above the ground and 5 feet below the tree branch it's hanging from.

Insects

TICKS

There are a few bugs to watch out for while hiking. Ticks are not a major concern, but they are around, especially in spring when the mountains are wet from snow-melt. Ticks drop out of trees onto hikers before finding a nice, warm, dark place to dig in. It's a good idea to do a quick tick check after any hike. Look particularly closely at the parts of your body that are difficult to see, like armpits and groin areas. If you find a tick lurking, remove it carefully. The longer it's embedded, the

HIKING GEAR CHECKLIST

- Backpack
- First-aid kit
- Flashlight or head lamp
- Food
- Hat (wide-brimmed)
- Insect repellent
- Lightweight jacket (waterproof, wind-resistant)
- Moleskin
- Pocket knife

- Rain jacket and pants
- Socks (extra pair)
- Sunscreen and sunglasses
- Trail map, compass, and/or GPS device
- Water (at least one gallon per person) or water filtration sytem
- Waterproof matches
- Whistle or signaling mirror
- Wildflower and/or bird identification guide

more likely it is to pass on Lyme disease. The best and only way to remove a tick is with tweezers. Pinch the tick as close to the skin as possible and pull gently but firmly on the tick without breaking off its body. You will need to be patient and pull for a while until the tick slowly backs out. If the tick has been embedded for more than 24 hours, or you have reason to believe you've contracted Lyme disease, see a doctor. The symptoms of Lyme disease include a circular rash around the site of the bite, lack of energy, headache, stiff neck, fever, chills, or muscle and joint pain.

MOSQUITOES

One of the beauties of living in an arid region is that mosquitoes are mostly absent. However, in the high mountains, especially where small lakes and ponds are prevalent, there can be spots where the mosquitoes are thick. The Uinta Mountains, with their marshy meadows and countless alpine lakes, are one example. Consider planning your Uinta hikes later in the summer, when the meadows have dried out and the mosquitoes have died back.

Recently, there's been concern about mosquitoes transmitting West Nile Virus. Although cases in Utah have been very isolated, they have occurred. Mosquito repellent does a good job of keeping these pests at bay. The most effective ones contain an ingredient called DEET (N, N-diethyl-m-toluamide). Other effective repellents include Picaridin (KBR 3023) and oil of lemon eucalyptus (p-menthane 3,8-diol, or PDM).

SALT LAKE CITY AND CENTRAL WASATCH

© MIKE MATSON

BEST HIKES

The Central Wasatch mountains are some of the

most accessible mountains in North America. More than 80 percent of Utah's population lives within 15 minutes of the Wasatch Range, with the lion's share of residents living in the Salt Lake Valley. These backyard peaks offer the closest – and some of the best – mountain recreation in the state. The Central Wasatch is home to seven major ski resorts in the Cottonwood Canyons and above Park City. Little and Big Cottonwood Canyons, located 20 and 25 miles south of downtown Salt Lake City, are home to four of these resorts: Brighton, Solitude, Snowbird, and Alta. The plentiful snow that contributes to these resorts' popularity is also the source of Salt Lake City's water supply. Well-maintained, paved roads lead up steep, rugged canyons to the ski areas and provide easy access, and in some cases public transportation, to dozens of beautiful hikes. The dramatic ridgeline on the Salt Lake side of the Wasatch Range features a lineup of highly visible peaks with trails leading to summit vistas overlooking the urban landscape below. With a little effort – in some cases a lot of effort – hikers can summit the peaks they see every day from their living room window. Prominent mountains such as Grandeur Peak, Mount Olympus, and Lone Peak all have trails starting near the valley floor.

On the Park City side of the Wasatch Range, the terrain is less rugged, but the hiking remains appealing. The Canyons, Park City, and Deer Valley Ski Resorts occupy the east side of the Central Wasatch and are home to a vast network of trails in and out of their boundaries. Some of these trails can be accessed by chairlifts, and others can be hiked directly from town. Family-friendly trails, such as the converted Rail Trail on the gently rolling Lost Prospector Trail, can be reached from Main Street without ever getting into a car.

The Central Wasatch remains surprisingly wild for being so close to so many people. The Forest Service has designated three wilderness areas in the Central Wasatch – Mount Olympus, Twin Peaks, and Lone Peak. These wilderness designations protect large parts of the range from further development. An impressive collection of wildlife occupies the central core of these mountains. Herds of mountain goats patrol the rocky granite cliffs in Little Cottonwood Canyon, moose browse the foliage along creek in Big Cottonwood Canyon, and mountain lions stealthily stalk the region's deer population.

Signs of human history in Central Wasatch make it a compelling place to explore. Mormon pioneers harnessed many of the range's creeks for drinking water and to power their mills. Many of the region's trails pass by remnants of the extensive silver mining in the range. Crumbling mine shafts marked by rusting machinery and huge piles of mine tailings are ubiquitous throughout the range.

The appeal of these wild mountains so close to home is the primary reason Salt Lake City has such a vibrant outdoor community. As these outdoors-minded souls continue to explore the range in new ways, and development pushes at its boundaries, the Wasatch Mountains will continue to evolve. At its core, though, these mountains will always have an appealing collections of trails.

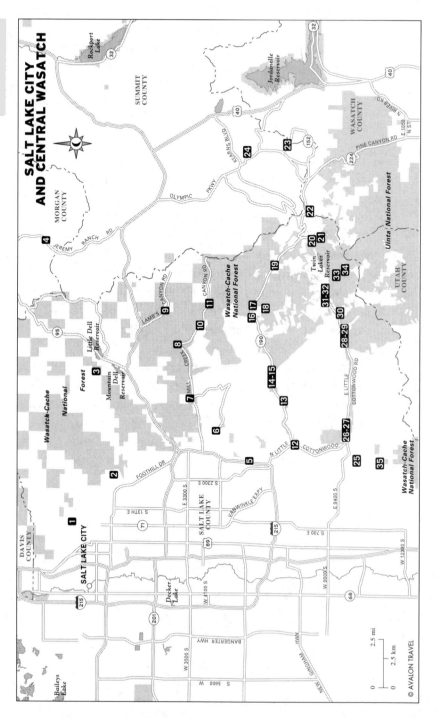

TRAIL NAME	LEVEL	DISTANCE	TIME	ELEVATION	FEATURES	PAGE
1 Ensign Peak	Easy	0.5–1 mi rt	30 min–1 hr	429 ft		31
2 Living Room	Easy/Moderate	2.3 mi rt	1.5–2 hr	1,213 ft		34
3 Emigration Canyon	Moderate	5.1 mi rt	3–4 hr	1,259 ft		37
4 Little Emigration Canyon	Easy/Moderate	8.0 mi rt	4–5 hr	1,433 ft		40
5 Mount Olympus	Butt-kicker	7.0 mi rt	5–7 hr	4,152 ft		44
6 Neff's Canyon	Moderate	5.5–6 mi rt	3 hr	2,667 ft		47
7 Grandeur Peak	Strenuous	5.5 mi rt	4–5 hr	2,729 ft		50
8 Mount Aire	Moderate	3.6 mi rt	2–3 hr	1,991 ft		53
9 Lambs Canyon	Moderate	4.0 mi rt	2–3 hr	1,520 ft		56
10 Alexander Basin to Gobbler's Knob	Strenuous	4.0 mi rt	4–5 hr	3,169 ft		59
11 Big Water Trail to Dog Lake	Moderate	5.3 mi rt	3–4 hr	1,482 ft		63
12 Ferguson Canyon	Moderate	3.8 mi rt	2–3 hr	2,253 ft		66
13 Stairs Gulch	Easy	1.25 mi rt	1 hr	1,184 ft		69
14 Twin Peaks of Broads Fork	Butt-kicker	8.6 mi rt	8–10 hr	5,120 ft		72
15 Lake Blanche	Moderate	5.8 mi rt	3 hr	2,720 ft		76
16 Mount Raymond via Butler Fork	Strenuous	7.8 mi rt	5–6 hr	3,115 ft		79
17 Desolation Lake via Mill D North Fork	Moderate	7.2 mi rt	3–4 hr	2,188 ft		83
18 Doughnut Falls	Easy	1.5 mi rt	1 hr	360 ft		86
19 Willow Heights	Easy	2.0 mi rt	1 hr	700 ft		88
20 Silver Lake	Easy	0.8 mi rt	30 min	30 ft		91
21 Brighton Lakes Trail	Moderate	4.6 mi rt	3 hr	1,594 ft		93
22 Guardsman Pass to Clayton Peak	Moderate	2.5 mi rt	2–3 hr	1,430 ft		97

TRAIL NAME	LEVEL	DISTANCE	TIME	ELEVATION	FEATURES	PAGE
23 Mid Mountain Trail	Moderate	11.5 mi rt	7–8 hr	1,512 ft		100
24 Lost Prospector	Moderate	4.3 mi one-way	2.5–3 hr	328 ft		103
25 Bells Canyon	Butt-kicker	8.3 mi rt	6–8 hr	5,040 ft		106
26 Temple Quarry	Easy	0.3 mile rt	15–30 min	85 ft		110
27 Little Cottonwood Trail	Moderate	6.8 mi rt	4 hr	1,545 ft		112
28 Red Pine Lake to the Pfeifferhorn	Butt-kicker	9.0 mi rt	7.5–9 hr	4,317 ft		115
29 White Pine Lake	Strenuous	9.5 mi rt	7–8 hr	2,851 ft		118
30 Snowbird Barrier Free	Easy	1.2 mi rt	30 min–1 hr	55 ft		121
31 Mount Superior	Strenuous	5.2 mi rt	5–6 hr	3,061 ft		124
32 Albion Meadows	Easy	3.5 mi rt	2 hr	1,085 ft		127
33 Catherine Pass	Moderate	2.0 mi rt	1 hr	800 ft		130
34 Cecret Lake	Easy	1.5 mi rt	1–2 hr	420 ft		133
35 Rocky Mouth Canyon	Easy	0.7 mi rt	30 min–1 hr	262 ft		136

1 ENSIGN PEAK
Ensign Peak Nature Park

BEST 🅒

🏃 ☀ 🚻 🚻

Level: Easy

Total Distance: 0.5-1 mile round-trip

Hiking Time: 30 minutes-1 hour

Elevation Change: 429 feet

Summary: A quick hike to an overlook above the State Capitol building and downtown Salt Lake City.

Want an overview of downtown Salt Lake City and the Salt Lake Valley? Do what the pioneers did on their first days upon arrival in the valley. Hike up to the 5,414-foot Ensign Peak and drink in views of the entire valley, including the State Capitol building and Great Salt Lake.

According to the historical plaque at the trailhead on July 26, 1847, two days after the Mormon Pioneers entered the Salt Lake Valley, Brigham Young and a group of his followers climbed to the top of this mountain and carefully surveyed the valley. One of them declared the peak Ensign Peak. According to the pioneers, the name comes from a biblical prophecy: "He will lift up an ensign unto the nations.... He lifteth up an ensign on the mountains" (Isaiah 5:26, 18:3). The peak has remained an important symbol for the Church of Jesus Christ of Latter-day Saints and is marked by a monument and nature park.

The trail up Ensign Peak is short, steep, and peppered with interpretive signs explaining the hike's historic significance. The trail's short distance and educational character make it an excellent experience for children. A small park with benches at the trailhead adds to its family-friendly feel.

From the circular park plaza, a paved trail leads north, uphill along a patch of Gambel oak trees. After a short distance the trail becomes dirt and steepens as it climbs the open south-facing hillside. A few short switchbacks lead west toward the summit, passing by a resting spot with concrete benches. Reaching the ridgeline, the trail bends back south to the summit monument.

Interpretive signs on the summit recount the site's history and provide information about the all-encompassing valley view. The view looks south across downtown and takes in everything from the city to the major summits along the Wasatch Range.

Options

Looking for a longer hike? A 1.1-mile section of the Bonneville Shoreline Trail connects the Ensign Peak Trail with the City Creek Canyon Trail (run a car shuttle beforehand to connect the two trailheads). To reach the junction with the Bonneville Shoreline Trail, continue 0.5 mile north uphill from Ensign Peak and turn right on the Bonneville Shoreline Trail. Turn right again when you reach City Creek to follow the City Creek Canyon Trail. Follow City Creek Canyon Trail 1 mile to the City Creek Canyon trailhead, where your car awaits. This trail combination adds up to a 3-mile one-way hike.

To reach the City Creek Canyon trailhead drive east (instead of west) on North Temple for 2.5 miles to 2nd Avenue. Continue on 2nd Avenue for 0.2 mile and turn left onto A Street. Drive 0.6 mile on A Street and turn left onto B Street. Continue 0.2 mile on B Street and then continue onto Bonneville Boulevard (where B Street becomes Bonneville Boulevard). Drive 0.6 mile to the City Creek Canyon entrance and trailhead.

Note: Cars are allowed to drive up City Creek Canyon on even numbered calendar days, but are not allowed on odd days, making odd days favorable for hiking.

downtown Salt Lake City from Ensign Peak

© MIKE MATSON

Directions

From State Street and North Temple in downtown Salt Lake City, drive west for one block to Main Street and turn right. Drive north for one block and turn right on 200 North. Drive 0.2 mile and continue straight onto East Capital Boulevard. Follow Capital Boulevard for 1.2 miles and turn left onto Ensign Vista Drive. Continue on Ensign Vista Drive for 0.3 mile until you reach the Ensign Peak trailhead, and park on the right side of the road.

GPS Coordinates: N 40°79.171' W 111°88.818'

Information and Contact

There is no fee. Leashed dogs are allowed. Maps are available at the Public Lands Information Center, 3285 East 3300 South (inside REI), Salt Lake City, UT 84109, 801/466-6411. For more information contact the Salt Lake City Parks Division, 1965 West 500 South, Salt Lake City, UT 84101, 801/972-7800, www.slcgov.com.

2 LIVING ROOM

BEST ◖

Wasatch-Cache National Forest

Level: Easy/Moderate

Total Distance: 2.3 miles round-trip

Hiking Time: 1.5–2 hours

Elevation Change: 1,213 feet

Summary: The Living Room comes complete with furniture assembled from rocks and the best view of the Salt Lake Valley of any living room in the city.

The foothills above the University of Utah are crisscrossed with a web of short trails extending off the central arterial trail, the Bonneville Shoreline Trail. A short, steep trail leading up to an overlook dubbed the Living Room is among

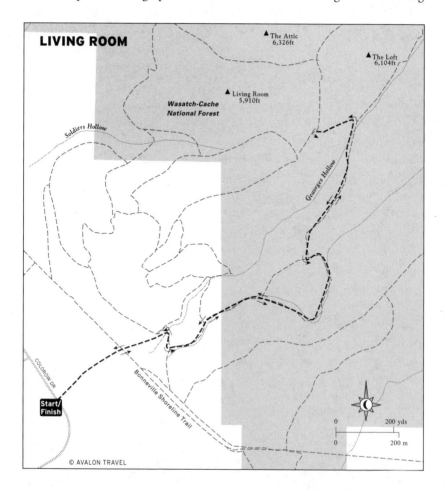

LIVING ROOM

The Attic
6,326ft

The Loft
6,104ft

Living Room
5,910ft

Wasatch-Cache
National Forest

Soldiers Hollow

Georges Hollow

COLOROW DR

Bonneville Shoreline Trail

Start/
Finish

0   200 yds

0   200 m

© AVALON TRAVEL

the sandstone arm chairs of the Living Room

the best of these offerings. The Living Room has a collection of sandstone furnishings, including armchairs, sofas, and a coffee table. It's a cool place for young kids to play on the rocks, and a popular destination for adults as well. Watching the sunset over the western mountains from the Living Room is a memorable experience; just remember to bring a headlamp along for the walk down. The hike up to the Living Room is enjoyable during any season, but fall and spring offer the most comfortable temperatures.

The trail to the Living Room is not signed, and can be a bit confusing to reach. The unmarked trailhead is on the east side of Colorow Drive. Start up the trail through a thick forest of Gambel oak. A large Russian olive tree grows over the trail, and you'll quickly cross a small spring trickling across the path. At 0.13 mile, the trail splits; take the left fork. After 75 feet, a trail enters from the left, but you will continue hiking up to the right. Shortly thereafter, at 0.2 mile, the trail crosses a wide dirt road covering an oil pipeline and then reaches the Bonneville Shoreline Trail at 0.22 mile. Turn right on the Bonneville Shoreline Trail and continue across the gully.

Joining the Bonneville Shoreline Trail briefly, the trail jogs south across a Gambel oak–filled ravine called Georges Hollow. On the south side of the ravine turn left onto a smaller, single-track trail and head up the drainage. For the first 0.75 mile the scrub oak and maple forest provides some shade for the trail. At 0.8 mile the trail leaves the drainage and climbs north toward the ridge. Following the ridge briefly, and then traversing to the north, the trail quickly rounds a corner and steps into the Living Room. Expect to share the popular Living Room with other hikers, especially at sunset.

Options

The Living Room can be combined with a hike along the Bonneville Shoreline Trail running north to south along the base of the Wasatch Mountains. The trail to the Living Room crosses the Bonneville Shoreline Trail at the beginning of the hike, 0.22-mile east of the trailhead. From here, turn left to hike north on the Bonneville Shoreline Trail. The trail can be hiked south for 1.25 miles to the trailhead at This is the Place Heritage Park, which adds 2.5 miles round-trip to the hike.

Directions

From Salt Lake City, take Exit 1 for Foothill Drive/Parley's Way. Continue straight for 3.3 miles on Foothill Drive and turn right onto Wakara Way. Drive 0.6 mile and turn right onto Colorow Road before entering Red Butte Garden. Continue 0.2 mile to the unmarked trailhead on the left side of the road. Park along Colorow Road just before the Huntsman Corporation building.

GPS Coordinates: N 40°75.915' W 111°82.135'

Information and Contact

There is no fee. Dogs are allowed on leash. Maps are available at the Public Lands Information Center, 3285 East 3300 South (inside REI), Salt Lake City, UT 84109, 801/466-6411. For more information, contact Salt Lake City Ranger District, Uinta-Wasatch-Cache National Forest, 125 South State Street, Salt Lake City, UT 84138, 801/236-3400, www.fs.fed.us.

3 EMIGRATION CANYON   BEST ◖

Parley's Canyon, Wasatch-Cache National Forest

Level: Moderate

Hiking Time: 3-4 hours

Total Distance: 5.1 miles round-trip

Elevation Change: 1,259 feet

Summary: A roller-coaster trail rises and falls along Emigration Canyon's ridgeline.

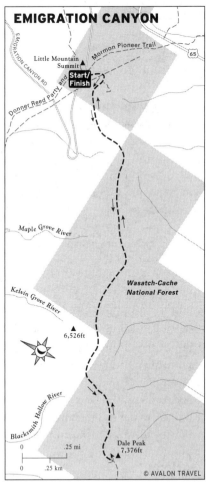

EMIGRATION CANYON

Hiking the Emigration Canyon Ridgeline embodies much of what's great about the mountains above Salt Lake City. The trail travels to a front-line view of the boundary between the urban sprawl of the Salt Lake Valley and the mountain wilderness that rises above it all. It's also one of the closest trails to downtown, making it a perfect quick escape from city life. With its relatively low elevation, starting at 6,227 feet, this trail is a good hike for cooler seasons, namely spring and fall.

Emigration Canyon was the final leg in the journey for the Mormon Pioneers when they arrived in the Salt Lake Valley in 1847. Although reminders of this history are not evident along the trail, it's still fun to be able to see the historic route from this elevated perspective.

The Emigration Trail follows the ridgeline from Little Mountain Summit to the 7,376-foot Dale Peak. The ridge walk enjoys expansive views the whole way, including Little Dell and Mountain Dell Reservoirs in Parley's Canyon.

The trail heads out of the west side of the parking lot near the restroom at Little Mountain Summit. The beginning of the trail has a bit of an industrial feel as it passes by a fenced-in utility compound and then a set of cell towers. The trail joins an old paved road briefly that transitions to a dirt road and finally a jeep track. Passing under a set of power lines at 0.5 mile, the trail leaves the human-altered landscape behind and enters a more natural-feeling landscape. The trail follows the ridge separating Emigration Canyon and Parley's Canyon, and views into both canyons are excellent from as early as the 0.5-mile mark. I-80 snakes up Parley's Canyon and the 36 holes of Mountain Dell Golf Course spread out beside the freeway and reservoirs. In Emigration Canyon large homes catch the eye, standing out against the otherwise-natural landscape. Vegetation is sparse

Emigration Canyon

along this part of the ridgeline with a few Gambel oak trees growing along the trail. Arrowleaf balsamroot wildflowers bloom in late spring and early summer, and even the occasional prickly pear cactus can be found tucked in among the grass and sagebrush.

At 1 mile from the trailhead you'll find yourself on a relatively steep hillside with Rocky Mountain maple trees mixed in with the Gambel oak. This unnamed peak stands 6,526 feet, or about 300 feet higher than the trailhead. Growing slowly in size as you progress up the ridge, the trees rise above head height on either side of the trail by 1.5 miles. Wire Mountain—or Big Beacon, as it's sometimes called because of its large square radio repeater on its summit—is visible to the northwest. Then at 1.75 miles the Salt Lake Valley comes into view for the first time. It's fun to watch the trees change with slowly rising elevation, with curl-leaf mountain mahogany starting to grow as you climb up Dale Peak. The summit views are impressive. Dale Peak's modest height is made up for by its central position, and views include everything from the valley floor cityscape to the Great Salt Lake to the surrounding Wasatch Mountain summits. Soak it all in before following the ridge back down to the car.

Options

The Emigration ridgeline also has a trail that heads east from the Little Mountain Summit parking lot. This is a popular mountain-biking trail, but is open to hiking as well. The trail leads 3.2 miles to Birch Spring Pass, making for a 6.4-mile round-trip hike.

Directions

From downtown Salt Lake City, drive south on State Street for 0.8 mile and turn left on University Boulevard. Drive 3.4 miles and turn left on Sunnyside Avenue. Continue 1 mile on Sunnyside Avenue until it turns into Emigration Canyon Road. Continue 6 miles up Emigration Canyon Road and turn right to keep following Emigration Canyon Road. Drive 1.7 miles to the parking lot on the right side of the road at Little Mountain Summit.

GPS Coordinates: N 40°77.472' W 111°71.846'

Information and Contact

Parley's Canyon, the canyon on the south side of the Emigration Canyon ridgeline, is a watershed and dogs are not allowed. Maps are available at the Public Lands Information Center, 3285 East 3300 South (inside REI), Salt Lake City, UT 84109, 801/466-6411. For more information, contact Salt Lake City Ranger District, Uinta-Wasatch-Cache National Forest, 125 South State Street, Salt Lake City, UT 84138, 801/236-3400, www.fs.fed.us.

❹ LITTLE EMIGRATION CANYON BEST ◖
Wasatch-Cache National Forest

🏕 🦌 ✈ 🌿 📷 🏠 👫

Level: Easy/Moderate **Total Distance:** 8.0 miles round-trip

Hiking Time: 4-5 hours **Elevation Change:** 1,433 feet

Summary: Little Emigration Canyon is part of the historic Mormon Trail, retracing the steps of the Mormon Pioneers from East Canyon to Big Mountain Pass.

Little Emigration Canyon is a trail rich in history. It's the eastern leg of the Mormon Pioneer National Historic Trail, a place where you can imagine the Brigham Young–led Mormon settlers in 1847 pulling their wagon trains over Big Mountain Pass—the final, but also highest pass, in their journey to the Salt Lake Valley. These early parties camped in a meadow next to the beaver ponds at the 1-mile mark on the trail. Legend has it that at Big Mountain Pass, where the party first enjoyed views of the Salt Lake Valley, Brigham Young declared the valley would be the place to establish their settlement. The trail was first established in 1846 by the infamous Donner-Reed Party on their way to California. It was in part the need to blaze a new trail through the Wasatch Mountains that slowed the party's progress, leading to their eventual demise trapped in California's Sierra Nevada Mountains in winter. The route continued to be used by the Pony Express and other pioneers coming west for the next 23 years, including 70,000 Mormons between 1846 and 1869.

Independent of its historical significance, the trail up Little Emigration Canyon is an enjoyable walk in its own right. The intermittent creek supports stands of aspen and cottonwood trees. Butterflies puddle where the trail crosses the creek. Beavers have built dams and ponds along the waterway, and open meadows are visited by other wildlife, including moose. The trail is one of the Wasatch Range's least steep routes and is a good hike for families and children.

The Little Emigration Canyon Trail

wildlfowers in Little Emigration Canyon

© MIKE MATSON

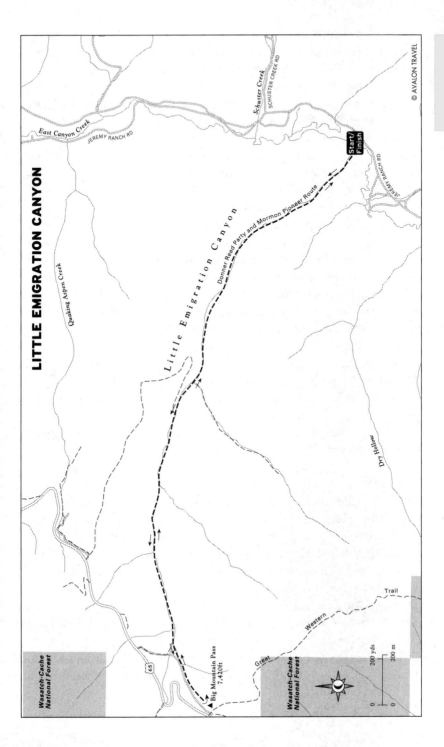

LITTLE EMIGRATION CANYON

© AVALON TRAVEL

East Canyon Creek

Schuster Creek

SCHUSTER CREEK RD

JEREMY RANCH RD

Start/ Finish

JEREMY RANCH RD

Donner Reed Party and Mormon Pioneer Route

Quaking Aspen Creek

Little Emigration Canyon

Dry Hollow

Trail

Western

Great

Big Mountain Pass 7,420ft

65

Wasatch-Cache National Forest

Wasatch-Cache National Forest

200 yds

200 m

0

0

starts at Mormon Flats in East Canyon. Leaving the gravel parking lot, it crosses East Canyon Creek via a wooden plank footbridge. The trail weaves through willows along the creek before entering the canyon at a gate through a barbed-wire fence. Sagebrush and grass cover the hills rising on either side of the canyon. Large cottonwood and quaking aspen trees provide shade along the trail.

At 1.3 miles mountain bikers have built a wooden ramp over a fallen log lying across the trail. There are several biker-built features like this along the trail. Mountain bikers like the Little Emigration Trail for its gentle grade and long, smooth descent, so be aware that they may come speeding around the corner.

The trail crosses the rocky creek bed repeatedly as it climbs gently up the canyon. In early summer, there's water in the creek, but it dries up as the season progresses. The creek is fed by snowmelt in early spring, and then by a natural spring in the dry months. The spring also fills the beaver ponds in the meadow at about 1.5 mile from the trailhead.

Wildflowers grow in clumps along the trail. Delicate columbine flowers can be found growing in the shade, and Indian paintbrush adds color to the open meadows. The trail continues to climb at a gentle grade toward the pass, with mile markers on brown flexi-poles providing distance updates.

The Little Emigration Canyon Trail climbs steeply for the last 0.25 mile to Big Mountain Pass. At the pass you'll be rewarded with views down to Parley's Canyon and of the Wasatch Mountains to the west. An interpretive trail sign gives a brief description of Mormon Pioneers journey and their decision to make the Salt Lake Valley their home. Big Mountain Pass is also a paved road—State Route 65 coming north from I-80 in Parley's Canyon.

Options

Little Emigration Canyon is a section of the longer Mormon Pioneer Trail, totaling 9 miles. The trail continues on down the west side of Big Mountain Pass to Little Dell Reservoir in Parley's Canyon. At 18 miles out-and-back, this trail is very long for a day hike. One option is to run a car shuttle and leave vehicles at both trailheads. This allows for a one-way 9-mile hike of the entire trail.

Directions

From Salt Lake City drive east on I-80 for 13 miles to the Exit 141 for Jeremy Ranch. Turn left off the exit ramp and go under the freeway. At the stop sign, turn left and take the next right onto Jeremy Ranch Road. Continue on this road until it forks, and stay left on East Canyon Road. Continue 4.9 miles and turn left into the gravel parking lot for Mormon Flat.

GPS Coordinates: N 40°81.564' W 111°58.477'

Information and Contact

There is no fee. Dogs are allowed on leash. Maps are available at the Public Lands Information Center, 3285 East 3300 South (inside REI), Salt Lake City, UT 84109, 801/466-6411. For more information contact the National Park Service's National Trails Intermountain Regional Staff in Salt Lake City, 324 South State Street, Suite 200, Salt Lake City, UT 84111, 801/741-1012, www.nps.gov/mopi.

5 MOUNT OLYMPUS   BEST (

Mount Olympus Wilderness Area, Wasatch-Cache National Forest

Level: Butt-kicker   **Total Distance:** 7.0 miles round-trip

Hiking Time: 5-7 hours   **Elevation Change:** 4,152 feet

Summary: Mount Olympus is one of Salt Lake City's steepest and most popular summit hikes.

There are many hikes that end with elevated views of the Salt Lake Valley, but there is only one Mount Olympus. With its dramatic northwest face, wildly twisted geology, and prominent position above the Olympus Cove neighborhood, the 9,026-foot Mount Olympus attracts the attention of countless hikers. It's one of the few mountains along the Wasatch Front recognized by virtually everyone—regardless of their level of interest in the outdoors.

Fittingly, one of the steepest trails in the entire range leads to its summit. Starting on Wasatch Boulevard, the trail climbs more than 4,000 feet in only 3.5 miles. Despite its steep grade, the trail is endlessly popular, with cars overflowing from its trailhead parking lot every day of the year. The hike can be hot in summer or blanketed in snow during winter, and still you'll find hikers along its many switchbacks—and for good reason. The majority of the hike is protected within the Mount Olympus Wilderness Area, and despite the many people and the drone of I-215, the mountain maintains a wild character. The hike offers a great aerobic challenge, even for the most physically fit hikers, and that adds to its appeal. The trail's biggest reward is its commanding summit views, which stretch for miles

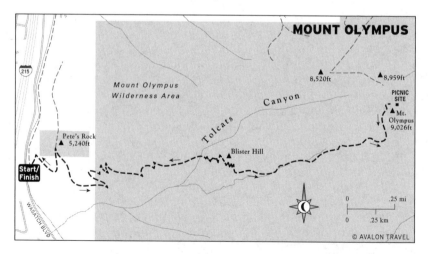

looking south from the summit of Mount Olympus

up and down the Salt Lake Valley. But for most, the right to say, "I've been to the top of Mount Olympus" is just as important.

The Mount Olympus Trail starts directly from the road, climbing a steep slope over a series of erosion-control steps. After 0.2 mile, the trail makes its first of many switchbacks as it continues to climb briskly up the open west face of the mountain. Climbing southeast from the first switchback, the trail crosses open rocky slopes as it gains elevation. In the first 1.5 miles the trail uses 10 switchbacks to ascend more than 1,500 feet. The reward for the steep grade: Valley views are sweeping from the very beginning of the trail, and only improve as your elevation increases. Juniper trees grow on the otherwise open slopes, providing brief patches of shade and nice spots to rest on hot days. At 0.75 mile the trail enters the Mount Olympus Wilderness Area. From here, the rocky path continues upward and to the east as it enters Tolcats Canyon. As you continue to climb higher, the hum of I-215 and the city fall off into the background, and the trail begins to feel more like a mountain hike than a steep walk in a city park. At 1.6 miles the trail crosses a small seasonal stream in Tolcats Canyon and begins to climb aggressively up the canyon. Gambel oak, Rocky Mountain maple, and curl-leaf mountain mahogany trees grow on these rocky slopes, shading the trail.

At 1.8 miles the trail pulls over the crest of the canyon and levels off slightly. Then at 2.4 miles the trail reaches the top of the ridge, walling in the south side of Tolcats Canyon. Views from here are wide open to the south of the ridge, looking south to Twin Peaks of Broads Fork above Big Cottonwood Canyon and the city of Sandy on the valley floor.

A short section of steep trail remains to the Mount Olympus summit. Head north, hiking steeply up a rocky gully and then through some large boulders on the west side of the summit pyramid. If you look closely for the trail here, no scrambling or rock climbing is required. The summit is marked by darkly varnished orange rock. Look to the north: You'll see the peak's north summit with downtown Salt Lake City just over the left shoulder. The entire Salt Lake Valley is visible from this vantage point, from Point of the Mountain marking its southern boundary to City Creek Canyon at the north end.

Options

From the Mount Olympus trailhead a short, 0.5-mile trail runs north along the Bonneville Shoreline bench above Wasatch Boulevard.

Directions

From Salt Lake City drive I-80 East for 5 miles and take the exit ramp for I-215 South. Continue south on I-215 to Exit 4 at 3900 South. At the base of the ramp, turn left and cross under the overpass. Turn right on Wasatch Boulevard and continue 2.5 miles to the Mount Olympus trailhead on the left side of the road. There's an elevated trailhead parking lot, but car break-ins are a problem here, so consider parking along the road where your car will be in plain sight.

GPS Coordinates: N 40°65.134' W 111°80.655'

Information and Contact

There is no fee. Dogs on leash are allowed. Maps are available at the Public Lands Information Center, 3285 East 3300 South (inside REI), Salt Lake City, UT 84109, 801/466-6411. For more information, contact Salt Lake City Ranger District, Uinta-Wasatch-Cache National Forest, 125 South State Street, Salt Lake City, UT 84138, 801/236-3400, www.fs.fed.us.

6 NEFF'S CANYON BEST

Twin Peaks Wilderness, Wasatch-Cache National Forest

Level: Moderate

Total Distance: 5.5-6 miles round-trip

Hiking Time: 3 hours

Elevation Change: 2,667 feet

Summary: Neff's Canyon is Salt Lake City's alpine dog park.

Located between Mount Olympus and Mill Creek Canyon, Neff's Canyon is a small, steep canyon that receives heavy traffic from dog walkers and hikers. The canyon is historically significant as the site of one of the early mills in the Salt Lake Valley. John Neff was a Mormon pioneer who built the first mills in the valley. His first one was on what is now called Mill Creek. The next canyon south also became a mill site and was named after Neff. The 13th-deepest cave in the United States, at 1,163 feet, is in Neff's Canyon. Located on the south side of the meadow at the top of the canyon, the cave is vertical in orientation and considered very dangerous. The entrance is gated and locked. Permission to enter the cave must be obtained by contacting the Uinta-Wasatch-Cache National Forest. Neff's Canyon is also the source of Mount Olympus Bottled Water. The company has been sourcing its natural spring water from Neff's Canyon since the 1890s.

The trail up Neff's Canyon is most popular with dog walkers and those looking for a quick workout. However, a few hikers actually follow the trail all the way to the upper meadow. The meadow is a peaceful place, surrounded by rugged peaks.

From the trailhead there are two trail options to start up Neff's Canyon. Both trails converge 0.8 mile up the canyon. The trail that drops down immediately into a grassy meadow on the south side of the parking lot offers a little more natural-feeling experience than the dirt road that leaves the far left side of the lot. The directions included here are for that trail. If you prefer the dirt road, it leaves from the left side of the parking lot and is very easy to follow.

Cross the grass meadow below the parking lot and duck into the trees. This version of Neff's Canyon gets less traffic than the dirt road, and offers a better hiking environment under the shade of the forest canopy. The trail climbs uphill, crossing some old water-diversion pipes and then paralleling an elevated creek bed on the right side of the canyon. In spring, this rocky streambed rushes with snowmelt, but most of the summer it's dry. The trail slowly draws closer to the dirt road as the canyon floor narrows, and hikers and dogs can be heard through the woods to the left of the trail. At 0.5 mile the trail crosses the creek. Then at 0.6 mile there's an intersection of trails, where it's difficult to know exactly which

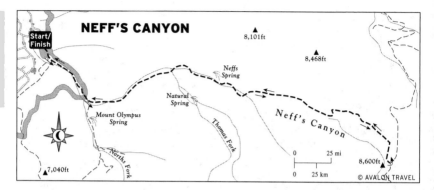

path to follow. Because there are multiple options here, and they're very similar in character, just choose a path and see where it leads. If you want to continue all the way up the canyon to the meadow, make sure to stick to the left side of the canyon when you choose your path, and eventually these trails will merge into one.

At about 2 miles the trail will enter the Mount Olympus Wilderness Area. The trail then climbs steeply upward for 0.25 mile. Large conifer trees protect the path and the stream, which is absent in the lower canyon, is now flowing freely to the left of the trail. Then at 2.2 miles you'll walk through a large aspen grove as the trail starts to climb steeply toward the meadow. The path becomes narrow as thick underbrush crowds in under the aspen. In the last 0.5 mile, the meadow views start to open up back down Neff's Canyon to the Salt Lake Valley, offering the first good vistas of the entire hike. Keep padding upward and you'll soon reach the upper meadow. Long grass, wildflowers, and butterflies meet in the meadow. Enjoy the solitude before heading back down to suburbia the way you came.

Options

From the upper east end of its meadow, ambitious hikers can follow a trail north that leads to the Thaynes Canyon Trail, which leads over a pass and into Mill Creek Canyon. From the meadow it's 3 miles to the Church Fork pull-off in Mill Creek Canyon.

Directions

From Salt Lake City drive I-80 East for 5 miles and take Exit 128 for I-215 South. Continue south on I-215 to Exit 4 for 3900 South. Turn left onto 3900 South and continue straight as 3900 South turns into Jupiter Drive South. Follow Jupiter Drive for 0.8 mile as it curves to the southeast and becomes Jupiter Drive East. Turn left on Oakview Drive and continue for 0.5 mile. Turn left again on Parkview and continue for 0.2 mile to Park Terrace Drive. Take a right on Park

© MIKE MATSON

Neff's Meadow, at the top of Neff's Canyon, is a very popular trail for dogs.

Terrace and drive 0.1 mile to White Way. Turn right onto White Way and drive 0.1 mile to the paved trailhead parking for Neff's Canyon.
GPS Coordinates: N 40°67.710' W 111°77.624'

Information and Contact

There is no fee. Dogs on leash are allowed. Maps are available at the Public Lands Information Center, 3285 East 3300 South (inside REI), Salt Lake City, UT 84109, 801/466-6411. For more information, contact Salt Lake City Ranger District, Uinta-Wasatch-Cache National Forest, 125 South State Street, Salt Lake City, UT 84138, 801/236-3400, www.fs.fed.us.

7 GRANDEUR PEAK   BEST **C**

Church Fork of Mill Creek Canyon, Wasatch-Cache National Forest

Level: Strenuous   **Total Distance:** 5.5 miles round-trip

Hiking Time: 4-5 hours   **Elevation Change:** 2,729 feet

Summary: Salt Lake City residents look up and see Grandeur Peak every day, but it's the 360-degree views down from the summit that make this hike one of the best in Mill Creek Canyon.

Grandeur Peak is one of Salt Lake City's most recognizable summits. Standing 8,299 feet, the peak's distinct triangular form separates Parley's Canyon from Mill Creek Canyon. Its prominent location and proximity to downtown Salt Lake City make it a sought-after summit. With easy, year-round access, Grandeur Peak is a trail many locals hike multiple times.

The Church Fork Trail is the most popular route up Grandeur Peak. The trail begins in the Church Fork Picnic Area of Mill Creek Canyon, ascends the Church Fork of Mill Creek, and then follows the ridgeline west to the Grandeur Peak's summit.

There are two parking areas for the Church Fork Trail. The first is at the trailhead, at the top of the picnic area. This trailhead parking lot is almost laughable in size, considering the popularity of the trail. It has room for only a few cars,

the view southwest from Grandeur Peak, including Mount Olympus and the Olympus Cove neighborhood

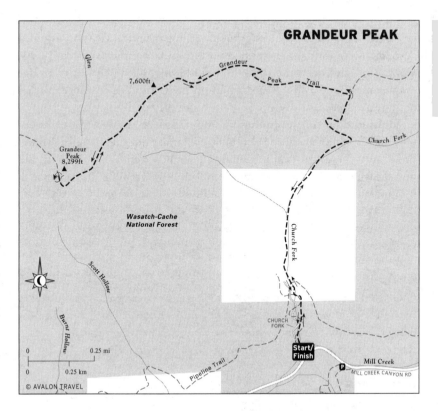

and fills quickly. The second parking area is on the north side of the Mill Creek Canyon Road just east of the turnoff for the picnic area. Parking along Mill Creek Canyon Road adds 0.2 mile to the hike.

From Mill Creek Canyon Road hike uphill through the picnic area to reach the trailhead. The wide, well-traveled Grandeur Peak Trail begins following Church Fork of Mill Creek uphill to the north from the picnic area. A dense mixed forest of box elder, Rocky Mountain maple, and white pine trees shade the path. At 0.3 mile from the road (0.1 mile from the official trailhead) the Grandeur Peak Trail intersects with the Pipeline Trail. Continue straight uphill at the junction. At 0.5 mile from the road the trail crosses the Church Fork on a wooden bridge beneath an impressive stand of large pine trees. Then at 1 mile from the road the trail leaves the creek and begins to climb a series of three long switchbacks up red dirt hillside.

The large trees give way to short Gambel oak and the trail becomes more exposed. Swallowtail butterflies swarm wildflowers along this part of the trail, and views begin to open up across Mill Creek Canyon to the upper ridges of Mount Olympus to the south. At 1.8 miles the trail becomes more rocky and exposed to the sun as it climbs to the ridgeline. Reaching the ridge, views are afforded down into Parley's Canyon to the north of I-80 and the Parley's Canyon Quarry. Downtown Salt Lake is also visible to the northwest. The trail follows the ridge to the summit, with curl-leaf mountain mahogany providing occasional patches of shade along the route.

To the south are impressive views of Mount Olympus's West Slabs with the Olympus Cove neighborhood below. A false summit teases hikers along the ridge. But a short, steep section of trail leads out around the west face of Grandeur and up to the summit. Enjoy the seemingly endless views. From the distant Oquirrh Mountains to the west to Mountain Dell Reservoir in Parley's Canyon to the east, there's plenty of panorama to take in. Return down the way you came, or if you've planned ahead and run a car shuttle to the base, take the trail coming up Grandeur's steep west face down into the city.

Options
Grandeur Peak has a very steep, direct trail up its west face, gaining 3,300 feet in two miles. This west-face trail can be combined with the Church Fork Trail for either the ascent or descent by running a car shuttle between the parking lots of the two trails. This allows for a one-way hike in either direction.

Directions
From Salt Lake City, drive I-80 East for 5 miles and take Exit 128 for I-215 South. Continue south on I-215 to Exit 4 for 3900 South. Turn left onto 3900 South and continue one block to Wasatch Boulevard. Turn left onto Wasatch Boulevard and drive one block to 3800 South/East Mill Creek Canyon Road. Turn right and continue 3 miles to the gravel parking area on the left side of the road at Church Fork Picnic Area.
GPS Coordinates: N 40°70.092' W 111°74.307'

Information and Contact
There is an entrance fee of $3 per vehicle; an annual pass is available for $40. Dogs on leash are allowed on even-numbered days and may be off leash on odd-numbered days. Maps are available at the Public Lands Information Center, 3285 East 3300 South (inside REI), Salt Lake City, UT 84109, 801/466-6411. For more information, contact Salt Lake City Ranger District, Uinta-Wasatch-Cache National Forest, 125 South State Street, Salt Lake City, UT 84138, 801/236-3400, www.fs.fed.us.

8 MOUNT AIRE
Mill Creek Canyon, Wasatch-Cache National Forest

🏕 🐕

Level: Moderate

Total Distance: 3.6 miles round-trip

Hiking Time: 2-3 hours

Elevation Change: 1,991 feet

Summary: A worthy summit with light traffic, Mount Aire offers a different experience from the most popular summit hikes along the Wasatch Front.

Easy access, a short trail, and a rewarding summit make Mount Aire a great after-work escape from urban life. Summit views include Parley's Canyon and I-80 to the north, Salt Lake City to the west, and the peaks of the central Wasatch Range to the south. It's also a good hike for dogs to burn off some pent-up energy. Mill Creek Canyon rules allow dogs off leash on the odd days of the month. The upper section of Mill Creek Canyon Road is closed until July 1.

The trail to Mount Aire's 8,621-foot summit wastes no time gaining elevation, leaving the small parking pull-off at Elbow Fork on the Mill Creek Canyon Road. In order to gain 2,200 feet in 1.6 miles, this trail must be steep, and you'll know within the first 10 minutes what you're in for. It's not a long trail, though, so enjoy the workout while it lasts!

A thick forest shades the trail as it ascends Elbow Fork. Large fir and pine trees mix with Rocky Mountain maple and stands of aspen. On the forest floor yellow arrowleaf balsamroot and other wildflowers line the trail. At 0.2 mile a trail branches off to the right leading to Lambs Canyon (dogs are not allowed in Lambs Canyon because it's part of the Parley's Canyon watershed). Stay left to continue toward Mount Aire. The trail is steep and rutted in places and thick brush occasionally crowds the path. After 1 mile you'll reach Mount Aire Pass. From the pass, limited views open up to the north, with Antelope Island visible in the Great Salt Lake. Mount Aire rises to the right above the pass. Without the creek, the forest dwindles above the pass, with a mix of Gambel oak and curl-leaf mountain mahogany growing on the dry, rocky hillside. The trail switchbacks repeatedly as it climbs Mount Aire's southwest-facing slope. Nearing the summit, at 1.4 miles, the first view into Parley's Canyon opens up to the north.

Mount Aire's summit views are rewarding, if not as sweeping as some Wasatch summits. From Mount Aire's high point you can pick out the peaks that divide Mill Creek Canyon from Big Cottonwood Canyon to the south, including Mount Raymond and Gobbler's Knob. To the west is Grandeur Peak, and to the east you'll look down over Lambs Canyon.

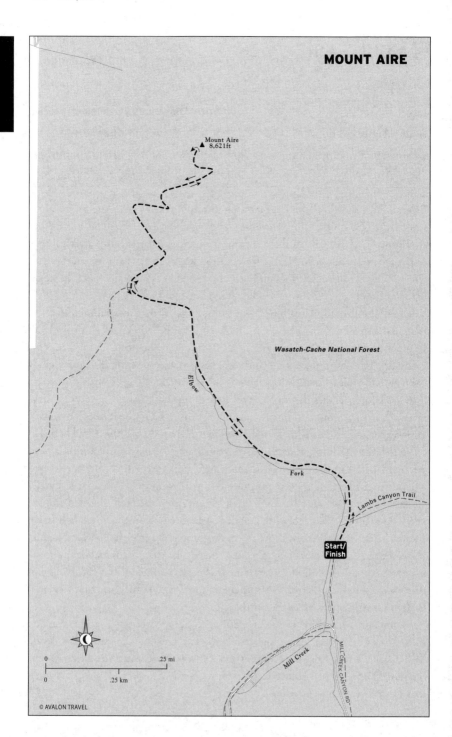

MOUNT AIRE

Mount Aire
▲ 8,621ft

Wasatch-Cache National Forest

Elbow

Fork

Lambs Canyon Trail

Start/
Finish

Mill Creek

MILL CREEK CANYON RD

0   .25 mi
0   .25 km

© AVALON TRAVEL

© MIKE MATSON

hikers near the summit of Mount Aire, with Mill Creek Canyon in the background

Options

By turning right at the junction 0.2 mile up the trail, it's possible to climb to Lambs Canyon Pass and then descend into Lambs Canyon. It's 3.5 miles to the Lambs Canyon trailhead. With a car shuttle, it's possible to hike from the Elbow Fork trailhead to the Lambs Canyon trailhead as a one-way hike.

Directions

From Salt Lake City drive I-80 East for 5 miles and take Exit 128 for I-215 South. Continue south on I-215 to Exit 4 for 3900 South. Turn left onto 3900 South and continue one block to Wasatch Boulevard. Turn left onto Wasatch Boulevard and drive one block to 3800 South/East Mill Creek Canyon Road. Turn right and continue 5.9 miles to the Elbow Fork trailhead on the left side of the road, where the road turns sharply to the right.

GPS Coordinates: N 40°70.899' W 111°68.989'

Information and Contact

There is an entrance fee of $3 per vehicle; an annual pass is available for $40. Dogs on leash are allowed on even-numbered days and may be off leash on odd-numbered days. Maps are available at the Public Lands Information Center, 3285 East 3300 South (inside REI), Salt Lake City, UT 84109, 801/466-6411. For more information, contact Salt Lake City Ranger District, Uinta-Wasatch-Cache National Forest, 125 South State Street, Salt Lake City, UT 84138, 801/236-3400, www.fs.fed.us.

9 LAMBS CANYON
Wasatch-Cache National Forest

Level: Moderate   **Total Distance:** 4.0 miles round-trip

Hiking Time: 2-3 hours   **Elevation Change:** 1,520 feet

Summary: A hike through a vibrant forest leads to a high mountain pass.

Lambs Canyon is a quiet drainage in an often-busy range, defined by mature trees and a trickling spring-fed creek. The hike goes up a forested valley to Lambs Canyon Pass with views down into Mill Creek Canyon. For those willing to make a car shuttle drop, the possibilities expand from the pass. It's easy to descend into Elbow Fork of Mill Creek Canyon or climb to Mount Aire from the pass.

The trail leaves Lambs Canyon Road and crosses a footbridge over the creek before heading into the forest. Paralleling a small creek, the trail climbs uphill through dense foliage. Large aspen, spruce, pine, and fir trees create a thick forest canopy, keeping the canyon shaded and cool during hot summer months. Deer can be found foraging along the creek in the thick undergrowth. You'll see everything from stinging nettles to cow parsnip to fireweed to thimbleberries growing along the stream's banks.

In late spring and summer, Lambs Canyon is a particularly good place to find butterflies, according to the Utah Lepidopterists' Society. The winged beauties

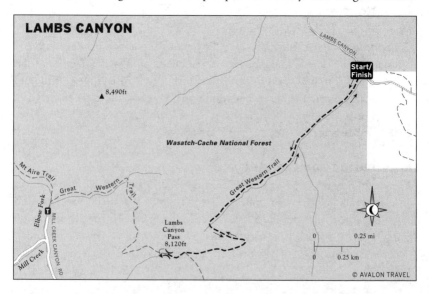

LAMBS CANYON

▲ 8,490ft

Wasatch-Cache National Forest

Mt Aire Trail

Great   Western   Trail

Great Western Trail

Start/Finish

Elbow Fork

MILL CREEK CANYON RD

Mill Creek

Lambs Canyon Pass 8,120ft

0   0.25 mi

0   0.25 km

© AVALON TRAVEL

view down Mill Creek Canyon, to the Salt Lake Valley, from Lambs Canyon Pass

are attracted to the perennial herb dogbain—an excellent source of nectar for three butterfly families: skippers, blues, and fritillaries.

At 1 mile the trail moves away from the spring, climbing uphill into a stand of old aspen trees. The forest opens up slightly, and wildflowers such as lupine and columbine can be spotted along the trail. At 1.5 miles the trail makes a large switchback, climbing more steeply for the last 0.5 mile to the pass. Then the path suddenly levels out and emerges from the forest at the 8,120-foot Lambs Canyon Pass. Views from the pass look out over the aspen tops into Mill Creek Canyon, and beyond to the Salt Lake Valley below. Return down the canyon the way you came, or consider hiking down into Mill Creek Canyon.

Options

From Lambs Canyon Pass the trail can be followed 2 miles down through the Elbow Fork drainage into Mill Creek Canyon. The trail ends at the Elbow Fork trailhead, which is the trailhead for the Mount Aire hike (see listing in this chapter). A car shuttle is required to make this one-way hike.

Directions

From Salt Lake City drive east on I-80 to Exit 137 for Lambs Canyon. From the exit ramp turn right on the Lambs Canyon Road and drive 1.6 miles to a small trailhead parking lot on the left side of the road. A Forest Service toilet and trail sign mark the trailhead.

GPS Coordinates: N 40°71.910' W 111°65.568'

Information and Contact

There is no fee. Dogs are not allowed because Lambs Canyon is a watershed. Maps are available at the Public Lands Information Center, 3285 East 3300 South (inside REI), Salt Lake City, UT 84109, 801/466-6411. For more information, contact Salt Lake City Ranger District, Uinta-Wasatch-Cache National Forest, 125 South State Street, Salt Lake City, UT 84138, 801/236-3400, www.fs.fed.us.

10 ALEXANDER BASIN TO GOBBLER'S KNOB

BEST

Mill Creek Canyon, Wasatch-Cache National Forest

Level: Strenuous

Total Distance: 4.0 miles round-trip

Hiking Time: 4-5 hours

Elevation Change: 3,169 feet

Summary: Climb to the summit of Gobbler's Knob through the lovely alpine meadows of Alexander Basin.

Ready for a workout? Reaching the summit of Gobbler's Knob through Alexander Basin will burn lots of calories. It's only 2 miles from the parking lot on Mill Creek Canyon Road to the top of Gobbler's Knob, but you gain more than 3,000 vertical feet. That's steep—really steep. Bring lots of water and a pair of trekking poles for this lung-burner. Note that the upper section of Mill Creek Canyon Road is open only from July 1 to November 1.

Once you accept the trail's straight-at-it approach, it's hard to deny the rugged beauty of Alexander Basin. The series of meadows in the trail's second mile are filled with blankets of wildflowers that are among the best in the state. There are no crowds or wildflower festivals here, and many days you might have the whole canyon to yourself. So enjoy the color on the way up, and then be blown away by the view at the top of Gobbler's Knob!

The Alexander Basin Trail heads uphill fast. Almost immediately the trail enters the Mount Olympus Wilderness and bolts directly uphill through the forest. Aspen and spruce shade the dirt trail, providing some relief from the heat during summer. At 0.5 mile the trail levels out for the first time, as the dense forest gives way to an open canopy of mature aspen. This is the beginning of a slow transition from woods to meadows that defines the rest of the hike. Then, at 0.9 mile, a trail leading up from Butler Fork merges with the Alexander Basin Trail. Take a left at this junction and continue uphill. Views begin to open up as the trees thin out. Looking back down toward Mill Creek Canyon, Mount Aire is visible on the northern skyline.

The trail climbs a series of natural steps into Alexander Basin. This is one wide avalanche gully, where most of the trees are small aspen or subalpine fir, and even those have been battered by years of sliding snow.

Horizontally fractured limestone cliffs mark the northeast side of Gobbler's Knob, rising above Alexander Basin on the right. As you climb into the upper bowl of the basin, you'll cross several limestone boulder talus fields. A steep section of trail weaves through a large stand of mature spruce trees before heading

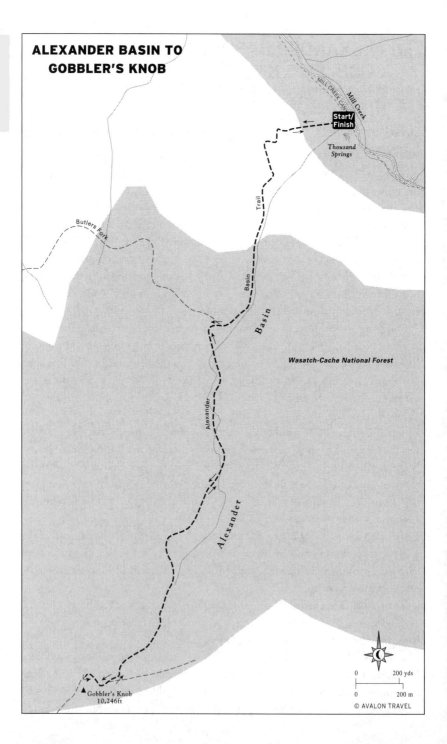

ALEXANDER BASIN TO GOBBLER'S KNOB

Mill Creek Cyn

Mill Creek

Start/Finish

Thousand Springs

Butlers Fork

Basin Trail

Basin

Alexander

Wasatch-Cache National Forest

Alexander

▲ Gobbler's Knob
10,246ft

0   200 yds
0   200 m

© AVALON TRAVEL

© MIKE MATSON

view from the summit of Gobbler's Nobb, looking across Big Cottonwood Canyon

up to the final saddle below Gobbler's Knob. Continue upward to the saddle and then hike right up the ridge to the summit.

Views from the saddle are spectacular. All of Big Cottonwood Canyon and the mountains around it stretch out before you to the east. Major summits such as Twin Peaks of Broads Fork and Kessler Peak rise on the south side of the canyon. Climbing a couple hundred more yards to the top of Gobbler's Knob will include extensive views west all the way out to the Great Salt Lake and the horizon beyond.

Options

From the summit of Gobbler's Knob, a trail also descends into Big Cottonwood Canyon to either the Butler Fork trailhead or the Mill B North Fork trailhead. By running a car shuttle to either of these trailheads, a one-way, cross-canyon hike is possible.

Directions

From Salt Lake City, drive I-80 East for 5 miles and take Exit 128 for I-215 South. Continue south on I-215 to Exit 4 for 3900 South. Turn left onto 3900 South and continue one block to Wasatch Boulevard. Turn left onto Wasatch Boulevard and drive one block to 3800 South/East Mill Creek Canyon Road. Turn right and continue 7.5 miles to the Alexander Basin trailhead on the right side of the road. **GPS Coordinates:** N 40°69.181' W 111°66.994'

Information and Contact

There is an entrance fee of $3 per vehicle; an annual pass is available for $40. Dogs on leash are allowed on even-numbered days and may be off leash on odd-numbered days. Maps are available at the Public Lands Information Center, 3285 East 3300 South (inside REI), Salt Lake City, UT 84109, 801/466-6411. For more information, contact Salt Lake City Ranger District, Uinta-Wasatch-Cache National Forest, 125 South State Street, Salt Lake City, UT 84138, 801/236-3400, www.fs.fed.us.

11 BIG WATER TRAIL TO DOG LAKE   BEST ◖

Mill Creek Canyon, Wasatch-Cache National Forest

Level: Moderate

Total Distance: 5.3 miles round-trip

Hiking Time: 3-4 hours

Elevation Change: 1,482 feet

Summary: Perfect for the dog days of summer, this shaded forest path offers a cool respite from the heat, complete with a dog swimming hole as its destination.

The Big Water Trail to Dog Lake is loved by two different user groups with equal passion. Mountain bikers love the trail for its gentle grade and wide, smooth path. Hikers with dogs frequent the same trail for its shaded path and dog-friendly mountain lake. Mill Creek Canyon rules allow dogs to hike its trails off leash on odd-numbered days of the month. Mountain bikers can ride the same trails, and dogs must be leashed, on even days. In addition to reaching Dog Lake, the Big Water Trail also accesses the crest between Big Cottonwood Canyon and Mill Creek Canyon. From Dog Lake, hikers can descend into Big Cottonwood via Butler Fork or Mill D, or hike east to Desolation Lake. Note that the upper section of Mill Creek Canyon Road is open only from July 1 to November 1.

The Big Water trailhead has an upper and lower parking lot, separated by 100 yards. Two different trails start from the two parking areas, but in 0.3 mile these trails merge into a single trail. These first sections of trail are similar in character, and climb at a gentle grade through a spruce and aspen forest. Once these trails merge, the pine needle–blanketed trail is wide, smooth, and shaded.

The trail switchbacks gently up Big Water Gulch. Starting at 0.3 mile the path comes out of the evergreen forest occasionally into groves of mature quaking aspen. The trail crosses Big Water Creek on wooden bridges at 0.9 mile and then again at 1.1 miles. Salmonberries grow along the side of the trail, and the forest opens up to allow limited views back down to Mill Creek Canyon. At 1.3 mile you'll come to a trail junction marked by a trail sign. Follow the sign and take the left fork to continue to Dog Lake. As the trail gains elevation, open groves of aspen partially shade the trail and lupine, aster, and Indian paintbrush can be seen growing in the thick blanket of green ground cover.

At 2.4 miles the Big Water Trail splits and provides two options to reach Dog Lake. Turn right for a slightly more direct route and continue 0.2 mile to the lake. The trail climbs a short, forested hill before descending quickly to the lake. The open shores of the lake are perfect for playing fetch with your dog or just relaxing.

Descend the way you came, or, if you don't have a dog along, consider dropping

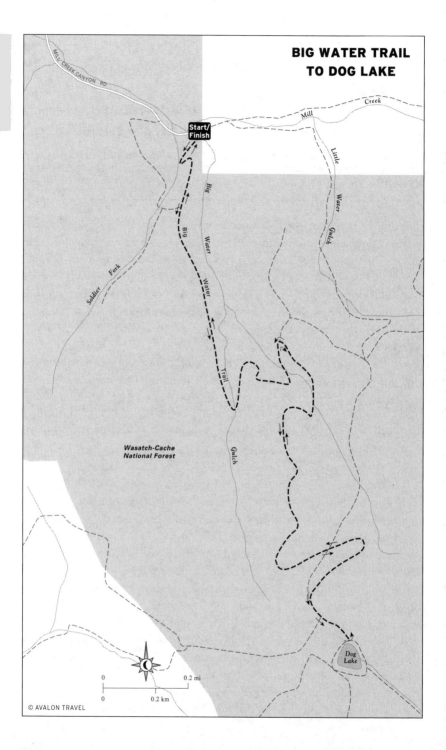

BIG WATER TRAIL
TO DOG LAKE

MILL CREEK CANYON RD

Mill Creek

Start/Finish

Little Water Gulch

Big Water

Big Water

Soldier Fork

Water Trail

Wasatch-Cache
National Forest

Gulch

Dog Lake

0   0.2 mi
0   0.2 km

© AVALON TRAVEL

into Big Cottonwood Canyon for a one-way trip.

Options

Dog Lake can also be reached from the Mill D North Fork Trail (see the listing for Mill D Trail to Desolation Lake) starting in Big Cottonwood Canyon. This option is 4.6 miles round-trip. However, dogs are not allowed in Big Cottonwood Canyon because it is a watershed.

Directions

From Salt Lake City drive I-80 East for 5 miles and take Exit 128 for I-215 South. Continue south on I-215 to Exit 4 for

Dog Lake at the top of the Big Water Trail

© MIKE MATSON

3900 South. Turn left onto 3900 South and continue one block to Wasatch Boulevard. Turn left onto Wasatch Boulevard and drive one block to 3800 South/East Mill Creek Canyon Road. Turn right and continue 7.7 miles to the Alexander Basin trailhead on the right side of the road.

GPS Coordinates: N 40°68.432' W 111°64.871'

Information and Contact

There is an entrance fee of $3 per vehicle; an annual pass is available for $40. Dogs on leash are allowed on even-numbered days and may be off leash on odd-numbered days. Maps are available at the Public Lands Information Center, 3285 East 3300 South (inside REI), Salt Lake City, UT 84109, 801/466-6411. For more information, contact Salt Lake City Ranger District, Uinta-Wasatch-Cache National Forest, 125 South State Street, Salt Lake City, UT 84138, 801/236-3400, www.fs.fed.us.

12 FERGUSON CANYON

BEST (

Wasatch-Cache National Forest

Level: Moderate

Total Distance: 3.8 miles round-trip

Hiking Time: 2-3 hours

Elevation Change: 2,253 feet

Summary: One of the heavily used smaller canyons along the Wasatch Front, Ferguson Canyon is popular with dog walkers, rock climbers, and hikers.

Rising above an affluent neighborhood just south of the mouth to Big Cottonwood Canyon, Ferguson Canyon offers a lovely, shady walk through the woods. The canyon is home to some uniquely featured granite-like rock walls where climbers come to escape the heat during summer months. The dense forest canopy shades the rock walls and trail, making the canyon a great place to exercise your dog as well. Farther up the canyon, a satisfying overlook takes in the Salt Lake Valley and the Oquirrh Mountains to the west. On summer afternoons paragliders can be seen flying on the rising thermals above the canyon's rim after launching near the trailhead.

The Ferguson Canyon Trail traverses north from the parking lot up a dirt road 0.2 mile to a white water tower at the canyon's mouth. After reaching the tower, the trail narrows and drops down onto the canyon floor and immediately enters the Twin Peaks Wilderness Area. Gambel oak and Rocky Mountain maple grow thickly along the creek.

For the first 0.5 mile the trail follows a narrow path through the trees by

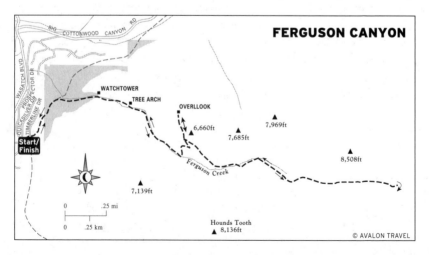

© MIKE MATSON

Gambel oak leaves at the entrance to Ferguson Canyon

granite boulders into the canyon. At 0.6 mile from the trailhead you'll encounter the first of a series of rock walls—called the Watchtower—where rock climbers scale a collection of short, sporty routes. The trail is wide here where climbers spread at the base of the cliffs. The trail crosses Ferguson Creek and climbs a steep, deeply eroded hillside for about 0.2 mile. Unfortunately there's nowhere else to reroute the trail, because the footing is difficult on the uphill and worse coming back down.

After crossing the creek once more, the trail switchbacks to the north away from the stream and climbs to a trail junction. The left fork leads 0.3 mile to a grand overlook of the Salt Lake Valley, and the right fork continues up the canyon 1.5 miles to a small meadow.

Options

The upper meadow of Neff's Canyon gets only a fraction of the visitors to the lower canyon and adds a nice 3-mile (round-trip) extension to the hike.

Directions

From Salt Lake City drive east on I-80 for 5 miles and merge onto I-215 South. Continue 6 miles and take Exit 6 for 6200 South. Turn left at the light at the bottom of the off-ramp and drive 1.7 miles south on 6200 South/Wasatch Boulevard. Continue past the mouth of Big Cottonwood Canyon for 0.3 mile and turn left onto Prospector Drive (7780 South). Take the immediate right and drive south for 0.3 mile. Turn left onto Timberline Drive and continue for one block. Parking spots are on the right side of the road.

GPS Coordinates: N 40°61.051' W 111°78.827'

Information and Contact

There is no fee. Dogs on leash are allowed. Maps are available at the Public Lands Information Center, 3285 East 3300 South (inside REI), Salt Lake City, UT 84109, 801/466-6411. For more information, contact Salt Lake City Ranger District, Uinta-Wasatch-Cache National Forest, 125 South State Street, Salt Lake City, UT 84138, 801/236-3400, www.fs.fed.us.

13 STAIRS GULCH

Big Cottonwood Canyon, Wasatch-Cache National Forest

Level: Easy

Hiking Time: 1 hour

Total Distance: 1.25 miles round-trip

Elevation Change: 1,184 feet

Summary: A short, steep trail leads up Stairs Gulch to a series of small waterfalls.

In winter, Stairs Gulch is one of the most dangerous avalanche gullies in the entire Wasatch Range. The 4,800-foot-long gully funnels snow down its steep chute from a huge starting zone high above. During the summer, when the avalanche danger has long passed, it offers a cool, shaded hike up to a charming series of small cascades.

Stairs Gulch is directly across Big Cottonwood Canyon from the Storm Mountain Picnic Area. Storm Mountain is a popular spot for rock climbers, who scale a variety of walls clustered around the central picnic area. The trail climbs quickly and offers great views down to Storm Mountain, taking in the mountain's wildly twisted geology. This short

looking down Stairs Gulch at Storm Mountain in Big Cottonwood Canyon

outing is an excellent way to break up a Sunday drive up Big Cottonwood Canyon or to gain a new perspective on the Storm Mountain area.

The Stairs Gulch Trail starts on the south side of the road directly across from the entrance to the Storm Mountain Picnic Area. The trail leads steeply uphill from the very beginning, following an old roadbed toward the mouth of Stairs Gulch. The trail is composed of charcoal-colored slate and is lined on either side by a mix of Rocky mountain maple, Gambel oak, and fir trees. You may hear rock climbers scaling the Challenge Buttress Wall that lies just across the creek from the trail.

At 0.3 mile the trail crosses the creek and enters the bottom of Stairs Gulch. Now climbing along the west side of the creek, the trail continues to gain elevation quickly as views begin to open up down to the north side of Big Cottonwood

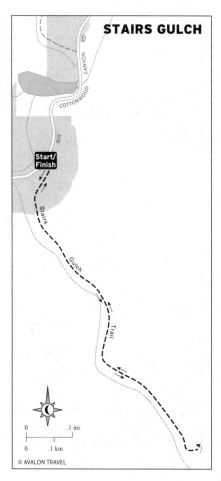

STAIRS GULCH

Start/
Finish

Stairs

Gulch

Trail

0   .1 mi
0   .1 km
© AVALON TRAVEL

Canyon. The route crosses the creek on large boulders several times in the next 0.3 mile as it negotiates the steep, narrow gully. Notice the wild hops growing in the gray gravelly soil along the trail. At 0.6 mile the trail reaches a small waterfall pouring into a small pool. This is as good a turnaround spot as any for this adventure. A faint trail continues above the waterfall up toward Twin Peaks, as Stairs Gulch is sometimes used as an alternative route to climbing the mountain from Broads Fork. However, this trail isn't maintained and doesn't present a great option when the snow has melted out, so consider making the waterfall your turnaround point and follow the trail down the way you came.

Options

Across from Stairs Gulch and Big Cottonwood Canyon Road is another short trail that's a good option if you're left looking to add on a few miles. The Mule Hollow Trail leads directly north from Big Cottonwood Canyon Road to an old, sealed-off, abandoned mine shaft. The trail is 2.2 miles round-trip and gains 1,215 feet in elevation. Find the trailhead located across Big Cottonwood Road on the other side of Big Cottonwood Creek from the Stairs Gulch Trailhead. (The trailhead is above the Storm Mountain Picnic Area on the north side of Big Cottonwood Creek.)

Directions

From Salt Lake City drive east on I-80 for 5 miles and merge onto I-215 South. Continue 6 miles and take Exit 6 for 6200 South. Turn left at the light at the bottom of the off-ramp and drive 1.7 miles south on 6200 South/Wasatch Boulevard. Turn left at the light and enter the mouth of Big Cottonwood Canyon.

Continue up Big Cottonwood Canyon Road for 2.8 miles and park on the right side of the road across from the Storm Mountain Picnic Area.
GPS Coordinates: N 40°62.381' W 111°74.318'

Information and Contact

There is no fee. Big Cottonwood Canyon is a watershed and dogs are not allowed. Maps are available at the Public Lands Information Center, 3285 East 3300 South (inside REI), Salt Lake City, UT 84109, 801/466-6411. For more information, contact Salt Lake City Ranger District, Uinta-Wasatch-Cache National Forest, 125 South State Street, Salt Lake City, UT 84138, 801/236-3400, www.fs.fed.us.

14 TWIN PEAKS OF BROADS FORK   BEST C

Big Cottonwood Canyon, Twin Peaks Wilderness,
Wasatch-Cache National Forest

Level: Butt-kicker   **Total Distance:** 8.6 miles round-trip

Hiking Time: 8-10 hours   **Elevation Change:** 5,120 feet

Summary: A challenging climb to the summit of the most prominent
mountain between Big Cottonwood Canyon and Little Cottonwood Canyon.

Rising between Little Cottonwood and Big Cottonwood Canyon, the Twin
Peaks massif stands guard over the steep, dramatic drainages that drop away to
the south and north. Twin Peaks of Broads Fork, not to be confused with the
nearby Twin Peaks of American Fork Canyon, is the highest and most prominent
peak on the eastern skyline of Salt Lake City. With an 11,330-foot East Summit,
and 11,328-foot West Summit rising nearly 7,000 feet above the valley floor,
Twin Peaks is easily recognizable from anywhere in the Salt Lake Valley. The
summit is a challenging hiking objective with a bit of scrambling across steep
rock mixed in. This exposed ridge hike shares many experiences with mountaineering, but requires no technical equipment or skills. Hikers will enjoy lofty
views in all directions, including the nearby Dromedary Peak to the east, the

looking west from the east summit of Twin Peaks to the west summit

Pfeifferhorn across Little Cottonwood Canyon to the south, and the entire Salt Lake Valley to the west.

The trail to the summit of Twin Peaks snakes up the Broads Fork drainage, starting at the busy S Curve/Mill B parking lot in Big Cottonwood Canyon. The trail is brutally steep, rising more than 5,000 feet in four short miles, although much of the elevation is gained in the last 1.5 miles as the trail climbs the Broads Fork's upper scree fields and Twin Peaks' summit ridge. The lower trail is still steep, but not any more punishing than many of the trails in the Wasatch Range.

The Broads Fork Trail starts at the far west end of the Mill B parking lot at the S Curve in Big Cottonwood Canyon. Starting through a conifer forest of spruce and fir trees, the trail heads southwest from the parking lot to reach the Broads Fork drainage. The first mile of trail is wide and sees heavy traffic. At 0.9 mile the trail reaches the cascading Broads Fork as it tumbles down through dark-colored rocks. A wide wooden bridge crosses the stream. From the bridge the trail narrows while it continues to climb relatively steeply through the forest. The evergreen trees begin to give way to mature stands of aspen before the trail breaks out into a meadow. The trail levels out briefly as it meanders through the small grass clearing. Continuing up the drainage, the route reaches a large beaver pond at

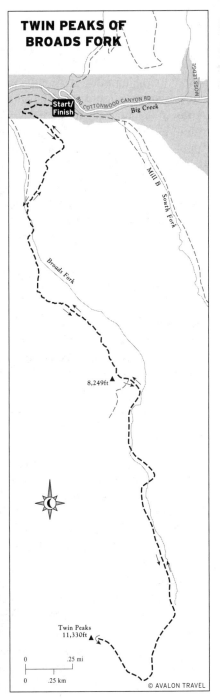

2.3 miles. This pond is classic moose habitat, so look closely for them in the thick willow trees that surround the water.

Above the beaver pond the maintained trail transitions into a sometimes-difficult-to-follow route to the summit of Twin Peaks. The rocky terrain in the cirque above the beaver ponds is dominated by large boulder fields and scree slopes. Watch carefully for rock cairns marking the path. It becomes faint in places, especially where it passes through the larger boulders. If you feel like you've wandered off the trail, continue heading up the cirque, aiming for the saddle between Twin Peaks and Dromedary Peak.

Cross the creek, leaving the pond across a haphazard collection of fallen logs, and traverse up the left side of the wetland. Now climbing into the lower part of the cirque, the trail hugs the very bottom of the V-shaped valley. Dark gray and rusty-red slate rock make up the interesting geology of this lower cirque. The slopes of Twin Peaks on the right, and Dromedary Peak on the left, are defined by steep rock walls.

Continue up through broken talus fields toward the saddle between the peaks. The best route up through the upper cirque is along the right side of the central talus field. Pick your route through the broken, often loose rock and aim for the right side of the notch. Near the top of the cirque look for a rock ledge marked by a small cairn on the right wall. Scramble carefully along this ledge to the saddle between Twin Peaks and Dromedary Peak. From this pass, which is part of the ridgeline dividing Big and Little Cottonwood Canyons, you'll be able to see the ridgeline scramble to the East Summit of Twin Peaks.

Follow the ridgeline west across black rock toward the summit. Pick your route carefully here—the ridge feels very exposed, with rock faces dropping off precipitously on both sides. The best route stays just on the south side of the ridge as it traverses across the steep terrain. Work your way over, with some easy rock climbing, or around the south side of the arête that bridges a false summit and the true summit ridge. From the top of this challenge it's a short walk up to the East Summit.

A short scramble leads across to the West Summit, which is two feet lower than the East Summit. Return carefully down the way you came.

Options

If you're looking for a blow-your-hair-back adventure and you're into exposed ridge-top scrambling, consider completing the Cottonwood Ridge Traverse. Climb Twin Peaks via the route described above and then traverse the ridge dividing Little and Big Cottonwood Canyons east. This route visits the summits of Sunrise, Dromedary, Monte Cristo, and Mount Superior, all above 11,000 feet in elevation. The route is 11.6 miles in length and sees very little traffic.

Directions

From Salt Lake City drive east on I-80 for 5 miles and merge onto I-215 South. Continue 6 miles and take Exit 6 for 6200 South. Turn left at the light at the bottom of the off-ramp and drive 1.7 miles south on 6200 South/Wasatch Boulevard. Turn left at the light and enter the mouth of Big Cottonwood Canyon. Continue up Big Cottonwood Canyon Road for 4.4 miles to the Mill B South/Lake Blanche trailhead on the right side of the road.

GPS Coordinates: N 40°63.347' W 111°72.393'

Information and Contact

There is no fee. Big Cottonwood Canyon is a watershed and dogs are not allowed. Maps are available at the Public Lands Information Center, 3285 East 3300 South (inside REI), Salt Lake City, UT 84109, 801/466-6411. For more information, contact Salt Lake City Ranger District, Uinta-Wasatch-Cache National Forest, 125 South State Street, Salt Lake City, UT 84138, 801/236-3400, www.fs.fed.us.

15 LAKE BLANCHE   BEST ◖
Big Cottonwood Canyon, Wasatch-Cache National Forest

Level: Moderate

Total Distance: 5.8 miles round-trip

Hiking Time: 3 hours

Elevation Change: 2,720 feet

Summary: Lake Blanche Trail leads to a glacial cirque filled with three picturesque alpine lakes: Lakes Blanche, Lillian, and Florence.

There was a time—most recently between 27,000 and 19,000 years ago during the last ice age—when glaciers filled the upper valleys in the Wasatch Range. Thousands of pounds of ice moved slowly down from the highest peaks, gouging out rock and sculpting the landscape into the dramatic forms we know and love today. Lake Blanche along with Lakes Lillian and Florence offer visual evidence of the sheer power of moving ice. These lakes sit at the base of a glacier-carved cirque, surrounded by rock scarred by glacier skid marks.

Looming above the water is the impressive Sundial Peak, a destination for rock climbers and mountaineers looking for challenging alpine routes. The glaciers have done beautiful work, making the Lake Blanche Trail one of the most popular trails in the Big Cottonwood Canyon, and in the Wasatch Mountains in general.

In addition to being one of the most aesthetically appealing hikes in the Wasatch, the Lake Blanche Trail is a pleasure to walk. Although it steadily gains elevation

Sundial Peak reflected in Lake Blanche

© MIKE MATSON

all the way to the lake, it's never too steep. A forest protects the lower half of the trail, providing relief from summer heat.

From the Mill B South Fork (S Curve) parking lot walk east along a paved trail next to Big Cottonwood Creek. Turn right at 0.25 mile where the Mill B South Fork joins Big Cottonwood Creek and the rocky Lake Blanche Trail branches off to the right side of the pavement. If you cross the bridge on the paved trail, you've missed the turn.

The Lake Blanche Trail crosses the creek at 0.4 mile and climbs a few short switchbacks away from the water to enter the Twin Peaks Wilderness Area. The trail remains on the east side of the creek for the rest of the hike. Salmonberries grow close to the water, and the forest starts to give way to open meadows at about 1.5 miles. Views back down the canyon begin to open up at about 1.7 miles and continue to improve as you progress toward the lake. The meadows are filled with Indian paintbrush, purple aster, and blue flax wildflowers. At 2.1 miles the trail switchbacks up the left side of the canyon across crushed gray rock. The switchbacks go through the edge of the boulder field at 2.6 miles before climbing the last 0.25 mile to the lake.

Orange, glacier-polished rocks that glow warmly in the afternoon sun surround Lake Blanche. The uniquely shaped Sundial Peak is reflected on the water's surface when it's calm. It's a

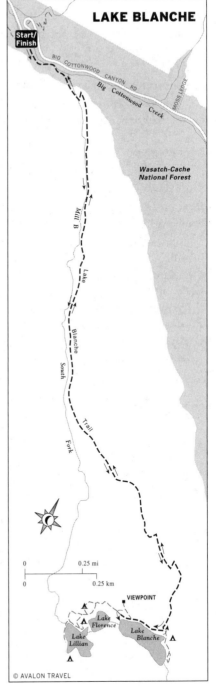

landscape photographer's dream. But you don't need a camera to appreciate this special spot. Soak in the scene before returning down the trail the way you came.

Options

Lakes Florence and Lillian aren't visible when you reach Lake Blanche. These two lakes are actually west of Lake Blanche about 200 yards down from the old dam on the lake's west end; they can be reached by hiking from the dam.

Directions

From Salt Lake City drive east on I-80 for 5 miles and take Exit 128 for I-215 South. Continue 6 miles and take Exit 6 for 6200 South. Turn left at the light at the bottom of the off-ramp and drive 1.7 miles south on 6200 South/Wasatch Boulevard. Turn left at the light and enter the mouth of Big Cottonwood Canyon. Continue up Big Cottonwood Canyon Road for 4.4 miles to the Mill B South/Lake Blanche trailhead on the right side of the road.

GPS Coordinates: N 40°63.347' W 111°72.393'

Information and Contact

There is no fee. Big Cottonwood Canyon is a watershed and dogs are not allowed. Maps are available at the Public Lands Information Center, 3285 East 3300 South (inside REI), Salt Lake City, UT 84109, 801/466-6411. For more information, contact Salt Lake City Ranger District, Uinta-Wasatch-Cache National Forest, 125 South State Street, Salt Lake City, UT 84138, 801/236-3400, www.fs.fed.us.

16 MOUNT RAYMOND VIA BUTLER FORK

Big Cottonwood Canyon, Wasatch-Cache National Forest

Level: Strenuous

Total Distance: 7.8 miles round-trip

Hiking Time: 5-6 hours

Elevation Change: 3,115 feet

Summary: A Big Cottonwood Canyon classic with panoramic views of the surrounding Wasatch Range.

When viewed from upper Big Cottonwood Canyon, Mount Raymond is one of the most commanding peaks in the canyon. Its dramatically steep southeast-facing cirque and prominent location along the Big Cottonwood Canyon/Mill Creek Canyon Ridgeline make it an attractive summit for hikers and peak baggers alike. Along the way, the trail offers outstanding views of Big Cottonwood Canyon and the major summits on the south.

By starting at the Butler Fork Trailhead, the route passes through the Walter F. Mueggler-Buter Fork Research Natural Area, a 1,270-acre area established in order to study a pristine stand of aspen. (Research scientist Walter Mueggler chose this area because it represents one of the least disturbed stands of aspen forest in the region.)

The trail up Butler Fork starts out from Big Cottonwood Canyon Road following the creek along the bottom of a steep ravine. Spruce and aspen trees provide patches of shade and the stream creates a pleasant environment with wildflowers and butterflies even in the mid-summer heat. At 0.3 mile the trail enters the Mount Olympus Wilderness Area and bends northwest through a thick stand of Engelmann's spruce trees. At 0.5 mile you'll enter a grove of mature aspen and reach a junction with a trail marker. Take the left fork here following the sign toward Dog Lake. Keep an eye out for moose throughout this section of trail, especially along the stream. Moose are frequently seen here stripping the leaves off the young aspen and willow trees growing near the water. This is also a likely spot to hear or see wild turkeys, which lend their name to nearby peak Gobbler's Knob.

Continue uphill to the west as the trail gradually becomes steeper, ascending through the aspen forest. At 0.8 mile the dirt path banks through a series of switchbacks before opening up to a nice view of upper Big Cottonwood Canyon. Columbine, lupine, and Indian paintbrush grow on either side of the trail. At 1.3 miles the trail gains a ridge and Mount Raymond comes into clear view to the west. A trail junction offers options left or right; turn right to continue towards Mount Raymond. (The left fork leads 0.2 mile to 8,707-foot Circle All Peak.) Walk the forested ridgeline to the northwest for 0.3 mile (1.5 miles from the trailhead)

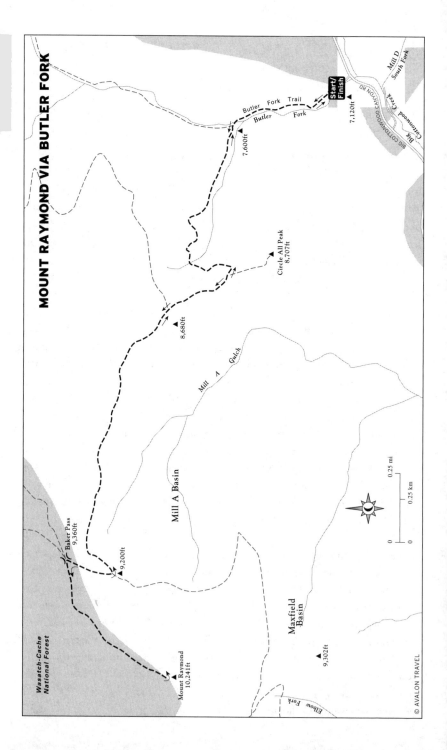

MOUNT RAYMOND VIA BUTLER FORK

Start/Finish
7,120ft

Mill D South Fork
Mill Creek
Big Cottonwood Canyon Rd
Big Cottonwood

Butler Fork Trail
Butler Fork
7,600ft

Circle All Peak
8,707ft

8,680ft

Mill A Gulch

Mill A Basin

Baker Pass
9,360ft
9,200ft

Wasatch-Cache
National Forest

Mount Raymond
10,241ft

Maxfield Basin

9,302ft

Elbow Fork

0   0.25 mi
0   0.25 km

© AVALON TRAVEL

Butler Fork Trail leading to Mount Raymond

to another trail junction. At this junction, take the left trail continuing towards Mount Raymond and Mill A Basin, the open cirque below the peak.

At 2.6 miles you'll emerge from the forest on the right side of Mill A Basin and another fork in the trail. Take the right fork and ascend 0.2 mile to Baker Pass, between the summits of Gobbler's Knob and Mount Raymond. From this pass, turn left and follow Mount Raymond's steep ridgeline to the southwest towards the summit. The ridge walk sports satisfying views northwest into Mill Creek Canyon. Limber pine and subalpine fir trees grow along the windswept divide. The trail grows faint as you climb closer to the summit. Follow the mountain's rocky spine closely, ducking around fir trees and scrambling across the protruding rocks. The final 0.25-mile to summit is exposed and can be windy on all but the calmest days, but the 360-degree views are worth the effort. Views extend from downtown Salt Lake City to Mill Creek Canyon and Big Cottonwood Canyon from this well-earned vantage point. Enjoy the summit and retrace your steps down the way you came.

Options

Leave a car at the Mill B South/Lake Blanche trailhead to make this a mostly one-way hike. As you descend from the summit to Baker Pass, turn right and retrace your steps. At the trail junction 0.2 mile downhill from Baker Pass, turn right instead of left and hike south through Mill A Basin. Continue 1.3 miles down through the cirque and turn left at the trail junction. Descend another 3.5

miles to the Mill B South/Lake Blanche Trailhead. This one-way option offers a 10.5-mile hike with the same 3,115 feet in elevation gain. It loses an additional 1,000 feet of elevation on the descent because the Mill B South/Lake Blanche Trailhead is lower on Big Cottonwood Road.

For the Mill B South/Lake Blanche Trailhead, drive 4.4 miles up Big Cotton-wood Canyon Road to the Mill B South/Lake Blanche Trailhead on the right side of the road.

Directions

From Salt Lake City drive east on I-80 for 5 miles and merge onto I-215 south. Continue another 6 miles and take Exit 6 for 6200S. Turn left at the light at the bottom of the off-ramp and drive 1.7 miles south on 6200S/Wasatch Boulevard. Turn left at the light to enter the mouth of Big Cottonwood Canyon. Continue up Big Cottonwood Canyon Road for 8 miles to the trailhead on the left side of the road. Park in the small pull-out at the trailhead.

GPS Coordinates: N 40°64.931' W 111°66.182'

Information and Contact

There is no fee. Big Cottonwood Canyon is a watershed and dogs are not allowed. Maps are available at the Public Lands Information Center, 3285 East 3300 South (inside REI), Salt Lake City, Utah 84109, 801/466-6411. For more information, contact Salt Lake City Ranger District, Uinta-Wasatch-Cache National Forest, 125 South State Street, Salt Lake City, UT 84138, 801/236-3400, www.fs.fed.us.

17 DESOLATION LAKE VIA MILL D NORTH FORK

Big Cottonwood Canyon, Wasatch-Cache National Forest

Level: Moderate

Total Distance: 7.2 miles round-trip

Hiking Time: 3-4 hours

Elevation Change: 2,188 feet

Summary: Tucked away in one of the quietest corners of Big Cottonwood Canyon's upper valleys, Desolation Lake is surrounded by wildflowers and frequented by wildlife.

The mountains between Big Cottonwood Canyon and Mill Creek Canyon are flanked by gentle slopes and lush, aspen-bordered meadows. The trail up Mill D North Fork to Desolation Lake visits a series of these lovely meadows, where moose forage among wildflowers and wade through beaver ponds. If spotting a moose in the Wasatch is on your to-do list, there's no better place to start than here. Desolation Lake can be reached by a number of routes from both canyons, but the Mill D Trail offers a scenic, straightforward option.

The Mill D North Fork Trail heads uphill from the paved roadside lot on Big Cottonwood Road. The trail runs parallel to the road for the first 0.5 mile, moving

Indian paintbrush blooms in front of Desolation Lake in Big Cottonwood Canyon

across dirt and small limestone rocks. It passes through thick Gambel oak and then a mature evergreen forest. At 0.5 mile the trail wraps around the corner to the left and heads north up the Mill D North Fork drainage. As the trail climbs up the canyon, it passes through a stand of ponderosa pine trees, which are rare in the Wasatch Range.

During the pioneer era the tributaries to Big Cottonwood Creek were harnessed for steam-powered sawmills to provide timber for Salt Lake Valley homes. Moving west to east up the canyon, these streams were simply named Mill A, B, C, and D. As the need for timber in the valley grew, mills were constructed farther up the canyon until they reached Mill D. Mill D was constructed in the summer

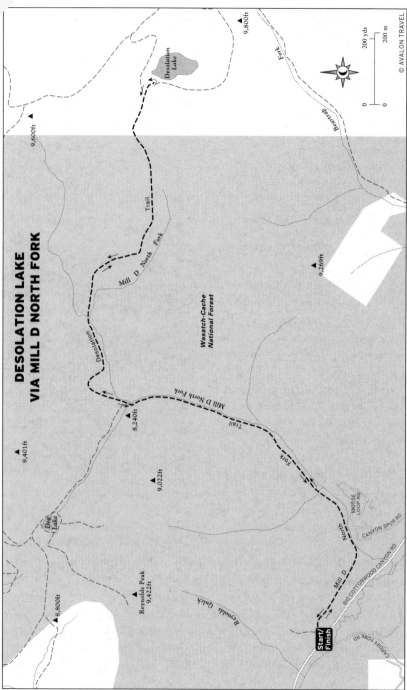

DESOLATION LAKE
VIA MILL D NORTH FORK

of 1856. The slopes of the Mill D North Fork Valley were logged for timber for the next 30 years.

Mill D is now home to a collection of cabins built starting in 1946. These cabins are on lots of Forest Service land and are across the stream from the trail. At 1.2 miles the trail drops down to the North Fork stream. You'll notice the trail merges here with a trail coming down from the cabins. Watch for deer hiding and grazing in thick undergrowth along the creek. At 1.75 miles you'll reach a trail junction with the Desolation Trail. Turn right to continue to Desolation Lake; note that Dog Lake can be reached by turning left.

The next 0.25 mile is the steepest section of the trail. The short climb brings you to an aspen-cloaked knoll, where views open up momentarily across Big Cottonwood Canyon. The grade levels off as the trail continues through mature aspen before opening up into a broad meadow. Look closely for moose in this meadow and in the small meadows farther up the trail. Circling around the meadow, the trail continues its gentle ascent toward Desolation Lake.

Options

This route to Desolation Lake can be turned into a loop trip by descending the 2.5-mile-long trail in Bear Trap Fork to Big Cottonwood Canyon Road. Parking a car shuttle at Silver Fork will allow for a one-way trip.

Directions

From Salt Lake City drive east on I-80 for 5 miles and take Exit 128 for I-215 South. Continue 6 miles and take Exit 6 for 6200 South. Turn left at the light at the bottom of the off-ramp and drive 1.7 miles south on 6200 South/Wasatch Boulevard. Turn left at the light and enter the mouth of Big Cottonwood Canyon (SR 190). Continue up Big Cottonwood Canyon Road for 9 miles. The trailhead will be on the left side of the road.

GPS Coordinates: N 40°64.988' W 111°64.817'

Information and Contact

There is no fee. Big Cottonwood Canyon is a watershed and dogs are not allowed. Maps are available at the Public Lands Information Center, 3285 East 3300 South (inside REI), Salt Lake City, UT 84109, 801/466-6411. For more information, contact Salt Lake City Ranger District, Uinta-Wasatch-Cache National Forest, 125 South State Street, Salt Lake City, UT 84138, 801/236-3400, www.fs.fed.us.

18 DOUGHNUT FALLS   BEST ◖

Big Cottonwood Canyon, Wasatch-Cache National Forest

Level: Easy   **Total Distance:** 1.5 miles round-trip

Hiking Time: 1 hour   **Elevation Change:** 360 feet

Summary: The unique feature of Doughnut Falls is a Big Cottonwood Canyon classic perfect for kids of all ages!

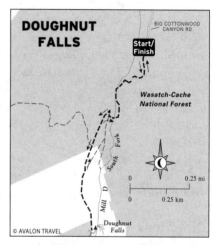

You've never seen a waterfall quite like Doughnut Falls. The cascade pours over a limestone ledge and falls directly through a doughnut-shaped hole that's been eroded from the rock. From the right angle with just the perfect amount of water, the creek appears to completely disappear inside the chasm.

The short hike to reach the falls has an easy grade, making it perfect for children or anyone looking for a relaxing stroll in the woods. Moose are frequently sighted near the trailhead, further adding to the hike's appeal.

Leaving the trailhead, a wide dirt path heads up the Mill D South Fork drainage through an aspen and spruce forest. In summer, hummingbirds buzz through the air in the meadows. At 0.4 mile the trail takes a hard right and crosses the creek to join an unpaved road. Just 0.1 mile farther, take the left fork in the road and the trail will drop abruptly down into a rock gully. The doughnut formation lies at the top of this gray limestone gorge. Working your way up to the intriguing falls takes some scrambling and shouldn't be attempted by young children. At higher water levels, like those found in spring or early summer, the rocks can be wet from spray created by the waterfall. If these conditions exist, it may be too dangerous to reach the doughnut part of the falls. But if conditions are safe, clamoring up there can be a really cool experience. The water pours directly through a 10-foot-wide circle in the rock and splashes down into a pool inside a cave below the hole. To reach the upper falls, cross the stream and scramble up the right side of the gully. If the water levels are high, it's possible to hike up the right side of the falls to gain a view of the doughnut hole from above. Take the steep trail leading up through the forest on the right side of the gorge, and work your way along the edge of the cliff until you can see the falls from above.

Options

It's possible to continue up the Mill D South Trail from Doughnut Falls to Cardiff Pass. The trail to the pass is 3.5 miles one way and passes by the site of the historic Cardiff Mine at 2.5 miles.

Directions

From Salt Lake City drive east on I-80 for 5 miles and merge onto I-215 South. Continue 6 miles and take Exit 6 for 6200 South. Turn left at the light at the bottom of the off-ramp and drive 1.7

Doughnut Falls pours through the doughnut hole in Cardiff Fork

© MIKE MATSON

miles south on 6200 South/Wasatch Boulevard. Turn left at the light and enter the mouth of Big Cottonwood Canyon. Continue up Big Cottonwood Canyon Road for 9 miles and turn right and continue 0.8 mile to the trailhead parking area.
GPS Coordinates: N 40°63.920' W 111°65.132'

Information and Contact

There is no fee. Big Cottonwood Canyon is a watershed and dogs are not allowed. Maps are available at the Public Lands Information Center, 3285 East 3300 South (inside REI), Salt Lake City, UT 84109, 801/466-6411. For more information, contact Salt Lake City Ranger District, Uinta-Wasatch-Cache National Forest, 125 South State Street, Salt Lake City, UT 84138, 801/236-3400.

19 WILLOW HEIGHTS
Big Cottonwood Canyon, Uinta-Wasatch-Cache National Forest

Level: Easy

Hiking Time: 1 hour

Total Distance: 2.0 miles round-trip

Elevation Change: 700 feet

Summary: A quiet walk on a lightly traveled trail reaches an open meadow and small lake.

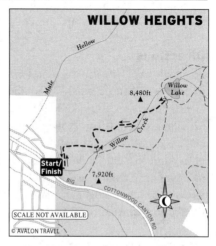

Among the gently sloping meadows found above the small community of Silver Fork on the northeast side of Big Cottonwood Canyon is a lovely little mountain lake called Willow Lake. Aptly named, Willow Lake is surrounded on three sides by thick vegetation, attracting moose and other wildlife. The open slopes of Solitude Ski Area are reflected on the lake's surface on calm days, creating a picturesque setting. This is an easy hike and quiet spot—the perfect outing for young kids or hikers looking for a relaxing walk in the woods.

Reaching the unmarked Willow Heights trail requires walking through a quiet neighborhood; park along Big Cottonwood Canyon and be respectful of the neighbors who live beside the trailhead.

From the pull-off parking area on Big Cottonwood Canyon Road, head northeast across the road and up Moose Tracks Lane 11430 East. Walk up a block and turn right onto Mountain Sun Lane 6490 South. Continue to the end of Mountain Sun Lane, where the pavement ends and the trail to Willow Heights begins. The trail isn't marked, but signs at the trailhead reading Conservation Area and Please Stay on Trail will indicate that you're in the right place.

The dirt path leads through an open grove of quaking aspen. The occasional granite boulder dots the trail, but the grade is mellow and the walking is easy. Young white pine trees grow among the aspen, and small clumps of wildflowers provide splashes of color. Utah wild pea, scarlet gilia, and lupine stand out as frequently seen flowers. Hummingbirds buzz through the air, attracted to the red

© MIKE MATSON

the peaks of Honeycomb Canyon and quaking aspen trees reflected in the waters of Willow Lake

blossoms on the scarlet gilia. At 0.4 mile from Big Cottonwood Road, the trail nears Willow Creek. Mountain bluebells grow in the thick brush along the water's edge. At 0.8 mile the trail reaches the first in a series of open meadows and crosses Willow Creek. Look for deer and moose tracks here at the shallow stream crossing. In less than 0.1 mile the trail enters a much larger meadow. At the top of the meadow, the trail forks; the left fork leads to Willow Lake and the right fork leads to a campsite above, overlooking the meadow. Going left, the trail ducks down quickly through a stand of willows and then to the small lake. Ducks swim on the lake's quiet waters, and signs of both beaver and moose are easy to spot. Early morning and or late evening are the best times to see either of these residents.

Options
From Willow Lake the trail can be followed another 0.8 mile to the northeast to Dry Lake.

Directions
From Salt Lake City drive east on I-80 for 5 miles and merge onto I-215 South. Continue 6 miles and take Exit 6 for 6200 South. Turn left at the light at the bottom of the off-ramp and drive 1.7 miles south on 6200 South/Wasatch Boulevard. Turn left at the light and enter the mouth of Big Cottonwood Canyon (SR 190).

Continue up Big Cottonwood Canyon Road for 11.3 miles and park on the right side of the road, 0.2 mile past the Silver Fork Lodge.
GPS Coordinates: N 40°63.315' W 111°60.960'

Information and Contact

There is no fee. Big Cottonwood Canyon is a watershed and dogs are not allowed. Maps are available at the Public Lands Information Center, 3285 East 3300 South (inside REI), Salt Lake City, UT 84109, 801/466-6411. For more information, contact Salt Lake City Ranger District, Uinta-Wasatch-Cache National Forest, 125 South State Street, Salt Lake City, UT 84138, 801/236-3400, www.fs.fed.us.

20 SILVER LAKE
Big Cottonwood Canyon, Wasatch-Cache National Forest

Level: Easy

Total Distance: 0.8 mile round-trip

Hiking Time: 30 minutes

Elevation Change: 30 feet

Summary: Silver Lake is Big Cottonwood Canyon's easy access mountain park – a popular place to spend an afternoon with a fishing pole or reading a book in the shade of the forest.

Silver Lake is a natural mountain lake at the top of Big Cottonwood Canyon nestled between Solitude and Brighton ski areas. A boardwalk trail with interpretive signs circles the lake and explores the wetland environment on the lake's northern shoreline. The lake becomes **Solitude Mountain Resort's Nordic Center** (www.skisolitude.com) during winter.

Although Silver Lake has an undeniably developed feel compared with most of the hikes covered in this area, its easy access and mountain setting

make it a very popular hike. Anglers and families come here to enjoy the beautiful mountain environment.

The short, level boardwalk trail loops around the lake's shoreline. If you plan on hiking up to Lake Solitude or Twin Lakes Reservoir, head right from the trailhead along the northwest shore of the lake. If not, then both directions are equally attractive. The trail is wide and easy to follow. The entire loop around the lake is a mile long. To reach the fishing pier head left from the trailhead; the pier is 0.2 mile down the boardwalk from the trailhead. Continuing down the south side of the lake you'll leave the boardwalk and enter the woods at 0.3 mile. There's a popular spot for fishing at 0.4 mile where the lake can be accessed from the shore.

Options

For hikers looking for a more challenging hike, separate trails extend to Lake Solitude (2.5 miles) and Twin Lakes Reservoir (1 mile) from Silver Lake's northwest shore.

Silver Lake

Directions

From Salt Lake City drive east on I-80 for 5 miles and merge onto I-215 South. Continue 6 miles and take Exit 6 for 6200 South. Turn left at the light at the bottom of the off-ramp and drive 1.7 miles south on 6200 South/Wasatch Boulevard. Turn left at the light and enter the mouth of Big Cottonwood Canyon. Continue up Big Cottonwood Canyon Road for 14.5 miles to the Solitude Mountain Resort Nordic Center.

GPS Coordinates: N 40°60.337' W 111°58.553'

Information and Contact

There is no fee. Big Cottonwood Canyon is a watershed and dogs are not allowed. Maps are available at the Public Lands Information Center, 3285 East 3300 South (inside REI), Salt Lake City, UT 84109, 801/466-6411. For more information, contact Salt Lake City Ranger District, Uinta-Wasatch-Cache National Forest, 125 South State Street, Salt Lake City, UT 84138, 801/236-3400, www.fs.fed.us.

21 BRIGHTON LAKES TRAIL   BEST C

Big Cottonwood Canyon, Wasatch-Cache National Forest

Level: Moderate   **Total Distance:** 4.6 miles round-trip

Hiking Time: 3 hours   **Elevation Change:** 1,594 feet

Summary: The Brighton Lakes Trail is one of the Central Wasatch's best hikes to a series of alpine lakes. As the trail climbs, the crowds thin and the lakes become more and more picturesque.

At the top of Big Cottonwood Canyon, tucked into the steep rocky terrain and hidden from view from the road, sits a chain of sparkling alpine lakes. Like steps on a giant staircase, Dog, Mary, Martha, and Catherine Lakes offer hikers progressively more impressive rewards as they explore farther up the trail. This trail is particularly enjoyable in autumn, when aspens growing in scattered clumps between huge gray granite boulders stand out in bright pockets of orange and gold. Although this is one of Big Cottonwood Canyon's most popular hikes, the crowds thin as the elevation and miles mount, leaving serenity at Catherine Lake on all but the busiest summer weekends.

The Brighton Lakes Trail begins beneath the Majestic and Crest Express chairlifts of Brighton Ski Resort. The trail's first segment is wide and well traveled, ascending through open ski slopes. After this initial 0.6-mile stretch, the path narrows as it ducks into a canopy of subalpine fir and leaves the human-altered ski resort behind. A few minutes after entering the forest, a signed junction points to a spur trail for Dog Lake. This short side trip leads to a quaint, pond-sized lake and wetland. Back on the main trail, the path follows the outlet stream for Lake Mary up through an uneven talus field and around a short dam. The reward upon arrival at Lake Mary is a breathtaking scene. The lake is surrounded by three towering peaks: Mount Millicent, Mount Wolverine, and Mount Tuscarora. The lake fills the bottom of a granite bowl, with mounds of fractured rock forming the uneven shoreline. On calm days, the glassy lake surface provides ample opportunities for landscape photographs.

Continuing up the trail along the left side of the lake, hikers will soon arrive at Lake Martha, tucked tightly into a deep bowl surrounded by forest and steep mountains. Lake Martha is protected by heavy vegetation—a favorite food source of Big Cottonwood Canyon's moose population. Look closely around the lake: When we visited in the early evening, a bull moose quietly hid in the dense underbrush by the lake's edge until we headed farther up the trail. Comfortable we were out of sight, the moose ventured out into the shallow lake to feed. From

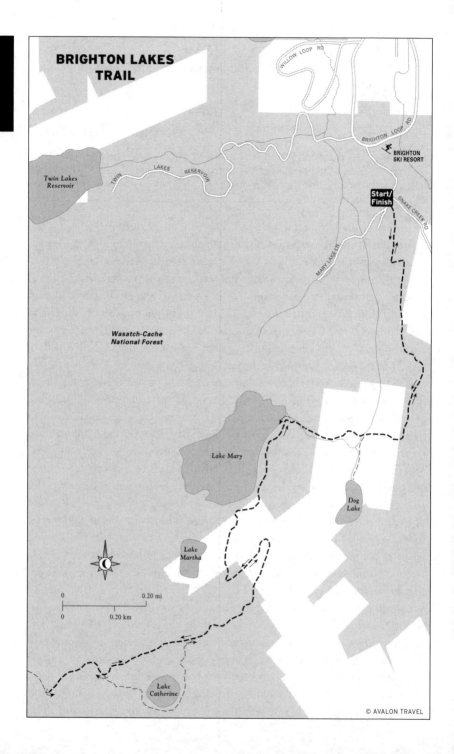

BRIGHTON LAKES TRAIL

WILLOW LOOP RD

BRIGHTON LOOP RD

BRIGHTON SKI RESORT

Twin Lakes Reservoir

TWIN LAKES RESERVOIR

Start/Finish

SNAKE CREEK RD

MARY LAKE LN

Wasatch-Cache National Forest

Lake Mary

Dog Lake

Lake Martha

0   0.20 mi
0   0.20 km

Lake Catherine

© AVALON TRAVEL

© MIKE MATSON

Mount Tuscarora reflected in Lake Mary on the Brighton Lakes Trail

Lake Martha the trail ascends steeply upward via a series of switchbacks to an exposed rocky ridge. From this vantage point excellent views extend back down to the lakes below. The trail forks at the ridge. Head left at the junction to reach Lake Catherine, this trail's crown jewel of alpine glory. The steep-sided Sunset Peak tumbles into the lake in rock talus fields. In early to midsummer, snowfields cling to the surrounding mountainsides. Look west toward Catherine Pass crossing the crest into Albion Basin and the upper reaches of Little Cottonwood Canyon.

Options

The Brighton Lakes Trail presents several options beyond the three lakes on the main trail. Dog Lake, the first side trail, offers a 500-yard diversion and is easily included with the three other main lakes in this chain. At Lake Mary, it's possible for hikers to head northwest for 1.1 miles to Twin Lakes Reservoir, on the opposite side of Mount Millicent. Finally, for hikers looking for a longer adventure, the trail continues for 2 miles on past Catherine Lake, through Catherine Pass and into Albion Basin. By leaving a car at the Albion Basin Road parking lot, hikers can make this a one-way trip and descend down Little Cottonwood Canyon.

Directions

From Salt Lake City drive east on I-80 for 5 miles and merge onto I-215 South. Continue 6 miles and take Exit 6 for 6200 South. Turn left at the light at the bottom of the off-ramp and drive 1.7 miles south on 6200 South/Wasatch Boulevard.

Turn left at the light and enter the mouth of Big Cottonwood Canyon. Continue up Big Cottonwood Canyon Road for 14.1 miles to Brighton Ski Area. The trailhead is in front of the Brighton Ski Resort.

GPS Coordinates: N 40°59.781' W 111°58.371'

Information and Contact

There is no fee. Big Cottonwood Canyon is a watershed and dogs are not allowed. Maps are available at the Public Lands Information Center, 3285 East 3300 South (inside REI), Salt Lake City, UT 84109, 801/466-6411. For more information, contact Salt Lake City Ranger District, Uinta-Wasatch-Cache National Forest, 125 South State Street, Salt Lake City, UT 84138, 801/236-3400, www.fs.fed.us.

22 GUARDSMAN PASS TO CLAYTON PEAK
Big Cottonwood Canyon, Wasatch-Cache National Forest

Level: Moderate

Total Distance: 2.5 miles round-trip

Hiking Time: 2-3 hours

Elevation Change: 1,430 feet

Summary: A high-elevation ridge walk along the crest of the Wasatch to the summit of Clayton Peak.

On paper, the trail from Guardsman Pass to Clayton Peak almost looks too good to be true. It's only 1.25 miles to the top of a 10,721-foot peak with commanding views of the Wasatch Range. The trail couldn't be much of a challenge, could it? Well, it is challenging, but this section of the Great Western Trail—which follows the Wasatch Crest along its north-to-south axis— is still one of the easiest hikes to the top of the Wasatch.

Clayton Peak sits on the eastern edge of the Big and Little Cottonwood Canyon's highest terrain. The perspective from Clayton's elevated summit helps tie together the geography seen so often from both the Salt

GUARDSMAN PASS TO CLAYTON PEAK

Start/Finish ▲ 9,880ft

Bloods Lake

▲ 10,420ft

Natural Spring

Wasatch Mountain State Park

Lackawaxen Lake

Wasatch-Cache National Forest

▲ Clayton Peak 10,721ft

0   0.25 mi

0   0.25 km

© AVALON TRAVEL

Lake City and Park City sides of the mountains. Straddling the dividing line between two distinctly different-feeling sides of the range, this view is like the final puzzle piece in a local's mental map of Salt Lake City's intimately loved mountains.

From the pull-off parking area at Guardsman Pass, the path to the 10,721-foot Clayton Peak starts off steep and rocky. The trail gains almost 1,500 feet in 1.25 miles, so go slowly and enjoy the view. Before reaching Clayton the trail climbs to the top of the peak known simply by its elevation—10,420. For this first 0.8-mile section the route ducks in and out of clumps of evergreens, mostly Engelmann spruce and subalpine fir. From the outset, this hike is all about the views, with open vistas to east and west. In the large alpine cirque to the east, a collection of mountain lakes sparkle blue in a blanket of green. The five closest lakes are known as the Blood Lakes, with the larger Silver Lake and Lake Brimhall farther east. To the west, the upper bowls of Big Cottonwood Canyons are visible, including the slopes of Solitude and Brighton Ski Resorts.

In midsummer this trail is buzzing with the sound of insects' wings. Butterflies are everywhere, and bees and hummingbirds cruise back and forth between clumps of wildflowers. At 0.5 mile the trail reaches the saddle and crosses over to the west side of the ridge. Beautiful limber pine trees grow along the ridge here, and the trail momentarily levels off. After traversing the west side of 10,420, the trail returns to the east side of the ridge. A trail comes up from the valley and joins the Great Western Trail at 0.75 mile. Stay right here to continue up Clayton Peak. At 0.9 mile the trail literally becomes a ridge walk, following the brown-and-gray rock spine of Clayton's lower ridge. Follow the trail as closely as you can as it weaves through the boulders. Before reaching the summit, you'll notice the top of the Great Western Express chairlift of Brighton Ski Resort below the trail.

Although many summits in the Wasatch Mountains offer sweeping views, the top of Clayton Peak is a particularly good place from which to comprehend the geography of the range. Views extend to landmarks in every direction, from the Heber Valley to the east, to Mount Superior in Little Cottonwood Canyon to the west, to Mount Timpanogos to the south. In a range surrounded by development and blanketed by ski areas, there's something particularly satisfying about seeing it all from such a wild vantage point.

the chairlift at Brighton Ski Resort, near the summit of Clayton Peak

© MIKE MATSON

Options

At 0.8 mile from the Guardsman Pass, a side trail leads 0.5 mile east down to the Blood Lakes.

Directions

From Salt Lake City drive east on I-80 for 5 miles and merge onto I-215 South. Continue 6 miles and take Exit 6 for 6200 South. Turn left at the light at the bottom of the off-ramp and drive 1.7 miles south on 6200 South/Wasatch Boulevard. Turn left at the light and enter the mouth of Big Cottonwood Canyon. Continue up Big Cottonwood Canyon Road for 13.8 miles and turn left onto Guardsman Pass Road. Continue 3 miles to the top of Guardsman Pass; the dirt parking area is on the right side of the road.

GPS Coordinates: N 40°60.521' W 111°55.620'

Information and Contact

There is no fee. Big Cottonwood Canyon is a watershed and dogs are not allowed. Maps are available at the Public Lands Information Center, 3285 East 3300 South (inside REI), Salt Lake City, UT 84109, 801/466-6411. For more information, contact Salt Lake City Ranger District, Uinta-Wasatch-Cache National Forest, 125 South State Street, Salt Lake City, UT 84138, 801/236-3400, www.fs.fed.us.

23 MID MOUNTAIN TRAIL
Park City

🏃 🐎

Level: Moderate

Total Distance: 11.5 miles round-trip

Hiking Time: 7-8 hours

Elevation Change: 1,512 feet

Summary: Park City's Mid Mountain Trail isn't so much about the destination as the journey.

The Mid Mountain Trail, sometimes called the 8,000-foot trail, approximately follows the 8,000-foot contour across the eastern side of the Wasatch Range above the town of Park City. Park City's mountains are blanketed by ski resorts, and the Mid Mountain Trail cuts right through the middle of all three: Deer Valley, Park City, and Canyons. Because it traverses the mountains, rather than climbing them, the trail offers a unique way to experience these resorts in the summer. Along the way it passes by old mining operations, under ski lifts, and by multimillion-dollar hotels. This is not your typical Wasatch Mountain trail.

In total, the Mid Mountain Trail snakes across 18.8 miles of terrain. Because that's a very long day hike, I've picked an 11-mile out-and-back section leading to an overlook of downtown Park City. This section starts at the Silver Lake Lodge in Deer Valley Resort and ends at a bench with a view in Park City Ski Area—the

overlooking Park City from the Park City Ski Area

© MIKE MATSON

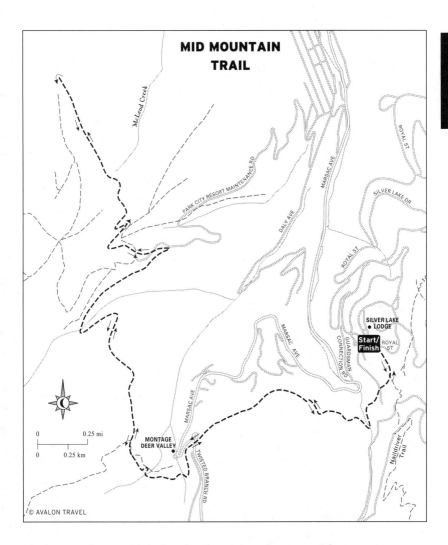

perfect spot for a mid-hike lunch. The trail can be accessed from many spots in Park City, so feel free to create your own adventure!

Starting at the parking lot for Silver Lake Lodge, walk by the right side of the lodge, past the right side of the Sterling Express chairlift, and down the gravel road to the right. The Mid Mountain Trail starts on the left side of the dirt road about 100 yards downhill from the Sterling lift.

Buffed smooth by thousands of mountain-bike tires, you won't find a better hiking surface than the Mid Mountain Trail. That also means that bikers ride this trail all the time, so be ready for them to come around the corner at any moment. The trail is intersected by dirt ski-area service roads, the first one coming at 0.8 mile. Head up the road 100 feet and rejoin the path on the road's right side. The trail alternates between open ski slopes and a mixed forest of aspen and spruce. At 1.25 miles you'll reach the first of many signed trail junctions; follow the signs for the Mid Mountain Trail.

At 2.4 miles the trail traverses around the huge, luxurious Montage Deer Valley hotel at the base of the Empire chairlift. Take the right fork in the trail and stay on the lower trail. The next mile winds through a mature grove of aspens. You'll cross another maintenance road at 4.2 miles. Then at 4.9 miles you'll follow a dirt road downhill for 100 yards under a ski lift before rejoining the single track on the left side of the road. At 5.2 miles you'll follow a dirt road uphill for about the same distance. At 5.6 miles the trail breaks out onto the open Crescent Ridge in Park City Mountain Resort. You'll see a bench on the right side of the trail, which offers a nice spot to enjoy a break and take in the commanding view of downtown Park City and the surrounding mountains. This is also a good place to turn around and head back.

Options

During the summer months, **Deer Valley Resort** (2250 Deer Valley Dr. South, 435/649-1000, www.deervalley.com) offers chairlift-served mountain biking trails. The trail system includes routes suitable for all kinds of riders—from beginner to expert. With full-suspension mountain bikes available for rent at Silver Lake Lodge (7600 Royal St.), you won't find a more convenient or high-quality introduction to mountain biking anywhere. A full-day bike pass for the chairlift costs $36.

Directions

From Salt Lake City drive east on I-80 for 21.6 miles to Exit 145 for Kimball Junction. From the exit ramp turn right onto SR 224 and drive 5.8 miles. Turn left onto Deer Valley Drive and continue 1.1 miles to the traffic circle. Take the second exit out of the circle for Marsac Avenue and continue 1.9 miles. Turn left onto the Guardsman Connection road and continue 0.3 mile to Royal Street. Turn right on Royal Street and drive 0.2 mile; park in the lot for Silver Lake Lodge on the right side of the road.
GPS Coordinates: N 40°62.275' W 111°48.934'

Information and Contact

There is no fee. Dogs are allowed on leash. A trail map is available online (www.parkcity.org). For more information, contact the Park City Municipal Corporation, 445 Marsac, Park City, UT 84060, 435/615-5001, www.parkcity.org.

24 LOST PROSPECTOR
Park City

🏕 🦌 ✈

Level: Moderate

Total Distance: 4.3 miles one-way

Hiking Time: 2.5-3 hours

Elevation Change: 328 feet

Summary: Lost Prospector offers an easy-access, low-elevation trail that traverses across Masonic Hill, just east of Main Street in Park City.

This Park City backyard trail is an autumn classic. Quaking aspen, Gambel oak, and Rocky Mountain maple trees line the trail and turn red, orange, and yellow in September and October. Traversing right above town, the trail's relatively low elevation keeps it free of early-season snow. Popular with beginner mountain bikers for its gentle grade, the trail is an unintimidating outing for hikers of all types.

Birders might spot black-billed magpies, white crowned sparrows, western meadowlarks, and horned larks in the mixed sagebrush and forest environments along the rolling hillside. The trail offers views down Main Street in historic Park City, and across the valley to the slopes of Park City Mountain Resort.

The trail is best hiked as a one-way excursion, parking a vehicle at both ends. From the small parking lot at Prospector Park, walk east along the paved path for 0.1 mile until it merges with the wider Rail Trail. Continue east on the Rail Trail for 0.6 mile. Despite the Rail Trail's proximity to the Kearns Boulevard, an excellent wildlife-watching opportunity presents itself. Between the trail and the road several beaver ponds with a large beaver lodge can be easily spotted. Just before you cross the bridge, look for the brown flexi-pole sign marking the Skid Row Trail. Turn right at the sign following the dirt path into the woods. Skid Row hardly lives up to its ominous name. Winding up through a maple and oak forest, the trail switchbacks gently back and forth, slowly gaining elevation. Mountain bikers usually ride the trail and this is their descent, so be aware that they could come around a corner at any time.

At 1.3 miles the trail reaches a junction with a trail sign. Take the right fork here, following the sign for Lost Prospector. The trail levels off, having already done most of its climbing. The dirt path rolls up and down, traversing the ridge westward above Park City High School. At 2.4 miles you'll reach another signed junction; continue straight to stay on the Lost Prospector Trail. Views open up 2–3 miles down to the high school and west toward downtown Park City. At 3.5 miles there is another trail junction; again continue straight, following the sign for the Lost Prospector Trail. This is the beginning of a beautiful stretch of trail through an aspen grove. At 3.8 miles views look down over Main Street to the ski slopes of Park City Mountain Resort. The trail ends at 4.3 miles on Aerie Drive.

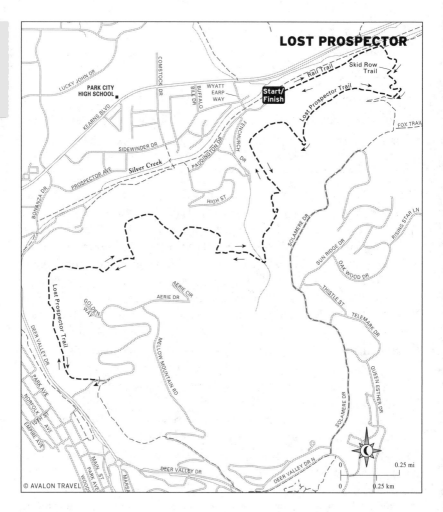

Options

It's possible to make a loop trip out of Lost Prospector by descending Aerie Drive, turning left, and following Deer Valley Drive to the Rail Trail. Then turn right on the Rail Trail and follow it back to Prospector Park.

Directions

To the Prospector Park trailhead: From Salt Lake City drive east on I-80 for 27 miles to Exit 146 and merge onto U.S. Highway 40 headed east. Continue 3.8 miles to Exit 4 for Park City. Turn right off the exit ramp onto Kearns Boulevard and drive 1.7 miles. Turn left on Wyatt Earp Way and turn left again into Prospector Park (2500 Wyatt Earp Way).

GPS Coordinates: N 40°66.804' W 111°48.543'

Lost Prospector Trail in Park City

To the Aerie Drive trailhead: From Salt Lake City drive east on I-80 for 23.5 miles to Exit 145 for Kimball Junction. Turn right off the freeway ramp onto State Route 224 and continue for 5.8 miles to Park City. Turn left onto Deer Valley Drive and drive 0.7 mile to Aerie Drive. Turn left on Aerie Drive and drive 0.2 mile to a small parking area on the right side of the road. The trail is across the street on the left side of the road.

GPS Coordinates: N 40°65.054' W 111°49.678'

Information and Contact

There is no fee. Dogs are allowed on leash. A map of the trail is available at the town of Park City's website. For more information contact the Park City Municipal Corporation, 445 Marsac, Park City, UT 84060, 435/615-5001, www.parkcity.org.

25 BELLS CANYON   BEST 【

Little Cottonwood Canyon, Wasatch-Cache National Forest

Level: Butt-kicker | **Total Distance:** 8.3 miles round-trip
Hiking Time: 6-8 hours | **Elevation Change:** 5,040 feet

Summary: A granite-walled canyon leads to a scenic waterfall, with the challenging option to continue to the Upper Bells Canyon Reservoir.

From the speeding traffic of cars cruising past on Wasatch Boulevard in Sandy to the secluded granite-rimmed bowl of the Upper Bells Canyon Reservoir, it's hard to find a greater transition in landscape and atmosphere in four miles than you'll experience in Bells Canyon. Although most hikers go only as far as the beautiful waterfall midway up the canyon, Upper Bells Canyon lures in those looking for adventure and solitude. It is perhaps one of the most secluded places in the central Wasatch. Wildflowers, mountain goats, and mosquitoes await those who venture up to the canyon's upper tier. Four appealing white granite towers rise on the north side of Bells Canyon and attract rock climbers seeking out long, challenging, adventurous routes.

From the paved parking lot on Wasatch Boulevard, the Bells Canyon Trail starts off in a suburban neighborhood in Sandy, south of the mouth to Little

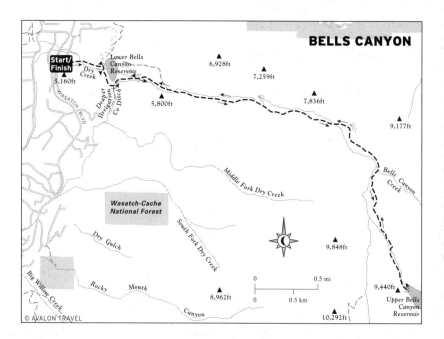

Cottonwood Canyon. It weaves first through landscaped yards and then quickly ascends a series of steep steps through granite boulders and Gambel oak trees. At 0.2 mile the trail rounds a corner, drops down a short hill, and crosses Bells Canyon Creek. This creek is also called the North Fork of Dry Creek and remains a nearly constant companion for the duration of this hike. Shortly, the trail reaches a distinct line of granite boulders marking the breached earthen dam that once held back the waters of Lower Bells Canyon Reservoir. Turn left at the trail sign and climb a small hill to a gravel road that circles the rim of the reservoir. In 1992,

Bells Canyon Waterfall in Bells Canyon

© MIKE MATSON

the dam for the Lower Bells Canyon Reservoir was breached by its owners, the Bells Canyon Irrigation Company, because of concerns about its structural integrity. A smaller lake still fills the lake bed but is no longer used for irrigation or drinking water. Follow the trail north and then east around the lake. Watch for a sign on the left side of the trail where the Bells Canyon Trail breaks off from the wider track. From here the trail enters the forest-blanketed canyon in earnest, with Rocky Mountain maple, Gambel oak, and aspen trees shading the path. As the trail steadily gains elevation, the sound of water falling over rocks never is far away. The trail enters the Lone Peak Wilderness Area at 1.25 miles.

At 2 miles, a wide fork in the trail marks a side trail to a lovely waterfall. From the waterfall the Bells Canyon Trail continues up the canyon two more steep miles to the Upper Bells Canyon Reservoir. The upper half of the trail receives far less traffic than the lower part, and offers a very different, more adventurous experience for those who continue on. Above the waterfall, the granite geology of the canyon becomes the center of attention, and the route itself becomes an exercise in route finding and eventually boulder hopping. The Bell Towers come plainly into view as the trail continues to steadily climb above the waterfall. Rock climbers will feel drawn to the many cracks and features these walls offer, and at least 30 routes have been climbed on the south-facing towers.

At 2.4 miles the trail emerges from the thick forest and offers its first good views back down the canyon to the Salt Lake Valley. With the steadily increasing elevation, more evergreen trees line the trail, including Engelmann spruce and subalpine fir. Around the 2.75-mile mark, the trail starts to cross a series of granite slabs that will dominate the landscape further for the remainder of the hike. Pad up these ancient rock slabs, looking carefully for rock cairns (small stacks of rocks) marking the trail. These cairns will mark the trail intermittently for the reminder of the hike. Blue flax and Wasatch penstemon wildflowers grow along the trail.

At 3 miles you'll walk through a meadow covered with bracken ferns. Then at 3.2 miles the trail crosses a creek descending from Thunder Bowl, a high alpine cirque on the north side of 11,154-foot South Thunder Mountain. Switchbacking steeply through subalpine fir trees with columbine, salmonberries, and Indian paintbrush, the trail continues upward through a long staircase of granite ledges. Continuing up the ridge, ancient limber pine trees grow where they can find a foothold in the exposed bedrock. The trail heads up the left side of the upper glacier-carved canyon, following the creek up through big granite boulders. At 4.1 miles you'll reach the Upper Bells Canyon Reservoir—or what was once a reservoir. The granite block dam that once held back the reservoir has been breached, and a gaping hole is punched through the center of it, leaving only the old natural lake at the bottom of the reservoir. Unfortunately the reservoir has left the old lake in poor condition, with a muddy shoreline and bathtub ring at the reservoir's high-water mark. It's still an impressive alpine environment, but you'll be disappointed if you're expecting a pristine lake.

Options
Many hikers choose to hike only to the beautiful waterfall, which is a worthy destination in itself. At 2 miles, take the fork to the side trail for the lovely falls, where clear water pours down a dark granite slab. Above the falls, the first of the Bell Towers, the white granite towers that mark the north ridge of the canyon, is visible through the forest canopy. Turn around here for a total hiking distance of 4 miles.

Directions
From Salt Lake City drive east on I-80 for 5 miles and merge onto I-215 South. Continue 6 miles and take Exit 6 for 6200 South. Turn left at the light at the bottom of the off-ramp and drive 1 mile south on 6200 South until it becomes Wasatch Boulevard. Continue on Wasatch Boulevard for 3.2 miles and take the right fork to stay on Wasatch Boulevard when Little Cottonwood Canyon Road branches off to the left. Continue 1.8 miles farther on Wasatch Boulevard to the small trailhead parking lot on the left side of the road.
GPS Coordinates: N 40°56.539' W 111°80.363'

Information and Contact

There is no fee. Little Cottonwood Canyon is a watershed and dogs are not allowed. Maps are available at the Public Lands Information Center, 3285 East 3300 South (inside REI), Salt Lake City, UT 84109, 801/466-6411. For more information, contact Salt Lake City Ranger District, Uinta-Wasatch-Cache National Forest, 125 South State Street, Salt Lake City, UT 84138, 801/236-3400, www.fs.fed.us or http://sandy.utah.gov.

26 TEMPLE QUARRY   BEST ⬤

Little Cottonwood Canyon, Wasatch-Cache National Forest

Level: Easy   **Total Distance:** 0.3 mile round-trip

Hiking Time: 15-30 minutes   **Elevation Change:** 85 feet

Summary: This paved interpretive trail explores the site where the Church of Jesus Christ of Latter-day Saints quarried stone to build the Salt Lake Temple in downtown Salt Lake City.

The Salt Lake Temple took 40 years to build, between 1853 and 1893. Quartz monzonite, which looks like light-colored granite, was quarried from the base of Little Cottonwood Canyon and used as the stone for the temple. Blocks were transported by oxen-pulled wagons initially, and then by railroad after 1873. The granite blocks weighed anywhere from three to five tons. It took wagons two days to deliver the granite blocks 20 miles from the Little Cottonwood Canyon to the temple.

The Temple Quarry Trail is paved and wheelchair accessible, and at a little less than half a mile, it's a great walk for toddlers and young children. Lined with interpretive signs outlining the site's role in building the temple, the trail offers a chance to learn a little piece of Salt Lake City's history in a beautiful mountain setting.

Leaving south from the paved parking lot, the Temple Quarry Trail leads down a little hill to the first interpretive sign. A mix of Rocky Mountain maple, Gambel oak, and fir trees partially shade the ribbon of asphalt. Follow the trail east as it loops past a small amphitheater with benches and then an observation deck overlooking Little Cottonwood Creek. Nice views of the steep granite walls on the south side of the canyon are visible from the viewing platform. Continue to the east end of the loop before returning to the parking lot alongside the Little Cottonwood Trail.

Options

It's easy to add on to the Temple Quarry Trail by heading up the Little Cottonwood Trail that shares trailhead parking with Temple Quarry Trail. The total hiking distance for these two trails is 7.1 miles round-trip.

quartz monzonite boulders along the Temple Quarry Trail

Directions

From Salt Lake City drive east on I-80 for 5 miles and merge onto I-215 South. Continue 6 miles and take Exit 6 for 6200 South. Turn left at the light at the bottom of the off-ramp and drive 1 mile south on 6200 South until it becomes Wasatch Boulevard. Continue driving south 3 miles to the base of Little Cottonwood Canyon. Turn right onto Little Cottonwood Canyon Road at the mouth of the canyon and then take an immediate left into the parking lot for the Temple Quarry/Little Cottonwood Trails.

GPS Coordinates: N 40°57.571' W 111°77.473'

Information and Contact

There is no fee. Little Cottonwood Canyon is a watershed and dogs are not allowed. Maps are available at the Public Lands Information Center, 3285 East 3300 South (inside REI), Salt Lake City, UT 84109, 801/466-6411. For more information, contact Salt Lake City Ranger District, Uinta-Wasatch-Cache National Forest, 125 South State Street, Salt Lake City, UT 84138, 801/236-3400, www.fs.fed.us.

27 LITTLE COTTONWOOD TRAIL

Little Cottonwood Canyon, Wasatch-Cache National Forest

Level: Moderate **Total Distance:** 6.8 miles round-trip

Hiking Time: 4 hours **Elevation Change:** 1,545 feet

Summary: A gently rising trail follows Little Cottonwood Creek up the canyon floor.

Starting at the base of Little Cottonwood Canyon, the Little Cottonwood Trail follows Little Cottonwood Creek up the canyon floor. Cottonwood, maple, and fir trees shade the wide path, making it an excellent choice on hot days. The white granite walls of Little Cottonwood Canyon rise over the trail, providing a dramatic backdrop for this peaceful mountain stroll. Following the moderate grade of the creek, this trail is popular with hikers of all types, from families of small children to trail runners. The trail is also an access trail for rock climbers headed to routes on the canyon's south walls, and a popular ride for mountain bikers.

Little Cottonwood Creek ranges from a raging river of white water during spring runoff to a clear, calm cascade dropping from pool to pool in the fall. Regardless of the water level, the creek helps make the trail a relaxing place to hike. Remains of the long human history of Little Cottonwood Canyon can be

© MIKE MATSON

the Little Cottonwood Trail at the base of Little Cottonwood Canyon

seen along the trail. From holes bored in the granite boulders by the pioneers to the now defunct mill sites along the creek, this trail offers constant reminders that Little Cottonwood Creek has been working hard for the residents of the Salt Lake Valley for hundreds of years.

Starting out from the east side of the Temple Quarry parking lot, the Little Cottonwood Trail begins as a smooth, crushed-granite path. After 0.6 mile the trail reaches a paved residential road leading down from Little Cottonwood Canyon Road. The trail joins the pavement for a short distance, until it reaches the powerhouse (0.1 mile), where it ducks around a gate left of the building and continues upstream.

The trail becomes rockier above the powerhouse, with white granite rocks breaking up the sand-and-dirt double track. At 1 mile the trail crosses Little Cottonwood Creek for the first time on a wide wooden bridge. Notice the house-sized boulder on the left side of the trail at 1.2 miles and the small round holes chiseled into the rock by Temple Quarry workers looking for suitable rock for the Salt Lake Temple in the 1860s and 1870s.

How does a boulder this big end up sitting by the river? Glaciers have sculpted Little Cottonwood Canyon periodically in the geologic past. Notice the U-shaped canyon walls near the base and the hanging valleys on the south side of the canyon. These are both sure signs of glaciation. Large

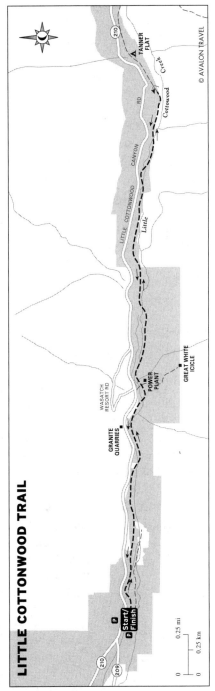

LITTLE COTTONWOOD TRAIL

© AVALON TRAVEL

boulders like this one get moved down-canyon on the slowly flowing ice, and then are deposited on the valley floor when the glaciers melt away.

A trail branches off the Little Cottonwood Trail on the right 2.2 miles from the trailhead. This side trail leads to a rock-climbing area called the Industrial Wall, and in winter, the base of the Great White Icicle, a popular ice-climbing feature. At 2.5 miles the trail crosses Little Cottonwood Creek on a wide bridge.

An old mill site with a partially standing granite-walled mill building marks the end of the trail. The ruins sit on the south side of the creek and cannot be reached from the trail. They do add a nice touch of history to the trail, even if viewed only from a distance. Turn around at the mill site and return to the Temple Quarry trailhead.

Options
At 2.75 miles a single-track trail branches off to the right of the main path. This winding loop is designed for mountain bikers and offers a more challenging downhill option than the wider main trail. It's a pleasant walk, and it adds less than 0.5 mile to the trail's total distance.

Directions
From Salt Lake City, drive east on I-80 for 5 miles and merge onto I-215 South. Continue 6 miles and take Exit 6 for 6200 South. Turn left at the light at the bottom of the off-ramp and drive 1 mile south on 6200 South until it becomes Wasatch Boulevard. Continue driving south 3 miles to the base of Little Cottonwood Canyon. Turn right onto Little Cottonwood Canyon Road at the mouth of the canyon, and then take an immediate left into the parking lot for the Temple Quarry/Little Cottonwood Trails.

GPS Coordinates: N 40°57.571' W 111°77.473'

Information and Contact
There is no fee. Little Cottonwood Canyon is a watershed and dogs are not allowed. Maps are available at the Public Lands Information Center, 3285 East 3300 South (inside REI), Salt Lake City, UT 84109, 801/466-6411. For more information, contact Salt Lake City Ranger District, Uinta-Wasatch-Cache National Forest, 125 South State Street, Salt Lake City, UT 84138, 801/236-3400, www.fs.fed.us.

28 RED PINE LAKE TO THE PFEIFFERHORN
BEST **C**

Little Cottonwood Canyon, Wasatch-Cache National Forest

Level: Butt-kicker

Total Distance: 9.0 miles round-trip

Hiking Time: 7.5–9 hours

Elevation Change: 4,317 feet

Summary: Red Pine Lake is a sparkling gem at the base of a granite bowl; hike and scramble onto one of the Wasatch Range's most impressive summits.

Hiking in the Wasatch Mountains doesn't get much better than this! The trail to Red Pine Lake starts in Little Cottonwood Canyon and ascends gently into a massive granite-boulder-strewn cirque. The pristine snowmelt-fed lake is adorned with wildflowers and shaded by stands of subalpine fir. Granite talus fields spill into the lake from a long rock ridge extending down from Thunder Mountain, giving the whole scene a wild, alpine feel. Continuing beyond the lake, hikers can clamor to the top of the Pfeifferhorn, an exposed, windswept summit with unbeatable views of the range's most dramatic landscapes.

The trail to Red Pine Lake shares its first mile with the White Pine Lake Trail. The path follows the grade of an old mining road through an aspen, spruce, and subalpine fir forest. The wide path follows a pleasant grade as it gently bends first west and then south toward the trail junction. At 0.9 mile the Red Pine Lake and White Pine

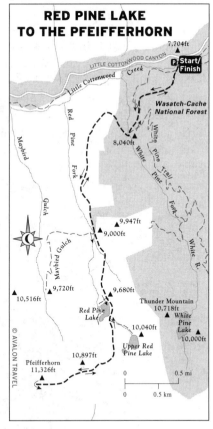

RED PINE LAKE TO THE PFEIFFERHORN

7,704ft

LITTLE COTTONWOOD CANYON

Little Cottonwood Creek

Start/Finish

Wasatch-Cache National Forest

Red Pine Fork

White Pine Trail

White Pine Fork

8,040ft

Maybird Gulch

Maybird Gulch

9,947ft

9,000ft

White R.

10,516ft

9,720ft

9,680ft

Thunder Mountain
10,718ft

Red Pine Lake

White Pine Lake

10,040ft

10,000ft

© AVALON TRAVEL

10,897ft

Upper Red Pine Lake

Pfeifferhorn
11,326ft

0   0.5 mi

0   0.5 km

Lake Trails diverge. The junction is marked by a Forest Service sign; take the right fork to Red Pine Lake. The right fork heads uphill and quickly crosses White Pine Fork Creek on a wooden bridge before bending around the ridge into Red

Pine Canyon. Salmonberries grow along the creek, and the purple blooms of Utah wild peas can be spotted along the trail. At 2.2 miles the trail wanders through an avalanche gully, marked by small trees with all their uphill branches stripped off by sliding snow. At 2.4 miles Red Pine Fork Creek can be heard and seen to the right of the path. Continuing steadily uphill through patches of forest and open rocky slopes, the trail reaches Red Pine Lake at 3.1 miles.

To continue on to the summit of the Pfeifferhorn, traverse around the left side of Red Pine Lake. Cross over the small stream and continue up the steep forested slope south of the lake. The boulder field to the left leads to upper Red Pine Lake, but to reach the Pfeifferhorn it's better to stay right in the spruce and subalpine fir. At 3.6 miles you'll reach a small alpine lake, or glacier tarn. The trail heads right from this lake, directly up the steep ridge. Climbing along this rocky ridge, the views go from impressive to spectacular, looking down to Red Pine Lake in the foreground and Twin Peaks of Broads Fork across Little Cottonwood Canyon to the north. At 3.9 miles you'll have gained the steep ridge and get your first glimpse of the Pfeifferhorn. Now at 10,900 feet and well above tree line, the grand scale of the Wasatch high country is spread out below you in all directions.

If it weren't for the enticing summit of the Pfeifferhorn, also called the Little Matterhorn, beckoning to the west, simply reaching this ridge-top vantage point would probably satisfy most adventure seekers. Gaining the ridge opens up views to the south that stretch from the impressive summits of Box Elder Peak and Mount Timpanogos to the distant Utah Lake on the valley floor and beyond to the western

© MIKE MATSON

Red Pine Lake (left) and Little Red Pine Lake (right) from the shoulder of the Pfeifferhorn

horizon. From here follow the ridgeline west toward the pyramid-shaped Pfeiffer-horn. This is a good place to identify the shallow gully on the southeast side of the Pfeifferhorn's rock cone; it is the easiest route to the summit. It is possible to follow the ridgeline all the way to this gully—scrambling across rocks and around rocks if necessary. And there is some exposure if you decide to stay on the apex of the ridge. Although no technical-climbing skills or ropes are necessary, you should be comfortable with exposure and move very carefully along this route. To avoid the exposed, scrambling option, drop down to the south side of the ridge and traverse the base of the rock spine. This option doesn't have the exposure, but it's not any easier than staying on the high route. Reaching the gully at 4.35 miles, scramble up the steep slope or up a steep snowfield, depending on the snowpack, to the summit. Trekking poles are a huge help anywhere above Red Pine Lake, but are worth their weight in gold on this final leg of the climb. The 11,326-foot summit of the Pfeifferhorn is a majestic spot. If conditions are right, it's the perfect place to enjoy a well-earned lunch. The views are incredible and include the peaks in Snowbird Ski Resort—Twin Peaks of American Fork, Mount Baldy, and Hidden Peak.

Options
At 2.5 miles from the parking lot a side trail branches off the Red Pine Lake Trail leading to Maybird Gulch. Maybird Gulch offers more solitude than Red Pine Lake as well as views of the Pfeifferhorn.

Directions
From Salt Lake City drive east on I-80 for 5 miles and merge onto I-215 South. Continue 6 miles and take Exit 6 for 6200 South. Turn left at the light at the bottom of the off-ramp and drive 1 mile south on 6200 South until it becomes Wasatch Boulevard. Continue driving south 3 miles to the base of Little Cotton-wood Canyon. Continue straight onto Little Cottonwood Road (Route 210) and drive 5.5 miles to the White Pine trailhead parking lot on the right side of the road. **GPS Coordinates:** N 40°57.494' W 111°68.111'

Information and Contact
There is no fee. Little Cottonwood Canyon is a watershed and dogs are not allowed. Maps are available at the Public Lands Information Center, 3285 East 3300 South (inside REI), Salt Lake City, UT 84109, 801/466-6411. For more information, contact Salt Lake City Ranger District, Uinta-Wasatch-Cache National Forest, 125 South State Street, Salt Lake City, UT 84138, 801/236-3400, www.fs.fed.us.

29 WHITE PINE LAKE

Little Cottonwood Canyon, Wasatch-Cache National Forest

Level: Strenuous

Total Distance: 9.5 miles round-trip

Hiking Time: 7–8 hours

Elevation Change: 2,851 feet

Summary: A long, gently rising trail leads to a turquoise-blue, snow-fed lake tucked between granite boulders and subalpine fir trees.

White Pine Lake is a Wasatch Mountain classic. This beautiful high-elevation lake completes a truly inspiring alpine setting. Granite boulders spill down to the lake from steep-sided Thunder Mountain. Dense pockets of wildflowers grow between the rocks, and trout jump on the water's surface.

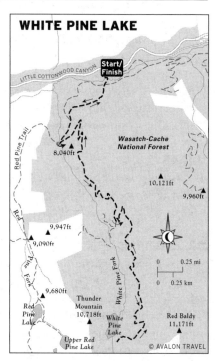

White Pine Lake is one of the most popular hikes in Salt Lake City's mountains. The trailhead, which is also the trailhead for Red Pine Lake, is packed during weekends and busy during weekdays for most of the summer season. By starting early or late you can avoid some of the crowds, but expect to see a lot of other hikers whenever you hit this trail. The trail is actually an old mining road built into White Pine Canyon around the turn of the 20th century. The road is slowly being reclaimed by nature and is quite enjoyable to walk. The gentle grade makes this relatively long trail feel less demanding than it really is.

Leaving the paved White Pine Trail parking lot, the trail quickly drops down to cross Little Cottonwood Creek on a sturdy bridge. Heading southwest, the old road gently climbs through an aspen and spruce forest toward a trail junction at 1 mile, where the White Pine and Red Pine Trails split. At the signed junction, head left up the old roadbed to White Pine Canyon. The trail switchbacks several times as it climbs from the junction into the canyon.

At 1.7 miles you'll get your first glimpse of White Pine Canyon itself as

Lupine and Indian paintbrush wildflowers bloom on the shores of White Pine Lake.

the trail levels off for the next 0.5 mile. The forest gives way to meadows with clumps of subalpine fir. Indian paintbrush grows in the meadows among thick grasses. A series of springs and small streams run across the trail at about 2 miles.

At 2.8 miles Thunder Mountain, which climbs precipitously above White Pine Lake, comes into view. Wide avalanche gullies extend down on the left of the trail from steep-sided Red Top Mountain. Beautiful meadows during summer, these slide paths can be extremely dangerous terrain during winter.

At 3.5 miles the trail winds its way up through a giant boulder field. An earthen dam marking White Pine Lake is visible on the right as you ascend this open bowl. Finally, the trail heads west through a gap in the rocks and looks down on White Pine Lake. Descend about 200 yards to the lake. A faint trail leads around the lake—with awesome wildflower displays on the east side of the water, and a gray boulder field on the west. When the water is lower, raccoon and deer tracks can be seen in the wet mud by the lake's edge.

Options

Ambitious hikers may consider hiking up the cirque to the south of White Pine Lake and through the saddle between 10,718-foot Thunder Mountain and 11,321-foot White Baldy. From the saddle, it's possible to descend into the Red Pine drainage and link up with the Red Pine Trail. This is off-trail adventure requiring a map and route-finding skills.

Directions

From Salt Lake City drive east on I-80 for 5 miles and merge onto I-215 South. Continue 6 miles and take Exit 6 for 6200 South. Turn left at the light at the bottom of the off-ramp and drive 1 mile south on 6200 South until it becomes Wasatch Boulevard. Continue driving south 3 miles to the base of Little Cottonwood Canyon. Continue straight onto Little Cottonwood Road (Route 210) and drive 5.5 miles to the White Pine trailhead parking lot on the right side of the road. **GPS Coordinates:** N 40°57.494' W 111°68.111'

Information and Contact

There is no fee. Little Cottonwood Canyon is a watershed and dogs are not allowed. Maps are available at the Public Lands Information Center, 3285 East 3300 South (inside REI), Salt Lake City, UT 84109, 801/466-6411. For more information, contact Salt Lake City Ranger District, Uinta-Wasatch-Cache National Forest, 125 South State Street, Salt Lake City, UT 84138, 801/236-3400, www.fs.fed.us.

30 SNOWBIRD BARRIER FREE

Snowbird Ski and Summer Resort, Little Cottonwood Canyon

Level: Easy

Total Distance: 1.2 miles round-trip

Hiking Time: 30 minutes–1 hour

Elevation Change: 55 feet

Summary: This paved, wheelchair-accessible path leads from the Snowbird Center to a wooden deck and viewing platform.

World famous as a ski resort for its quality and quantity of snow, Snowbird Ski Resort is a worthy summer destination as well. The Snowbird Barrier Free Trail offers a paved, wheelchair-accessible interpretive experience. Leaving directly from the upper deck of the Snowbird Center, the trail traverses under the tram and leads 0.6 mile to a wooden observation deck. The deck enjoys views of Little Cottonwood Canyon's sights, including the impressive south face of Mount Superior. Along the way, kid-friendly interpretive signs explain the flora and fauna that call these ski slopes home. Possible wildlife sightings include moose, mule deer, Uinta ground squirrels, and even mountain goats. This easy, mostly level trail is a perfect hike for young children or resort visitors looking to explore the world outside their hotel.

Park in the lot for the Snowbird Center and walk up through the building to the top floor. From the deck at the top of the Snowbird Center walk out toward the Peruvian chairlift at the base of the ski slopes. The Barrier Free Trail starts just to the right of the Peruvian lift. The paved trail traverses to the west below the ski slopes, passing stands of Engelmann spruce and subalpine fir. In midsummer Indian paintbrush, lupine, western coneflower, and columbine grow along the sides of the path. At 0.3 mile the trail passes under the Wilber chairlift. Continue on along the ribbon of pavement for another 0.3 mile to the observation deck. The deck provides views all the way down Little Cottonwood Canyon. From this perspective it's easy to see that this distinctly U-shaped valley was carved by glaciers during the last ice age. Looking across the canyon you'll see Hellgate Cliffs up-canyon on the right and Mount Superior straight ahead.

From the observation deck turn around and follow the pavement back to the Snowbird Center.

Options

If you're looking for a trail at the top of Snowbird, rather than the base, then ride the tram to the top of Hidden Peak and walk the 1.5-mile Mount Baldy Trail.

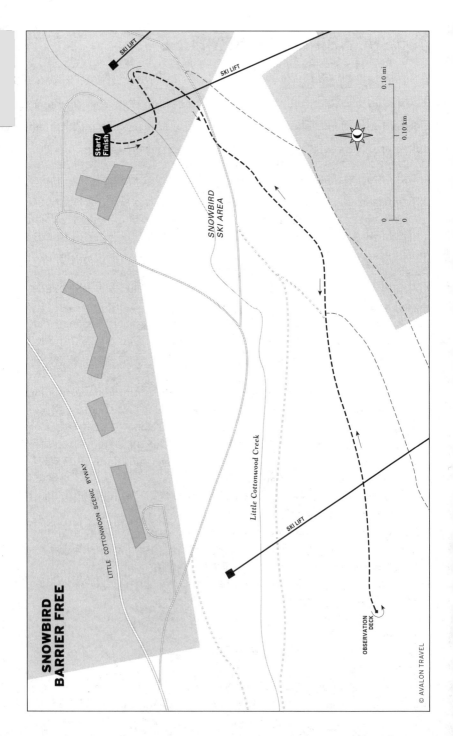

SNOWBIRD
BARRIER FREE

SKI LIFT

SKI LIFT

Start/Finish

SNOWBIRD SKI AREA

Little Cottonwood Creek

LITTLE COTTONWOOD SCENIC BYWAY

SKI LIFT

OBSERVATION DECK

0.10 mi

0.10 km

0

0

© AVALON TRAVEL

the observation deck at the end of the Snowbird Barrier Free Trail

Directions

From Salt Lake City drive east on I-80 for 5 miles and merge onto I-215 South. Continue 6 miles and take Exit 6 for 6200 South. Turn left at the light at the bottom of the off-ramp and drive 1 mile south on 6200 South until it becomes Wasatch Boulevard. Drive 3.2 miles and continue onto Little Cottonwood Road. Follow Little Cottonwood Road for 8 miles and turn right into Entry 2 for Snowbird. Park in the main parking lot for Snowbird Center.

GPS Coordinates: N 40°58.102' W 111°65.674'

Information and Contact

There is no fee. Little Cottonwood Canyon is a watershed and dogs are not allowed. A summer trail map for Snowbird Resort can be downloaded as a PDF file from the website. For more information contact the Snowbird Activity Center, Snowbird Center, Level Three, 801/933-2147, ext. 4147, www.snowbird.com.

31 MOUNT SUPERIOR

Little Cottonwood Canyon, Wasatch-Cache National Forest

Level: Strenuous

Hiking Time: 5-6 hours

Total Distance: 5.2 miles round-trip

Elevation Change: 3,061 feet

Summary: An exposed summit hike to one of the Little Cottonwood Canyon's best-known peaks.

Looking north across Little Cottonwood Canyon from Snowbird Ski Resort, there's no more impressive peak than Mount Superior. With its long, steep, south face and striking red-colored rock, Mount Superior begs to be skied in the winter and hiked in the summer.

As far as Wasatch summits go, climbing Mount Superior is actually one of the less strenuous hikes. It does require some scrambling on the exposed summit ridge, however, and careful route finding. Although this isn't a hike for beginners or those who don't enjoy heights, it can be one of the most enjoyable summit hikes in the entire Wasatch Range. Mount Superior divides Little Cottonwood Canyon and Big Cottonwood Canyon, so views from the summit extend down both of these canyons as well as across the entire central part of the range.

Mount Superior is home to one of the Wasatch range's mountain-goat herds, who live on the peak's steep, exposed terrain. Look for them on the trail along the upper ridgeline, or farther down the mountain on the wide-open rock talus slopes.

To hike to the summit of Mount Superior, follow the Cardiff Pass Trail uphill from the northwest corner of the parking lot at the Alta Guard Station. The trail climbs steeply uphill for the first 0.1 mile until it intersects a dirt maintenance road. Turn left and walk down the dirt road for 0.5 mile and then turn right on

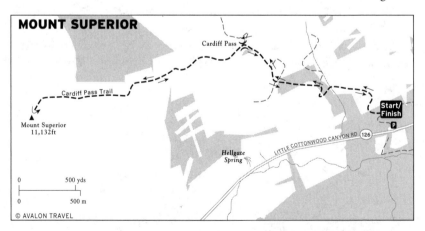

MOUNT SUPERIOR

Cardiff Pass

Cardiff Pass Trail

Mount Superior
11,132ft

Start/
Finish

LITTLE COTTONWOOD CANYON RD 126

Hellgate
Spring

| 0 | 500 yds |
| 0 | 500 m |

© AVALON TRAVEL

© MIKE MATSON

the mailbox summit register on Mount Superior

the trail/dirt road leading uphill. This old mining road slowly transitions into a trail, albeit a double-track mining road for most of the way up to Cardiff Pass. Lupine and Indian paintbrush grow on the open slopes above and below the trail as it winds steeply upward. This trail weaves through the old mine sites that first brought miners to Alta in the 1870s. The Big Emma Mine site is just to the right of the trail where it starts near the Alta Guard Station, and the Flagstaff Mine is above the trail on the right for the first mile of the trail. The impressive southeast face of Mount Superior dominates the skyline to the west.

By 1 mile the views from the trail are already impressive. They take in everything from the Alta and Snowbird Ski Resorts to the distant 11,326-foot Pfeifferhorn to the southwest. At 1.3 miles the trail leaves the old mining road and heads left uphill on a single track. The trail continues to climb steeply beneath a single set of power lines that lead up to Cardiff Pass at 10,000 feet. From the pass you can look all the way down Cardiff Fork to Big Cottonwood Canyon to the north. From the pass turn left and follow the trail to the west along the ridgeline. The trail traverses west of an unnamed 10,277-foot summit and continues along the ridge toward Mount Superior. Hearty limber pine trees grow along the windswept ridge. Closely following the spine of the ridge, the trail climbs steadily toward the summit. It takes careful observation to follow the most-used trail through this exposed, rocky scramble, so take your time and seek out the best route to the summit. Although no rock climbing is necessary through this section, it does have an intimidating, exposed feel to it, so move carefully and enjoy the setting!

A gray mailbox tucked into the rocks marks the summit of 11,132-foot Mount Superior. Just to the west is the 11,033-foot Monte Cristo. It can be reached by continuing to scramble west along the ridge. Retrace your route back down the way you came to return to the car.

Options

In winter, backcountry skiers often ski across Cardiff Pass from Little Cottonwood Canyon, down the Cardiff Fork drainage to the Big Cottonwood Canyon Road. For an epic summer adventure it's possible to hike this same route and summit Mount Superior along the way. This trail link-up requires a car shuttle, leaving a car at the parking lot for Doughnut Falls/Cardiff Fork in Big Cottonwood Canyon. After summiting Mount Superior and returning to Cardiff Pass, simply go left at the pass and hike down Cardiff Fork six miles to the trailhead.

Directions

From Salt Lake City drive east on I-80 for 5 miles and merge onto I-215 South. Continue 6 miles and take Exit 6 for 6200 South. Turn left at the light at the bottom of the off-ramp and drive 1 mile south on 6200 South until it becomes Wasatch Boulevard. Continue driving south 3 miles to the base of Little Cottonwood Canyon. Continue straight onto Little Cottonwood Road (Route 210) and drive 8.3 miles to the parking area to the left of the Alta Guard Station at the end of the pavement on Little Cottonwood Canyon Road.
GPS Coordinates: N 40°59.022.' W 111°63.909'

Information and Contact

There is no fee. Little Cottonwood Canyon is a watershed and dogs are not allowed. Maps are available at the Public Lands Information Center, 3285 East 3300 South (inside REI), Salt Lake City, UT 84109, 801/466-6411. For more information, contact Salt Lake City Ranger District, Uinta-Wasatch-Cache National Forest, 125 South State Street, Salt Lake City, UT 84138, 801/236-3400, www.fs.fed.us.

32 ALBION MEADOWS

Little Cottonwood Canyon, Wasatch-Cache National Forest

Level: Easy

Total Distance: 3.5 miles round-trip

Hiking Time: 2 hours

Elevation Change: 1,085 feet

Summary: Walk among wildflowers and gaze up at big mountains under the chairlifts of Alta Ski Area.

Albion Meadows Trail leads hikers from Alta's base area up to the Albion Basin Campground. The trail wanders by clumps of subalpine fir trees and through open meadows dominated by a colorful blend of Jacob's ladder, Indian paintbrush, lupine, and asters. Each July at the peak of the bloom, the Annual Wasatch Wildflower Festival visits Albion Meadows. Steep-sided peaks with menacing names such as the Devil's Castle and Hellgate Cliffs surround this alpine wonderland. Moose are often spotted foraging along the headwaters of Little Cottonwood Creek. And mine tailings, from Alta's early years as a mining hamlet, are still visible on the slopes above the trail. This rich blend of scenery, wildlife, and history make the trail an enjoyable outing, despite the obvious development of the ski area. Interpretive "Ske-cology" signs detail the wildlife living in this meadow environment. Possible wildlife sightings include porcupines, moose, yellow-bellied marmot, mule deer, and mountain goats.

The Albion Meadows Trail starts at the end of the paved Little Cottonwood Canyon Road at the large parking area on the right side of the road. Look for a small trailhead sign listing Albion Meadows, Germania Pass, and Cecret Lake. The trail descends quickly from the road and joins a gravel road in the Alta Ski Area. The road continues gently uphill past a ski-area building before passing between two large logs with a trail sign at 0.3 mile. Granite boulders dot the meadow, and pockets of subalpine fir trees break up the otherwise open valley floor. In these patches of evergreens expect to spot black rosy finch, red crossbill, Clark's nutcracker, and other birds.

It's interesting to note that at the peak of the mining activity in Alta in the 1870s there were no trees left in these meadows. All the trees had been cut down and used to support the mineshafts or for buildings in the town. Since then the town of Alta has launched an extensive tree-planting campaign, and the upper canyon now has a nice mix of forest pockets and open meadows.

The trail passes by Alta's Cecret chairlift as it continues up the canyon. At 1.6 miles you'll cross the headwaters of Little Cottonwood Creek. At 2 miles the Albion Meadows Trail will form a T into the Cecret Lake Trail. From here you may continue on to Cecret Lake or turn around and return to the parking lot.

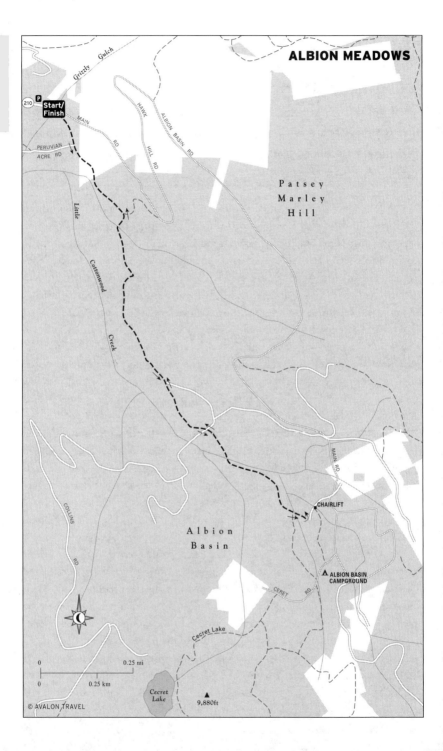

Options

It's easy to link the Albion Meadows Trail up with the Cecret Lake Trail that continues 0.75 mile to Cecret Lake from the Albion Basin Campground. This will make the entire outing 5 miles round-trip.

Albion Meadows in the Alta Ski Area

Directions

From Salt Lake City drive east on I-80 for 5 miles and merge onto I-215 South. Continue 6 miles and take Exit 6 for 6200 South. Turn left at the light at the bottom of the off-ramp and drive 1 mile south on 6200 South until it becomes Wasatch Boulevard. Continue driving south 3 miles to the base of Little Cottonwood Canyon. Continue straight onto Little Cottonwood Road (Route 210) and drive 8.3 miles to the parking area to the right of the Alta Guard Station at the end of the pavement on Little Cottonwood Canyon Road.

GPS Coordinates: N 40°59.022' W 111°63.909'

Information and Contact

There is no fee. Little Cottonwood Canyon is a watershed and dogs are allowed. Maps are available at the Public Lands Information Center, 3285 East 3300 South (inside REI), Salt Lake City, UT 84109, 801/466-6411. For more information contact Salt Lake City Ranger District, Uinta-Wasatch-Cache National Forest, 125 South State Street, Salt Lake City, UT 84138, 801/236-3400, www.fs.fed.us.

33 CATHERINE PASS
Little Cottonwood Canyon, Wasatch-Cache National Forest

Level: Moderate

Total Distance: 2.0 miles round-trip

Hiking Time: 1 hour

Elevation Change: 800 feet

Summary: A high-elevation romp through lush wildflower meadows to the saddle between the upper reaches of Little Cottonwood Canyon and Big Cottonwood Canyon.

It is hard to find a better example of the best Salt Lake City's mountains have to offer than the short, rewarding hike to Catherine Pass from Albion Basin. Add on an extension to the summit of Sunset Peak and you'll fall in love with the Wasatch Mountains all over again. Wildflower-dappled meadows and soaring summit views combine for a high-alpine experience that is difficult to match inside the state of Utah. Throw in the possibility of seeing a moose along the trail and you have one of the best short hikes in this guide.

The Catherine Pass Trail starts from a gravel parking lot 2 miles up the Alta Summer Road under the Albion chairlift. The wide dirt path rolls over open, sometimes rocky terrain blanketed by a green ocean of plant life. Wildflowers line the trail, and mountain bluebells, lupine, Indian paintbrush, and white aster fill the color wheel. Big peaks surround Albion Basin. Devil's Castle is the

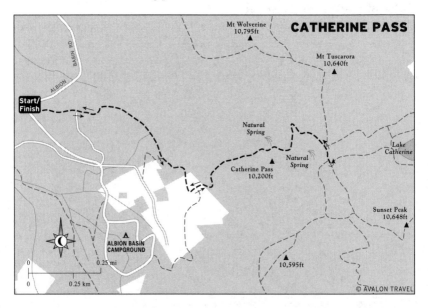

Catherine, Martha, and Mary Lakes from Catherine Pass

prominent dark limestone mountain directly across the basin from Catherine Pass Trail, and Mount Wolverine is the large peak on the left as you climb toward the pass. At 0.7 mile you'll reach a signed junction in the trail. The right fork leads back down into Albion Basin; take the left fork to continue to Catherine Pass. The trail remains wide and easy to follow as it rises through clumps of subalpine fir trees into a lovely meadow at 0.9 mile. Mount Wolverine walls in the meadow to the north, and a small stream trickles to the right of the trail. At 1.1 miles the trail crosses this small brook and leaves the meadow, starting a short section of switchbacks leading toward Catherine Pass. At 1.3 miles you've made it to Catherine Pass and can enjoy views into the upper reaches of Big Cottonwood Canyon, including the pristine Catherine Lake.

Options

There are several ways to extend this hike from Catherine Pass, including dropping down to Catherine Lake and continuing on to the Brighton Lakes Trail, which includes Catherine, Martha, Mary, and Dog Lakes on the way to the Brighton Ski Area parking lot. With a car shuttle this makes for an excellent cross-canyon hike from Little Cottonwood Canyon to Big Cottonwood Canyon. Another great extension to the Catherine Pass Trail is to continue up to the 10,648-foot summit of Sunset Peak. From the pass the trail to the summit is not difficult or even particularly steep, but it offers wonderful views to the ridge tops of the surrounding Wasatch Peaks. To say the views are sweeping is an understatement.

Directions

From Salt Lake City drive east on I-80 for 5 miles and merge onto I-215 South. Continue 6 miles and take Exit 6 for 6200 South. Turn left at the light at the bottom of the off-ramp and drive 1 mile south on 6200 South until it becomes Wasatch Boulevard. Continue driving south 3 miles to the base of Little Cottonwood Canyon. Continue straight onto Little Cottonwood Road (Route 210) and drive 10 miles to the parking lot on the right side of the Albion Basin Summer Road.

On weekends and holidays during the summer months the town of Alta runs a free shuttle from the end of the pavement on Little Cottonwood Canyon Road to the parking lot for the Catherine Pass trailhead. The parking lot fills quickly, so the shuttle is the safest bet. The shuttle comes about every 15 minutes and helps reduce traffic in Albion Basin. Keeping traffic to a minimum reduces dust along the unpaved Albion Basin Road.

GPS Coordinates: N 40°58.277' W 111°61.810'

Information and Contact

There is no fee. Little Cottonwood Canyon is a watershed and dogs are not allowed. Maps are available at the Public Lands Information Center, 3285 East 3300 South (inside REI), Salt Lake City, UT 84109, 801/466-6411. For more information, contact Salt Lake City Ranger District, Uinta-Wasatch-Cache National Forest, 125 South State Street, Salt Lake City, UT 84138, 801/236-3400, www.fs.fed.us.

34 CECRET LAKE   BEST ◖
Little Cottonwood Canyon, Wasatch-Cache National Forest

Level: Easy   **Total Distance:** 1.5 miles round-trip

Hiking Time: 1-2 hours   **Elevation Change:** 420 feet

Summary: Alta's easy-access alpine lake is a kid-friendly introduction to the beauty of Little Cottonwood Canyon.

Located in the shadow of Alta Ski Area's chairlifts, Cecret Lake is a bite-sized treat of Albion Basin's summer-time splendor. This short walk samples the best of the alpine meadow beauty found at the top of Little Cottonwood Canyon. In midsummer, the wildflower displays here are at their peak and on par with some of the best in North America.

Cecret Lake's family-friendly trail is a great first hike for toddlers and small children. Interpretive signs provide information about the surrounding environment, including the wildflowers, insects, and other wildlife found here. The gently sloped, wide-open path has room for kids to play, is easy to follow, and provides an alpine lake as a reward at its end.

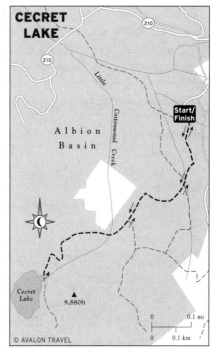

The Cecret Lake Trail heads southwest from the parking lot through open meadows dotted by patches of alpine fir and spruce trees. Mountain bluebells and Indian paintbrush line the trail as it heads toward the forbidding Devil's Castle. At 0.3 mile take the left fork of the trail. At 0.5 mile, the trail begins to gain elevation a little more quickly and becomes rockier as it climbs toward Cecret Lake. (Look for rock climbers on the cliffs to the left of the trail.) Two quick switchbacks lead you to the lake at 0.7 mile. The Devil's Castle and Sugarloaf Mountain rise quickly from the lake, giving the place a dramatic alpine feel.

Cecret Lake is anything but secret—in fact, it's one of the busiest hikes in the Wasatch Mountains. In order to accommodate a small parking lot at the trailhead, the town of Alta provides a free shuttle on weekends from the ski area's parking lot (at the end of the pavement on Little Cottonwood Canyon Road) to the trailheads on the Albion Basin Road. Two shuttles constantly drive back and forth on the 2.5-mile road, arriving about every 15–30 minutes at each stop. The Albion Basin Road is gated and closed to cars in early summer, until sometime in July.

Options

If the short hike to Cecret Lake doesn't leave you feeling satisfied, you can continue to the 11,051-foot Sugarloaf Mountain. The trail skirts the east side Cecret Lake and continues south up Sugarloaf Mountain, switchbacking steeply up a ridge to a saddle between the Devil's Castle and Sugarloaf Mountain. Follow the ridgeline west to the summit of Sugarloaf Mountain. The trail from the lake to the summit is an additional 1.1 miles for a total distance of 3.7 miles.

Directions

From Salt Lake City, drive east on I-80 for 5 miles and merge onto I-215 South. Continue 6 miles on I-215 South and take Exit 6 for 6200 South. Turn left at the light at the bottom of the off-ramp and drive 1 mile south on 6200 South until it becomes Wasatch Boulevard. Continue driving south 3 miles to the base of Little Cottonwood Canyon. Continue straight onto Little Cottonwood Road

the Cecret Lake Trail, Albion Basin in the Alta Ski Area

© MIKE MATSON

(Route 210) and drive 11.3 miles to the parking lot for the Cecret Lake trailhead at the end of the road.

On weekends and holidays during the summer months, the town of Alta runs a free shuttle from the end of the pavement on Little Cottonwood Canyon Road to the parking lot for the Cecret Lake trailhead. The parking lot fills quickly, so the shuttle is your safest bet. The shuttle arrives about every 15 minutes and helps reduce traffic in Albion Basin. Keeping traffic to a minimum also reduces dust along the unpaved Albion Basin Road.

GPS Coordinates: N 40°57.756' W 111°61.335'

Information and Contact

There is no fee. Little Cottonwood Canyon is a watershed and dogs are not allowed. Maps are available at the Public Lands Information Center, 3285 East 3300 South (inside REI), Salt Lake City, UT 84109, 801/466-6411. For more information, contact Salt Lake City Ranger District, Uinta-Wasatch-Cache National Forest, 125 South State Street, Salt Lake City, UT 84138, 801/236-3400, www.fs.fed.us.

35 ROCKY MOUTH CANYON

City of Sandy, Wasatch-Cache National Forest

🦌 🕸 🐕 👫

Level: Easy

Total Distance: 0.7-mile round-trip

Hiking Time: 30 minutes–1 hour

Elevation Change: 262 feet

Summary: A short trail leads to a unique, hidden canyon with a waterfall.

Rocky Mouth Canyon is one of the Wasatch Mountains' hidden treasures. Most people who recreate in Little Cottonwood Canyon have driven by it many times and don't even known it's there. But tucked into the trees behind an upscale Sandy neighborhood is a small canyon and waterfall. This hike requires little effort, yet offers a great place for kids to play or for adults to relax and enjoy one of nature's unique spots.

From the parking lot, the Rocky Mouth Canyon Trail ascends a set of wooden steps through Gambel oak trees. Look for deer foraging quietly in the woods by the trailhead. At the top of the stairs, head right along the sidewalk and follow the street as it bends back around to the left (north). The trail continues two blocks later, on the uphill side of the street, as it completes the bend. You can see the mouth of the canyon above the houses to the right. The trail is marked by a brown trailhead sign.

Follow the path as it parallels the left side of a black wrought-iron fence. At the top of the fence the trail leaves suburbia behind and quickly enters nature. Rocky Mountain maple trees line the trail before it abruptly enters the canyon mouth 0.3 mile from the trailhead. Granite boulders mark the canyon entrance. Scamper up a short series of boulders on the canyon floor to reach what can be described as a miniature slot canyon.

A 50-foot cascade of water pours down the back of canyon wall, and steep cliffs wall in the chasm on three sides. The pouring water and confined, slotlike geography create a cool microclimate within the canyon, offering a great place to

the waterfall in Rocky Mouth Canyon

visit on hot summer days. Little kids will love playing in the water where it runs through a shallow pool at the base of the falls.

Return down the trail the way you came.

Options

The Bells Canyon Trail lies three miles north on Wasatch Boulevard and offers a butt-kicking climb of 8.3 miles round-trip with a shorter 4-mile option to a lovely waterfall.

Directions

From Salt Lake City, drive south on I-15 for 12 miles to Exit 292 for 11400 South. Take a left off the Exit on 11400 South and drive 2.7 miles. Turn right on 1700 East and drive 0.3 mile. Turn left onto Wasatch Boulevard and drive 2.3 miles. The trailhead will be on the right side of the road. Note: Park in the trailhead parking lot on Wasatch Boulevard. Don't park in the neighborhood above on Eagle View Drive.

GPS Coordinates: N 40°54.547' W 111°80.687'

Information and Contact

There is no fee. Dogs are allowed on leash. For more information contact the City of Sandy Parks and Recreation, Sandy City Hall, 10000 Centennial Pkwy, Sandy, UT 84070, 801/568-7100, http://sandy.utah.gov.

NORTHERN WASATCH

© MIKE MATSON

BEST HIKES

Like the jagged edge of a serrated knife, the

Wasatch Mountains rise boldly out of a salty desert, definitively marking the western edge of the Rocky Mountain chain. The Wasatch stands in proud defiance of the endless expanse of the basin and range desert to its west. More than just a geographic transition, these peaks help define, sustain, and characterize the two million people living in their shadow. For Wasatch Front residents, the mountains are an unavoidable part of daily life. Whether by simply providing a scenic backdrop to live beneath, catching the snow that will become our drinking water, or providing local jobs in Utah's $650-million-per-year ski industry, Salt Lake City would be a very different place without its mountains. So it makes perfect sense that many of Utah's best hikes are found in this range.

The Wasatch Mountains are divided into three regions: the Northern Wasatch, from Ben Lomond north of Ogden to the northern edge of Salt Lake City; the Central Wasatch Core, from City Creek Canyon above downtown Salt Lake City to Lone Peak above the town of Alpine; and the Southern Wasatch, from Lone Peak to the southern terminus of the range.

The Northern Wasatch Mountains stand guard over the wide expanse of the Great Salt Lake. Major summits like steep-faced Ben Lomond and Willard Peak climb more than 4,000 feet from the valley floor to elevations over 9,000 feet. Between these peaks and the lake lie the cities of Ogden, Taylorsville, Farmington, and Bountiful. Although the hikes in this stretch of mountains hold special significance for those living at their base, they are well worth the short drive for Salt Lake City residents as well. With nearly a mile of vertical relief, the peaks offer hikers unparalleled views of the Great Salt Lake. (Summer sunsets over the lake are particularly spectacular.)

The massive change in elevation between the valley floor and mountaintops allows for a complex ecosystem of plants and wildlife. Expect to encounter everything from thick stands of quaking aspen and Engelmann's spruce, to small bunches of stunted subalpine fir near tree line, to open, wildflower-dappled slopes in the high country. The deciduous forests that blanket the foothills and deep-cut canyons are characterized by broad-leafed box elders, Rocky Mountain maples, and the slow-growing but ever-present Gambel oak trees.

The deep canyons cutting into these dramatic mountains hold secrets of their own. Lovely forest walks lead to plunging waterfalls where the stream's water supports a wonderful web of life – from towering, ancient white pine trees to brightly colored butterflies. From the tops of massive peaks to the depths of hidden canyons, there's a lot to be discovered in the Northern Wasatch.

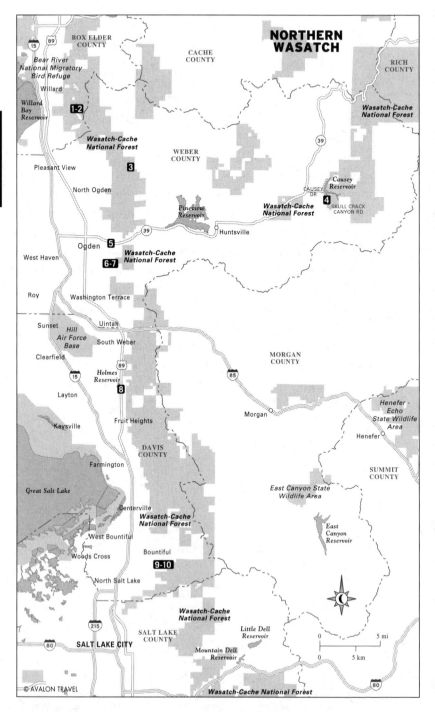

TRAIL NAME	LEVEL	DISTANCE	TIME	ELEVATION	FEATURES	PAGE
1 Willard Peak	Easy/Moderate	1.6 mi rt	1-1.5 hr	564 ft		144
2 Ben Lomond from Inspiration Point	Moderate	4.8 mi rt	3-4 hr	290 ft		147
3 Ben Lomond via the North Skyline Trail	Butt-kicker	16 mi rt	10-12 hr	2,880 ft		150
4 Skull Crack Trail	Moderate	4.5 mi rt	2-3 hr	1,279 ft		153
5 Birdsong Trail	Easy	1-2.3 mi rt	1 hr	518 ft		156
6 Malans Peak via Taylor Canyon	Moderate	5.5 mi rt	3-4 hr	2,814 ft		159
7 Waterfall Canyon	Moderate	3 mi rt	1.5-2 hr	1,500 ft		162
8 Adams Canyon	Moderate	3-3.5 mi rt	2-3 hr	1,683 ft		165
9 Kenny Creek Trail	Moderate	4.5 mi rt	2.5-3 hr	2,850 ft		168
10 Mueller Park	Moderate	6.2 mi rt	3-4 hr	1,571 ft		171

1 WILLARD PEAK
Wasatch-Cache National Forest

Level: Easy/Moderate

Hiking Time: 1–1.5 hours

Total Distance: 1.6 miles round-trip

Elevation Change: 564 feet

Summary: A short, ridgeline scamper to the highest peak in the Northern Wasatch Range.

Willard Peak is the highest peak in Weber County at 9,763 feet and the highest peak in the northern section of the Wasatch Range. Although it's higher than nearby Ben Lomond, it receives far less attention.

Despite its noteworthy height, Willard Peak is an easy climb. The drive to the trailhead, however, is more challenging than the hike. The road from the town of Mantua to Inspiration Point covers 13 bumpy, rutted miles of dirt road. A high-clearance vehicle is a must, and four-wheel drive is highly recommended. Motorcycles or ATVs will also have no problem reaching Inspiration Point. The long, winding road definitely thins out the crowd, so if you make it as far as Inspiration Point, expect hiker traffic to be relatively light.

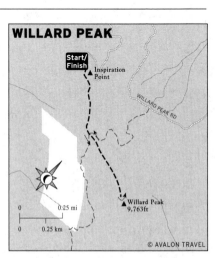

Willard Peak, and the ridgeline that connects to Ben Lomond to the south, is home to one of the Wasatch Range's larger herds of mountain goats. You'll also see a variety of hawks and ravens soaring in the consistent updrafts rising off the ridge. The rewards for reaching Willard Peak's summit are substantial. The peak's position above the Willard Bay area of the Great Salt Lake, and its steep western slope, make for a summit vista that has an edge-of-the-world feel. It's also a great spot from which to enjoy the sunset, because the trail is short and it's easy to make it back to the car before total darkness. Plus, it's hard to beat unobstructed sunset views to the western horizon from almost 10,000 feet. The western flank of Willard Peak was the site of an iron mine, called the Eldorado Mine, that opened in 1873 and was operated by Israel Elliott Brown.

The trail from Inspiration Point to Willard Peak's summit is the true definition of a ridge walk. From the gravel parking area at Inspiration Point the trail descends the ridge to the south. Limber pine trees grow in charcoal-gray soil, and lupines grow along the wind-buffeted slopes. The large open bowl below the ridgeline to the east is Willard Basin. You'll notice terraces cut into its slopes. This is where 700 miles of terraces were constructed in a project headed by the Civilian Conservation Corps and the Soil Conservation Services to curtail extensive flooding and soil erosion during the 1920s and 1930s.

At 0.4 mile from the trailhead a trail merges in from the right. Take the left fork here, staying on the east side of the ridge. At the next fork, just 50 yards farther, take the right trail and stay high along the ridge. The trail continues to cling closely to the ridge as it ascends steeply up Willard's northern flank. Work your way up through a section of treeless purple shale rock. Higher up, groups of limber pine and subalpine fir grow just below the summit on the ridgeline. The trail weaves through them, stepping around scraggly trees and through boulders just below the summit. In places where the faint trail is difficult to follow, look for blue splotches of paint on the rocks.

Willard Peak's summit has a unique rock chasm spanning its length. Looking much like a crevasse found on a glacier, the break in the rock is only a few feet across, but very deep. If you have small children or dogs with you, this is a place to exercise caution. Views from the summit look down to Willard Bay, a freshwater reservoir on the east side of the Great Salt Lake. To the north is Inspiration Point with Willard Basin on its eastern flank. And to the south is the ridgeline leading the eye toward Ben Lomond, with Mount Ogden in the distance.

© MIKE MATSON

view from the summit of Willard Peak with Willard Bay in the Great Salt Lake below

Options

Willard Peak can also be climbed as part of a two-summit hike with Ben Lomond. After climbing Willard Peak, descend Willard Peak via the same ridge you climbed. At the base of the ridge, turn left and follow the trail south to reach Ben Lomond, rather than returning to Inspiration Point to the north. This option offers a 6-mile round-trip hike.

Directions

From Salt Lake City drive north on I-15 for 52 miles and take Exit 362 for U.S. Highway 89/91. Continue right at the fork, following signs for Brigham City/Logan, and merge onto U.S. Highway 91 North. Continue north for 5.5 miles on U.S. Highway 91 and take the exit for Mantua. Drive 0.2 mile and continue onto 100 South. Drive 0.5 mile on 100 South and turn right onto Main Street. Continue on Main Street for 0.1 mile; it turns into Willard Peak Road. After 1 mile, turn left to stay on Willard Peak Road and continue for 13 miles.

Note: Willard Peak Road is deeply rutted and rocky. Attempt it only if you have a high-clearance vehicle, ATV, or motorbike. Expect the 13 miles to take at least an hour to drive.

GPS Coordinates: N 41°23.455' W 111°59.159'

Information and Contact

There is no fee. Dogs are allowed on leash. Maps are available at the Public Lands Information Center, 3285 East 3300 South (inside REI), Salt Lake City, UT 84109, 801/466-6411. For more information, contact the Ogden Ranger District, Uinta-Wasatch-Cache National Forest, 507 25th Street, Suite 103, Ogden, UT 84401, 801/625-5112, www.fs.fed.us.

2 BEN LOMOND FROM INSPIRATION POINT

Wasatch-Cache National Forest

BEST 🌙

🚶 🦌 ✈ 🦌

Level: Moderate

Total Distance: 4.8 miles round-trip

Hiking Time: 3-4 hours

Elevation Change: 290 feet

Summary: This is the easiest way to the summit of Ben Lomond, the Northern Wasatch's best-known peak.

Ben Lomond is one of the crowning jewels of the Northern Wasatch and one of the most recognized peaks along the Wasatch Front. Its claim to fame: According to local legend the peak was the inspiration for the mountain in the Paramount Pictures logo. Paramount's founder William Hodkinson grew up in Ogden and sketched the peak from his memory on a napkin during an early business meeting. The mountain's steep western face and prominent position above Ogden make it both easy to recognize and a coveted summit for peak baggers. The peak was named after another, similar-looking mountain in the Munro Range of the Scottish Highlands. The word *Ben* or *Beinn* means mountain in Gaelic, which explains why the mountain is listed simply as Ben Lomond on maps.

Ben Lomond can be climbed by several routes. The trail from Inspiration Point is by far the easiest route to the summit. It also has the added advantage of passing by Willard Peak, the tallest peak in Weber County and the Northern Wasatch Range. So if reaching county high points or peak bagging in general is something you enjoy, this hike offers two nice prizes for the effort of one. What's the catch? The 13-mile dirt road leading to the trailhead at Inspiration Point is in very poor condition; it is extremely rocky and deeply rutted, requiring a high-clearance vehicle.

Once you've completed the drive, the trail to Ben Lomond is a pleasure to walk. The entire trail follows an exposed ridge above tree line. Views are panoramic the whole way, and except on weekends, you're likely to have the whole

the summit plaque and register on Ben Lomond

© MIKE MATSON

trail to yourself. Although the trail does rise and fall with the ridge, it's nearly flat in comparison with other trails that climb Ben Lomond from thousands of feet below.

Descend the ridge from the parking lot at Inspiration Point, to the saddle between Inspiration Point and Willard Peak. (To avoid any confusion, Inspiration Point is also called Willard Mountain, which is a different mountain from Willard Peak altogether.) At 0.4 mile the trail splits, with one trail leading to the right across the ridge to the west and another leading up Willard Peak to the east. Cross the ridge on the right-hand trail to continue toward Ben Lomond. The trail will meet another spur trail coming up the slope from the west at 0.5 mile. Stay high on the trail and continue straight, traversing under Willard Peak. Downhill from the trail to the west is the historic Eldorado Mine site. Scattered limber pine trees are about the only trees growing in this rocky alpine environment. Wildflowers, stunted sagebrush, and bunch grass fill in the thin soil around the rock. The mountain is one of the best places to find wildlife in the Northern Wasatch. A herd of mountain goats range back and forth between Ben Lomond and Willard Peak to the north.

At 1.4 miles the trail rounds a bend, providing the first views of the summit of Ben Lomond. Hawks and ravens soar on the thermal updrafts rising off the long, consistent ridgeline. Look for a large herd of mountain goats grazing near this part of the trail. They can often be spotted in

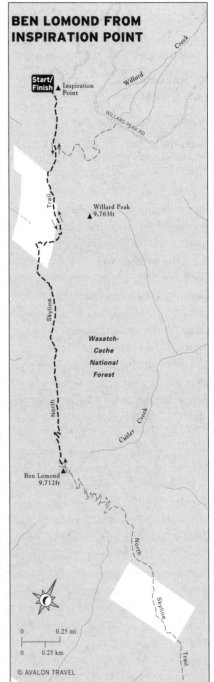

BEN LOMOND FROM INSPIRATION POINT

Start/Finish ▲ Inspiration Point

Willard Creek

WILLARD PEAK RD

Willard Peak ▲ 9,763ft

Trail

Skyline

North

Wasatch-Cache National Forest

Cutler Creek

Ben Lomond 9,712ft

North

Skyline

Trail

0   0.25 mi
0   0.25 km

© AVALON TRAVEL

the trees to the west of the trail or in the open bowl on the east side of the ridge. At 2.1 miles the trail begins to climb gently toward the summit of Ben Lomond. The rocky trail bends through a few short switchbacks just to the east of the summit before topping out on Ben Lomond 2.4 miles from the trailhead. A metal box and plaque mark the summit, providing information about the peak's unique name and Peter Skeen Ogden, who discovered Ogden in 1828. Enjoy this breathtaking spot before following the ridgeline back to Inspiration Point.

Options

If you're interested in an epic day-hike, consider connecting this route to Ben Lomond's summit with the Skyline Trail, which leads to Ben Lomond's summit from the south. The best way to combine these two hikes is to leave a car at the North Divide Trailhead (at the base of the Skyline Trail in North Ogden Canyon) and drive to the Inspiration Point Trailhead. By starting at Inspiration Point, the trail is mostly level to Ben Lomond's summit followed by a long downhill, making the 21-mile round-trip distance much more manageable. These two trails meet just to the east of the summit of Ben Lomond. To connect the two trails, simply take the right fork in the trail and descend to the south, rather than following the trail back towards Inspiration Point to the north.

Directions

From Salt Lake City drive north on I-15 for 52 miles and take Exit 362 for U.S. Highway 89/91. Continue right at the fork, following signs for Brigham City/Logan, and merge onto U.S. Highway 91 North. Continue north for 5.5 miles on U.S. Highway 91 and take the exit for Mantua. Drive 0.2 mile and continue onto 100 South. Drive 0.5 mile on 100 South and turn right onto Main Street. Continue on Main Street for 0.1 mile; it turns into Willard Peak Road. After 1 mile turn left to stay on Willard Peak Road and continue for 13 miles.

Note: Willard Peak Road is deeply rutted and rocky. Attempt it only if you have a high-clearance vehicle, ATV, or motorbike. Expect the 13 miles to take at least an hour to drive.

GPS Coordinates: N 41°23.455' W 111°59.159'

Information and Contact

There is no fee. Dogs are allowed on leash. Maps are available at the Public Lands Information Center, 3285 East 3300 South (inside REI), Salt Lake City, UT 84109, 801/466-6411. For more information, contact the Ogden Ranger District, Uinta-Wasatch-Cache National Forest, 507 25th Street, Suite 103, Ogden, UT 84401, 801/625-5112, www.fs.fed.us.

3 BEN LOMOND VIA
THE NORTH SKYLINE TRAIL   BEST (

Wasatch-Cache National Forest

Level: Butt-kicker

Total Distance: 16 miles round-trip

Hiking Time: 10-12 hours

Elevation Change: 2,880 feet

Summary: This long and grueling route to the summit of 9,712-foot Ben Lomond rewards hikers with sweeping views to both the west and east side of the Northern Wasatch Mountains.

This is the most popular trail to the summit of Ben Lomond, and it's what you'd expect for a mountain of its physical stature. Climbing Ben Lomond via the North Skyline Trail is a full-day affair. The trail is long, steep, and challenging. The route is actually a section of the massive Great Western Trail, which is 4,455 miles in length and weaves through Arizona, Idaho, Montana, Utah, and Wyoming. This section of trail to the summit, known as the North Skyline Trail, begins at North Ogden Pass (North Ogden Divide) in North Ogden Canyon.

Starting at the paved parking lot, the trail begins with 10 long switchbacks climbing out of the canyon. At first it's a smooth dirt track, curving through a Gambel oak and maple forest—but as the single track climbs, it becomes rockier, and although there are patches of shade provided by trees, it is mostly exposed.

the view south from the summit of Ben Lomond

© MIKE MATSON

The trail is open to mountain bikers, motorcycles, and horses, so be aware of their presence and be ready to share the trail with other users. On that note, rattlesnakes like the sun-drenched, rocky slopes too, so keep an eye out for them as well. Hummingbirds frequent the yellow mule ear and other wildflowers along this hillside and can be heard buzzing and chattering along the trail. Manzanita shrub, pinyon pine, and juniper trees are common as the elevation increases. Views are impressive even in the first couple of miles. To the east the Pineview Reservoir can be seen in the Ogden Valley, and North Ogden is visible to the west.

As the trail works progressively up the endless switchbacks, they become longer in length until finally, at 2.5 miles, they top out of the canyon and gain the southern end of the long ridge that includes Chilly Peak and Ben Lomond Peak. Scattered Indian paintbrush wildflowers dot the ridge, and the open landscape has a distinctly alpine feel. The trail works northwest up the ridge before dropping onto the eastern slopes, where snowfields can linger well into June. Stands of stunted quaking aspen grow along the trail. At about 3.5 miles the trail enters a forest of pine and Engelmann spruce and levels off. The view changes dramatically as the trail crosses over to the west side of the ridge at 4 miles. All of the Northern Wasatch Front is visible to the west, and Ben Lomond comes into view for the first time from the trail.

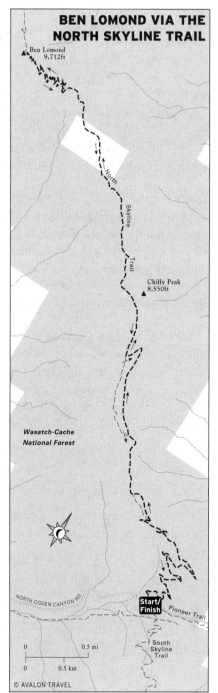

BEN LOMOND VIA THE NORTH SKYLINE TRAIL

Ben Lomond 9,712ft

North Skyline Trail

Chilly Peak 8,550ft

Wasatch-Cache National Forest

NORTH OGDEN CANYON RD

Start/ Finish

Pioneer Trail

South Skyline Trail

0   0.5 mi

0   0.5 km

© AVALON TRAVEL

Gently rolling, and gaining only about 400 feet, the next 1.5 miles are high-country bliss. Snarled old subalpine firs dot the ridgeline, and clumps of wildflowers cling to the thin alpine soil.

Options

The North Skyline Trail (starting at the North Divide Trailhead) can be followed farther north from the summit of Ben Lomond to the summit of Willard Peak and beyond to Willard Basin. By leaving a vehicle at the Willard Basin Trailhead it is possible to do this trail as a 21-mile one-way hike.

Directions

From Salt Lake City, drive north on I-15 for 25.1 miles to Exit 349/UT 134. Turn right onto UT 134/2700 North; at 0.3 mile, 2700 North turns into 2600 North. Continue on 2600 North for 2.7 miles, turn left onto 1050 East, and drive 0.7 mile. Turn right onto 3100 North and drive 0.5 mile, then continue on the North Ogden Canyon Road for 4.1 miles. The trailhead parking lot will be on the right.
GPS Coordinates: N 41°32.023' W 111°89.927'

Information and Contact

There is no fee. Dogs on leash are allowed. Maps are available at the Union Station Information Center, 2501 Wall Avenue, Ogden, UT 84401, 801/625-5306. For more information, contact the Ogden Ranger District Office, Uinta-Wasatch-Cache National Forest, 507 25th Street, Ogden, UT 84401, 801/625-5112, www.fs.fed.us.

4 SKULL CRACK TRAIL
Wasatch-Cache-National Forest

Level: Moderate

Hiking Time: 2-3 hours

Total Distance: 4.5 miles round-trip

Elevation Change: 1,279 feet

Summary: A scenic trail runs above the south shore of the steep-walled Causey Reservoir.

According to the National Forest Service, Skull Crack Trail gets its name from two hunters: James Slater and Marinus Johansen. Legend goes that one of their mules became unruly while they were in the canyon hunting. Johansen struck the mule over the head so hard with his gun barrel that he cracked the mule's skull.

The Causey Reservoir is named after Thomas Causey, who operated a sawmill at Causey Creek and the South Fork. The earthen dam, constructed between 1962 and 1966, creates the reservoir on the South Fork of the Ogden River. The canyon walls around the lake are particularly steep, making the lake very deep, and scenic. Skull Crack Trail runs above the south shore of the lake and leads to a dispersed campground where the Right Fork of the Ogden River enters the reservoir. The trail is a great backpacking trip for kids, and is popular with the local Boy Scouts. The campground can be reached by boat as well, though the lake doesn't have a dedicated boat launch and only nonmotorized boats are allowed. There's fishing on the lake for rainbow, cutthroat, and brown trout.

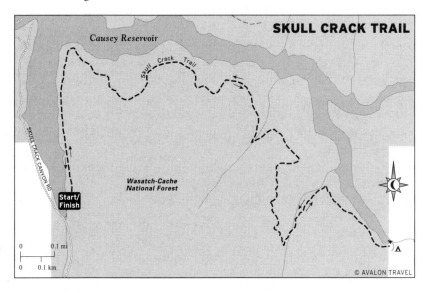

the Causey Reservoir, as seen from Skull Crack Trail

The Skull Crack Trail leaves a gravel parking lot at the end of the lake's southwest finger. It closely follows the shoreline at first, passing through big sagebrush and Gambel oak trees. The red dirt trail rises gently, slowly gaining elevation above the lake's shoreline. At 0.5 mile there's a fork in the trail; take the right fork to stay high above the lake. Where the trail makes a wide right-hand turn, the conifers grow among the deciduous trees, with large Douglas fir trees framing the view of the lake.

At 1.4 miles the forest gives way to open sagebrush slopes and excellent views spread out across the canyon to where the Left Fork of the Ogden River flows into the lake. In the early morning when the lake's waters are calm, the steep rock walls reflect on the surface, painting a beautiful mirror image. As the trail approaches the eastern end of the lake, it starts descending quickly through a short series of switchbacks. It continues to lose elevation until it reaches a campground. From the campground, simply follow the trail back out the same way you came.

Options

Skull Crack Trail can also be done as short backpacking trip. At the end of the trail, on Causey Reservoir's east arm, there is a campsite that's suitable for 2–4 tents. The Right South Fork of the Ogden River feeds into the reservoir at the campground, providing a source of fresh water (this water should be treated before drinking; during spring and periods of heavy runoff, it can be laden with sediment).

Directions

From Salt Lake City drive north on I-15 for 16 miles and take Exit 324 for U.S. Highway 89 North. Drive 10.6 miles on U.S. Highway 89 and take Exit 92 for State Route 167 toward Huntsville. Continue 4.4 miles and follow State Route 167 as it turns left. Drive 1.6 miles farther and turn left onto Trappers Loop Road. Continue for 9.5 miles and turn right onto Ogden Canyon Road/State Route 39. Follow Ogden Canyon Road/State Route 39 for 1.8 miles and turn right to stay on State Route 39. Follow State Route 39 for 8.4 miles and turn right onto Causey Drive. Continue 1.6 miles and turn right onto Skull Crack Canyon Road, marked by a sign for Causey Estates. Drive 1 mile and turn left into the parking lot for the Skull Crack Trailhead.

GPS Coordinates: N 41°28.902' W 111°58.282'

Information and Contact

There is no fee. Dogs on leash are allowed. Maps are available at the Union Station Information Center, 2501 Wall Avenue, Ogden, UT 84401, 801/625-5306. For more information, contact Ogden Ranger District Office, Uinta-Wasatch-Cache National Forest, 507 25th Street, Ogden, UT 84401, 801/625-5112, www.fs.fed.us.

5 BIRDSONG TRAIL
Wasatch-Cache National Forest

Level: Easy

Hiking Time: 1 hour

Total Distance: 1-2.3 miles round-trip

Elevation Change: 518 feet

Summary: Birdsong Trail is a pleasant stroll through a diverse forest at the mouth of Ogden Canyon.

Birdsong Trail offers a quiet, peaceful alternative to the many heart-pounding, summit-seeking ascents along the Wasatch Front. It is a place to notice the little things in nature. Cold, clear springs flowing out of the ground. The sounds of songbirds serenading each other in the dense woodlands. And microclimates so different and close to each other that a water-thirsty redwood tree and desert-loving prickly pear cactus can be found within 100 yards of each other. The trail is a great place for families too; young children can explore nature and feel empowered by finishing the entire hike on their own.

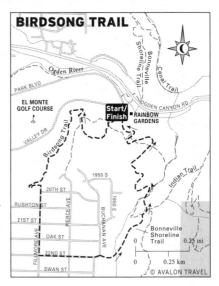

The Birdsong Trail can be done as an out-and-back walk or a loop trail, and may be started at either the Rainbow Gardens Gift Shop or at the 22nd Street Trailhead. The heart of the trail—and the place with the highest density of birds—lies in the thick stands of trees encircling the meadow just west of the Rainbow Gardens parking lot. From Rainbow Gardens head south out of the lot on the crushed gravel trail and into the thicket of Russian olive and cottonwood trees, willow, maple, and oak. It's here in the woods that you'll see and hear some of the following birds: yellow-breasted chat, chipping sparrow, blue-gray gnatcatcher, Bullock's oriole, black-headed grosbeak, Virginia's warbler, and gray catbird. The trail rises as it circles the meadow, staying in the woods for the first 200 yards before climbing onto a bluff overlooking the grassland. Here prickly pear cacti grow between big sagebrush in a typical western desert plant community. The trail makes a 0.25-mile loop around the top of this overlook, providing a view of the El Monte Golf Course to the west and Ogden Canyon to the east. At the far point in the loop, a fork in the trail offers an option to continue south toward the 22nd Street Trailhead. Head right to hike toward 22nd Street, or left to make the small loop back to Rainbow Gardens. If you continue to the right, the Birdsong Trail meanders southwest through more forest and then through a short section of sagebrush before ending at the intersection of 20th Street and Fillmore in the Olympus Heights neighborhood. From here walk four blocks south and three blocks east through the neighborhood to return to the 22nd Street Trailhead. To complete the loop from the 22nd Street Trailhead, hike north along the Bonneville Shoreline Trail, following the green signs for the Rainbow Trail (with the Birdsong Trail listed below in fine print). From the trailhead you'll walk up a short trail to merge with the large Bonneville Shoreline Trail. Follow this trail for 0.1 mile and turn left, then go downhill for 0.75 mile to the Rainbow Gardens Gift Shop.

Options

This trail has two official trailheads: one at Rainbow Gardens and the other at the 20th Street Trailhead for the Bonneville Shoreline Trail. The shortest option is to simply walk the trail through the woods from the Rainbow Gardens parking lot to the top of the bluff and return the way you came. The trail can be done as a loop from either trailhead as well.

Directions

From Salt Lake City drive north on I-15 for 35.3 miles and take Exit 341 for 31st

overview of the Birdsong Trail with Ben Lomond in the background

Street/UT 79. Take the right fork and merge onto 31st Street/UT 79. Follow 31st Street for 1.2 miles and turn left onto U.S. 89/Washington Boulevard. Drive 0.1 mile and take a right onto 30th Street. Continue on 30th Street for 1.2 miles and turn left onto 1200 East/Harrison Boulevard. Drive 1.4 miles on Harrison Boulevard and turn right onto 20th Street. Continue on 20th Street for 125 feet and take the first left onto Valley Drive and stay on Valley Drive for 1.2 miles. Turn right into the Rainbow Gardens parking lot.

GPS Coordinates: 41°23.619' 111°93.077'

Information and Contact

There is no fee. Dogs on leash are allowed. The USGS Map for Ogden covers this area. For more information, contact Rainbow Gardens, 1851 Valley Drive, Ogden, UT 84401, 801/621-1606, www.rainbowgardens.com.

6 MALANS PEAK VIA TAYLOR CANYON

BEST C

Wasatch-Cache National Forest

Level: Moderate

Total Distance: 5.5 miles round-trip

Hiking Time: 3-4 hours

Elevation Change: 2,814 feet

Summary: This shaded forest hike leads to a stunningly beautiful lookout point that allows for sweeping views of the Northern Wasatch Front.

Shaded by a lush forest for most of the route, Malans Peak Trail is an excellent choice for hot summer days. Although it is actually a sub-ridge of the much higher Mount Ogden, Malans Peak's commanding position above the city makes it a natural destination for hikers.

The Malans Peak Trail starts out from Ogden's 29th Street Trailhead as a gravel path leading up and south to the Bonneville Shoreline Trail. At 0.2 mile the trail joins the Bonneville Shoreline Trail. Take the left path, following the green trail signs for Taylor Canyon South Trail. After 0.1 mile there will be a second fork in the trail with a short post marking the Taylor Canyon South Trail. Take the right fork headed into the woods. The smooth dirt trail enters the Gambel oak and Rocky Mountain maple forest and heads uphill and north toward Taylor Canyon. At a third junction, two trails cross in an X; continue uphill and to the right, following the sign for Taylor Canyon. At 1 mile, the trail crosses Taylor Creek (or the dry creek bed) on a wooden

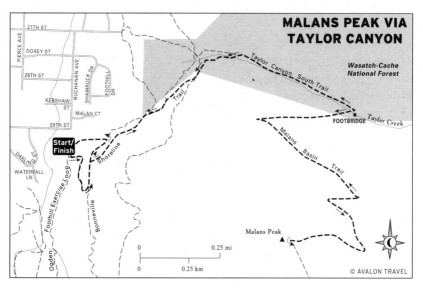

MALANS PEAK VIA TAYLOR CANYON

© MIKE MATSON

the view south from the overlook on the summit of Malans Peak

bridge to the north side of the creek to enter Taylor Canyon. The trail continues along the left side of the creek until it reaches another junction and footbridge at 1.4 miles. Take the right fork here, following the sign for Malans Basin Trail. From here the trail climbs steeply up the south side of Taylor Canyon. After passing an interesting limestone cliff, the trail continues up to its first impressive viewpoint at 2 miles. The route ducks back into dense vegetation and heads east toward Mount Ogden. A mix of conifers, maple, oak, and chokecherry creates a forest canopy that closes in around the trail. Pine needles blanket the wide path. The trail has one last switchback before leading back west to the craggy overlook of Malans Peak.

The view is one of the best along the Wasatch Front, spreading out from the town of Ogden to include the Great Salt Lake to the west, Antelope Island and the Stansbury Mountains to the southwest, and the prominent peaks of the Northern Wasatch Range, including Ben Lomond and Willard Peak, to the north. There's no question that it's a worthy destination in itself, but the more ambitious can add to the adventure by continuing on to Malans Basin and the historic site of the Malan Heights Resort, a small hotel, sawmill, and seven log cabins that were built in 1893. The resort burned in a fire in 1913 and is now marked by an interpretive sign and the old iron boiler from the sawmill. It's a popular spot to spend the night on short backpacking trips.

Options
Extend this hike by continuing up the trail to Malans Basin at 3 miles or even to the summit of Mount Ogden at 10 miles one-way.

Directions

From Salt Lake City, drive north on 1-15 for 35.3 miles and take Exit 341A. Drive east on 31st Street to Washington Boulevard. Turn left on Washington Boulevard and continue one block to 30th Street. Turn right on 30th Street and go east for 1.2 miles to Tyler Avenue. Turn left on Tyler Avenue and drive one block to 29th Street. The trailhead parking lot is at the end of 29th Street.

GPS Coordinates: 41°21.101' 111°93.184'

Information and Contact

There is no fee. Dogs on leash are allowed. The USGS Map for Ogden covers this area. Malans Peak is on private property; however, it is open to the public. There is no direct contact information.

7 WATERFALL CANYON

BEST 🄲

Uinta-Wasatch-Cache National Forest

🚻 🛶 🐎 👫

Level: Moderate	**Total Distance:** 3.0 miles round-trip
Hiking Time: 1.5-2 hours	**Elevation Change:** 1,500 feet

Summary: A short, steep trail leads to a hidden 200-foot-high waterfall with views to the valley floor below.

Waterfall Canyon is a relatively short, challenging hike leading to the impressive Malan Falls. During the summer, Malan Falls is a wispy curtain of water falling from ledge to ledge over broken brown cliffs. Ogden locals hike up to the falls to cool off in the misty shower and to enjoy the beautiful natural amphitheater. Butterflies flit along the creek, birds sing in the lush forest, and hikers from all walks of life shuffle up and down the rocky trail. This is a popular hike for families with children and a great hike for dogs. In winter, the crowds disappear and the falls build into a formidable bulging icicle. During extremely cold periods in winter, the ice becomes strong enough for ice climbers to test their skills here. The falls were first climbed in 1971 by local climbing pioneer Jeff Lowe; it represented the most technically difficult climb of its kind.

The Waterfall Canyon Trail begins on the east side of Ogden at the 29th Street Trailhead. From the parking lot, follow a short section of gravel trail leading uphill to the Bonneville Shoreline Trail. To continue to Waterfall Canyon,

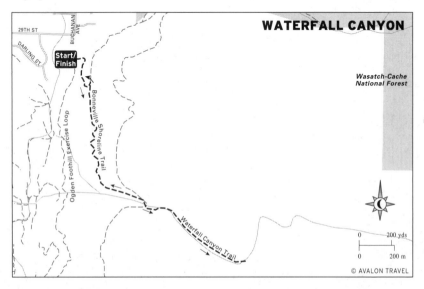

© MIKE MATSON

the falls in Waterfall Canyon

join the Bonneville Shoreline Trail by turning right at the green trail sign and hike south 0.5 mile to the entrance to the canyon. This wide, open section of trail rises gently through Gambel oak trees and offers views of Ogden and the northern arm of the Great Salt Lake. Prickly pear cacti grow in clumps in the sandy soil, and it is not unusual to spot rattlesnakes moving through the underbrush or warming themselves on the rocks. (Keep a wary eye out, especially if you brought your dog along.)

After passing two rusty old water tanks, the trail wraps gently around the hillside and into Waterfall Canyon. At 0.6 mile and the mouth of the canyon, the trail crosses a wooden bridge and parallels the south side of the creek. The trail then becomes rocky and steep as it climbs alongside the cascading stream. Large conglomerate boulders make for interesting geology, and the lush forest is full of winged creatures—from songbirds to dragonflies and butterflies. Large yellow swallowtail butterflies, with their large yellow-and-black-striped wings, are easy to identify, but more commonly expect to see European whites and the tiny blue azure along the trail.

The path crosses the stream again over another footbridge. Back on the north side of the drainage now, the trail continues over rocky terrain through a dense forest until the waterfall comes into view. From here, it becomes a scramble up loose rocks to the base of the falls.

For great photos, consider bringing a tripod on this hike. Using the tripod for camera stability, set the camera for the slowest shutter speed possible to let the falling water blur. Shutter speeds slower than 1/15 of a second will produce the best results.

Options

The Waterfall Canyon Trail can be combined with the Malans Peak Trail, descending Taylor Canyon to create a 7-mile loop. This option involves some steep scrambling to climb out of the rock gully on the right side of Waterfall Canyon, required to join the Malans Peak Trail. From there, the trail ascends to Malans Basin and can be followed north to the 6,916-foot Malans Peak. From Malans

Peak, follow the trail downhill (north) into Taylors Canyon to connect with the Bonneville Shoreline Trail; this trail heads south to finish the loop at the 29th Street Trailhead.

Waterfall Canyon Trail can also be combined with a hike to the north or south along the Bonneville Shoreline Trail.

Directions

From Salt Lake City, drive north on I-15 for 35.3 miles and take Exit 341A. Drive east on 31st Street to Washington Boulevard. Turn left on Washington Boulevard and continue one block to 30th Street. Turn right on 30th Street and go east for 1.2 miles to Tyler Avenue. Turn left on Tyler Avenue and drive one block to 29th Street. The trailhead parking lot is at the end of 29th Street.

GPS Coordinates: 41°21.101' 111°93.184'

Information and Contact

There is no fee. Dogs on leash are allowed. Maps are available at the Union Station Information Center, 2501 Wall Avenue, Ogden, UT 84401, 801/625-5306. For more information, contact the Ogden Ranger District, Uinta-Wasatch-Cache National Forest, 507 25th Street, Suite 103, Ogden, UT 84401, 801/625-5112, www.fs.fed.us.

8 ADAMS CANYON
Wasatch-Cache National Forest

Level: Moderate

Hiking Time: 2-3 hours

Total Distance: 3-3.5 miles round-trip

Elevation Change: 1,683 feet

Summary: Adams Canyon Trail follows the North Fork of Holmes Creek through a shaded forest to a picture-perfect waterfall.

If bigger isn't always better, then the waterfall at the top of Adams Canyon just might be for you. The cascade isn't the tallest or the largest you'll encounter. In fact, it doesn't even have an official name. But it's a beautiful falls and a great destination for a hike.

The Adams Canyon Trail doesn't start off in glorious fashion. Leaving from an unmarked dirt parking lot, it skirts a chain-link fence around a water-holding pond. Then it abruptly climbs a hot, sandy hill through a mazelike series of short, steep switchbacks. But by 0.7 mile where the Adams Canyon Trail meets the Bonneville Shoreline Trail, the aesthetics of the trail have improved considerably. And they only get better as the route enters Adams Canyon itself. Stay left of the creek where the two trails meet and continue into the forested confines of Adams Canyon.

The trail stays close to the creek for almost the entire trip up the canyon. Dragonflies and butterflies flit through the air along the watercourse. Butterfly species found here include the Weidemeyer's Admiral with its dark brown wings with white highlights, the western tiger swallowtail with its bumblebee

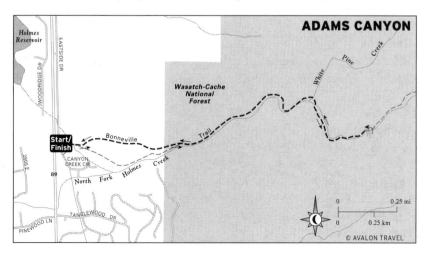

color scheme, and the tiny yet beautiful Reakrit's blue. The stream's water sustains a lush forest highlighted by some truly impressive ancient white pine trees. With trunks three feet in diameter, these are trees you'd expect to find in a coastal rain forest in Southeast Alaska, not Northern Utah.

Adams Canyon waterfall

Ascending the canyon, the trail sticks to the left side of the creek, skirting around spots where the creek's banks have been washed out by high water. After 0.75 mile of hiking in the canyon itself, or about 1.5 miles total, the trail crosses a wooden footbridge and heads up the south side of Holmes Creek. The route gets steeper above the bridge crossing, and hikers must clamor over several large rocks on the canyon's right side. Nothing is too dangerous here, but going slowly is a good idea. It's worth bringing a pair of trekking poles for this upper portion of the trail; they may come in handy for crossing the creek below the waterfall as well. After going by a series of small wood-choked waterfalls, the trail bends around a rock wall and reveals the upper Adams Canyon waterfall. Depending on the season and water level of the creek, crossing the stream to the left side of the falls may or may not be a good idea. After soaking in the beauty, return down the canyon the way you came.

Options

Hikers looking to extend their trip can head south down the Bonneville Shoreline Trail, which meets the Adams Canyon Trail at the mouth of Adams Canyon.

Directions

From Salt Lake City drive north on I-15 for 16.2 miles to Exit 324/U.S. Highway 89 and follow signs for I-84 East/South Ogden. Continue north on U.S. Highway 89 for 6.2 miles. Turn right onto Eastside Drive, continue for 85 feet, and turn right again to stay on Eastside Drive. Continue 0.3 mile and turn left into the unpaved trail parking lot.

GPS Coordinates: 41°06.636' 111°90.946'

Information and Contact

There is no fee. Dogs on leash are allowed. Maps are available at the Public Lands Information Center, 3285 East 3300 South (inside REI), Salt Lake City, UT 84109, 801/466-6411. For more information, contact the Salt Lake Ranger District, Uinta-Wasatch-Cache National Forest, 6944 South 3000 East, Salt Lake City, UT 84121, 801/733-2660, www.fs.fed.us.

9 KENNY CREEK TRAIL   BEST C
Wasatch-Cache National Forest

Level: Moderate   **Total Distance:** 4.5 miles round-trip

Hiking Time: 2.5-3 hours   **Elevation Change:** 2,850 feet

Summary: Kenny Creek Trail follows a historic, brush-choked route to the remnants of a pioneer-era mining cabin.

Despite sharing trailheads from the same parking lot, the Kenny Creek Trail and Mueller Park Trail could not be more different in character. On the Mueller Park Trail you'll pass dozens of other users, including mountain bikers. Along the Kenny Creek Trail, don't be surprised if you don't see another soul, much less a mountain biker. The Mueller Park Trail is wide and well maintained. The Kenny Creek Trail is overgrown in places; sometimes the brush and grass is so thick, you won't be able to see your feet. Both trails have their advantages—the trick is finding what's best for you. The advantages to Kenny Creek include solitude, the potential for seeing wildlife such as deer and elk, and the visible history of a 100-year-old miner's cabin. On the downside, the trail maintenance on the Kenny Creek Trail is lacking in places. Wear long pants to avoid scratched-up legs.

Kenny Creek Trail starts on the north side of the Mueller Park Road 0.3 mile beyond the park entrance station, across from the parking lot for sites 1–7 in the Mueller Park picnic area. The trenchlike, dirt trail gains elevation quickly, following the creek until it crosses the stream at 0.3 mile. Box elder, Rocky Mountain maple, Gambel oak, and white pine trees predominate in the

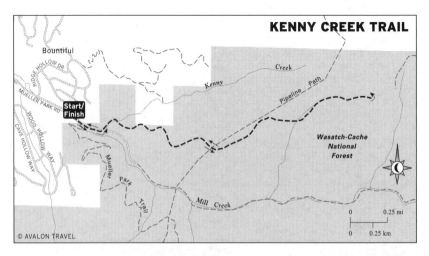

© MIKE MATSON

the Kenny Creek Trail with the Great Salt Lake and Oquirrh Mountains on the horizon

low-slung forest shading the trail. After a switchback up a steep hill the trail opens up into the first of a series of grassy meadows. Although clumps of maple trees still provide shade, underbrush encroaches on the trail, and the shoulder-height grass makes the meadows feel a little claustrophobic. At 1.1 miles the forest gives way to a short-grass meadow, and views open up to the west. The cities of Woods Cross and Bountiful, along with the Great Salt Lake and Antelope Island, are all visible on a clear day. You'll also notice the scar left from the recently built natural gas pipeline known as the Apex Expansion Project. The pipeline, owned by Kern River Gas Transportation Company, is a 28-mile extension of a pipeline from North Canyon to Salt Lake International Airport. It's part of a larger pipeline running from Wyoming to California. Cross the barren swath left from the construction and head back into the Gambel oaks. Yellow mule ear and Wasatch penstemon wildflowers grow in thick clumps, and the vegetation is closer to the ground here, allowing for more expansive views as you climb higher up the mountainside. Across the canyon to the south look for the Mueller Park Trail as it crosses the exposed ribbon of pipeline.

As the trail continues to gain elevation, it becomes rocky in sections. Keep an eye out for grouse roaming the underbrush and deer and elk on the exposed slopes of the mountain. Just when you start to wonder if this trail will lead to anywhere in particular, you'll hike through a stand of old aspens at 2.25 miles. Beyond the aspens are the toppled logs of a pioneer-era miner's cabin and the tailings from his mine. From the cabin return down the way you came.

Options

The trailhead for the Mueller Park Trail (see listing in this chapter) is right across the street and offers a longer 6.2-mile option.

Directions:

From Salt Lake City drive north on I-15 for 4.2 miles to Exit 312 and merge onto U.S. 89/Beck Street. Continue to follow U.S. 89 for 3.3 miles. Turn right onto 2600 South and drive 0.6 miles to Orchard Drive. Continue straight onto Orchard Drive and drive 0.9 mile to 1800 South. Take 1800 South for 2.4 miles to the entrance to Mueller Park where it turns into Mueller Park Road.

GPS Coordinates: 41°86.436' 111°83.758'

Information and Contact

There is no fee. Dogs on leash are allowed. Maps are available at the Public Lands Information Center, 3285 East 3300 South (inside REI), Salt Lake City, UT 84109, 801/466-6411. For more information, contact the Salt Lake Ranger District, Uinta-Wasatch-Cache National Forest, 6944 South 3000 East, Salt Lake City, UT 84121, 801/733-2660, www.fs.fed.us.

10 MUELLER PARK

Wasatch-Cache National Forest

Level: Moderate

Total Distance: 6.2 miles round-trip

Hiking Time: 3-4 hours

Elevation Change: 1,571 feet

Summary: A smooth, twisting track through a quiet, shady forest reaches an elevated overlook of the Great Salt Lake.

If you're looking for a peaceful walk in the woods, here it is. This trail is a tunnel through a dense green forest with a gentle grade and smooth tread—the type of trail you could walk once a week all summer and fall more in love with every time.

The well-maintained path is a favorite of trail runners and mountain bikers, but it's a wonderful walk as well, especially if you enjoy identifying the copious communities of plant species encountered along the way. At the end of this section of trail, an overlook with two wooden benches looks down on Big Rock, a large rock face protruding from the forest. The panorama includes a view of the Great Salt Lake and Antelope Island on the western horizon.

Heading south out of the paved parking lot, a wooden footbridge crosses Mill

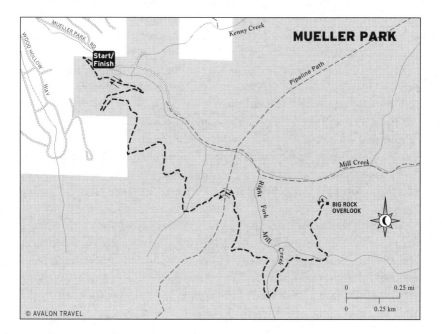

© AVALON TRAVEL

the city of Bountiful, with the Great Salt Lake behind it, from the Mueller Park Trail

Creek immediately before beginning up a forested slope. The pine needle–blanketed trail is wide in the first mile as it navigates a series of short, gentle switchbacks. Mature Gambel oak, Rocky Mountain maple, and box elder tree branches stretch across the trail, reaching for all the available sunlight. Even on hot days, it's relatively cool on this part of the trail. The trail has been buffed smooth by thousands of mountain bike tires, and wide berms mark the tight corners where bikers bank their turns.

At 0.9 mile, the forest opens up to offer a glimpse of Big Rock, the destination for this section of the trail. Look up the canyon and notice the large gray rock standing out in stark contrast to the green forest canopy. As the trail gains elevation, it exits the forest periodically to allow views of the surrounding mountains. You'll notice the scar left from the recently constructed natural gas pipeline known as the Apex Expansion Project. The pipeline, owned by Kern River Gas Transportation Company, is a 28-mile extension of a pipeline from North Canyon to Salt Lake International Airport. It's part of a larger pipeline running from Wyoming to California.

At about 1.5 miles the trail crosses a small tributary to Mill Creek, descending from Cave Peak. In the next mile, the trail levels and crosses a series of wood-plank bridges, first for a seeping spring and then over the Right Fork of Mill Creek. From the creek, the trail works north for 0.4 mile to the Big Rock overlook, marking the end of this section of the trail. Turn around and return to the car from Big Rock for the 6.2-mile out-and-back distance.

Options

For hikers looking for a longer hike, the Mueller Park Trail continues another 3 miles to the Ruby Flat for a 13-mile out-and-back. Beyond Ruby Flat, the trail can actually be linked up with North Canyon, including a section of pavement at the bottom of North Canyon to make a 13-mile loop.

Directions:

From Salt Lake City, drive north on I-15 for 4.2 miles to Exit 312 and merge onto U.S. 89/Beck Street. Continue to follow U.S. Highway 89 for 3.3 miles. Turn right onto 2600 South and drive 0.6 mile to Orchard Drive. Continue straight onto Orchard Drive and drive 0.9 mile to 1800 South. Take 1800 South for 2.4 miles to the entrance to Mueller Park where it turns into Mueller Park Road. **GPS Coordinates:** 41°86.436' 111°83.758'

Information and Contact

There is no fee. Dogs on leash are allowed. Maps are available at the Public Lands Information Center, 3285 East 3300 South (inside REI), Salt Lake City, UT 84109, 801/466-6411. For more information, contact the Salt Lake Ranger District, Uinta-Wasatch-Cache National Forest, 6944 South 3000 East, Salt Lake City, UT 84121, 801/733-2660, www.fs.fed.us.

SOUTHERN WASATCH

© MIKE MATSON

BEST HIKES

The Southern Wasatch Mountains are a peak

bagger's paradise. Located south of Salt Lake City and east of the cities of Alpine, Lehi, Orem, and Provo, the Wasatch Range's highest summits can be found here, along with its most popular hikes. Mount Nebo is the southernmost peak in the Wasatch Range, and the highest at 11,928 feet. Mount Nebo attracts many visitors because of its height, but it isn't the area's most popular hike. That distinction belongs to Mount Timpanogos. "Timp," as it's affectionately called, reaches 11,750 feet and is by far the most-climbed peak in the state of Utah. The rocky massif dominates the skyline of Provo with its broad, seven-mile-wide ridgeline, punctuated by three distinct summits. Horizontal bands of limestone and quartzite give the mountain a distinctive zebra-stripe profile. These dark-colored vertical bands of rock are too steep to hold snow during winter, creating a beautiful visual contrast after storms. Other attractive mountains such as Box Elder and Squaw Peak attract the attention of summit seekers in this part of the range as well.

The Southern Wasatch has plenty to offer in the way of compelling shorter hikes, too. Mount Timpanogos is circumnavigated by the Alpine Loop Scenic Byway, which leads to an interesting variety of high-quality hikes. Along this route families can go spelunking – the National Park Service leads tours in an underground squeeze-way at the Timpanogos Cave National Monument – or walk to the quiet, secluded shores of Silver Lake. Right above the town of Provo, Brigham Young University's Y Mountain beckons both families and college kids with its irresistible, 380-foot-tall white letter Y.

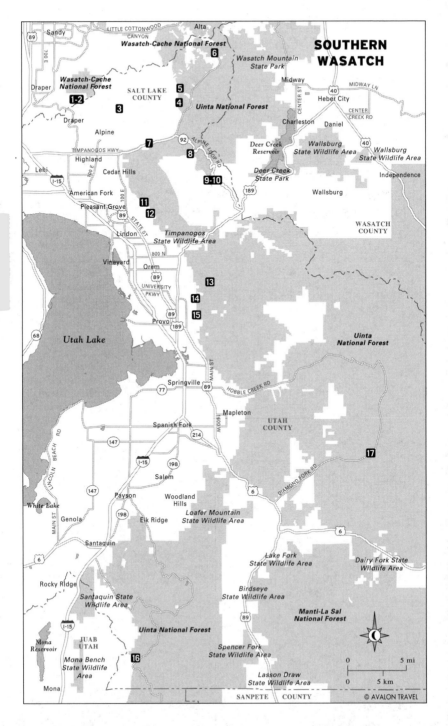

TRAIL NAME	LEVEL	DISTANCE	TIME	ELEVATION	FEATURES	PAGE
1 Lone Peak on the Jacob's Ladder Trail	Butt-kicker	10.5 mi rt	8-10 hr	5,702 ft		180
2 Ghost Falls	Easy	2.6 mi rt	1-2 hr	436 ft		184
3 Dry Creek Canyon to Horsetail Falls	Moderate	4.0 mi rt	2-3 hr	1,965 ft		187
4 Box Elder	Butt-kicker	9.4 mi rt	7-8 hr	4,704 ft		189
5 Silver Lake from Silver Flat Reservoir	Moderate	4.1 mi rt	2-3 hr	1,522 ft		193
6 Pittsburg Lake	Moderate	3.0 mi rt	2-2.5 hr	1,512 ft		196
7 Timpanogos Cave National Monument	Moderate	2.5 mi rt	3-3.5 hr	1,197 ft		199
8 Timpooneke Trail	Butt-kicker	12.7 mi rt	9-10 hr	4,937 ft		202
9 Aspen Grove Trail	Butt-kicker	12.0 mi rt	8-10 hr	4,900 ft		205
10 Stewart Falls	Easy	3.8 mi rt	2 hr	342 ft		208
11 Grove Creek	Moderate	4.0 mi rt	2.5-3 hr	3,132 ft		211
12 Battle Creek Falls	Easy	1.1 mi rt	30 min-1 hr	465 ft		214
13 Buffalo Peak	Easy	1.0 mi rt	30 min-1 hr	278 ft		216
14 Squaw Mountain	Moderate	7.0 mi rt	3.5-4 hr	1,965 ft		218
15 Y Mountain	Easy	1.6 mi rt	1 hr	1,115 ft		221
16 Mount Nebo via the North Peak Trail	Butt-kicker	9.3 mi rt	6-8 hr	3,530 ft		224
17 Fifth Water Hot Springs	Moderate	4.6 mi rt	2.5-3 hr	984 ft		227

1 LONE PEAK ON THE JACOB'S LADDER TRAIL

BEST 🌙

Uinta National Forest

Level: Butt-kicker

Total Distance: 10.5 miles round-trip

Hiking Time: 8-10 hours

Elevation Change: 5,702 feet

Summary: A steep, challenging hike to the summit of one of the most appealing peaks in the Wasatch Range.

Lone Peak is one of the Wasatch Range's most aesthetically pleasing mountains. Steep granite walls, a stunningly beautiful alpine cirque, and its prominent position along the Salt Lake Valley's southern skyline sets Lone Peak apart as a Wasatch highlight. In 1977, the Lone Peak Wilderness was created as part of the Endangered American Wilderness Act to protect these 30,088 acres. The wilderness designation—and its high, difficult-to-reach upper slopes—keep the mountain's

LONE PEAK ON THE JACOB'S LADDER TRAIL

© MIKE MATSON

Wildflowers bloom in Lone Peak Cirque.

character as wild as any spot in the Wasatch Range. A resident herd of mountain goats is often seen in Lone Peak Cirque or along its craggy ridges. The granite-like quartz monzonite rock found on the walls of Lone Peak Cirque is sought out by rock climbers for its long, appealing cracks. Some of the best high-altitude, alpine rock routes in the state are found here.

There are several trails up Lone Peak, and they all have their faults. Steep, heavily eroded sections mar each trail, and all the options are long and challenging. The Jacob's Ladder Trail seems to be the best option, and the trailhead is easy to find.

Jacob's Ladder Trail starts by switchbacking gently through Gambel oaks and Rocky Mountain maples. The first 1.3 miles of trail are used by mountain bikers for the downhill run of a loop trail coming up from Corner Canyon—you'll notice the banked curves and the imprints of knobby tires in the dust. Enjoy the gentle grade, because the trail becomes progressively steeper as it winds up the canyon. The single track quickly leaves the shade of the oaks to join a wide jeep track coming across from Traverse Ridge, the fingerlike mountain extending down to the valley floor. The trail follows the ridgeline as it gains elevation, alternating between sharp rocky sections and smooth dirt. In some places, the path is wide enough for a semitruck, whereas in others it's just a narrow ribbon. By 0.9 mile, the views are already spectacular—look west across the valley to the Oquirrh Mountains and south to Utah Lake. Several jeep trails come up from the right to join the trail; ignore these options and continue uphill along the ridge.

At 1.7 miles the trail begins climbing up a very steep hillside, leaving the ridge below. This part of the trail is in very poor shape. In fact, it feels more like a steep, deeply eroded gully than a proper trail. Climb steadily upward and have faith—things get better as the elevation increases. By 2.25 miles the worst of the gully climb is behind you, and you'll come out into a clearing with well-earned views.

At 2.5 miles Lone Peak Cirque comes into view to the northeast. The Draper Ridge Trail comes in from the west at 2.9 miles, joining the Jacob's Ladder Trail at an unmarked junction. The trail works its way up a broad ridge called Ennis Peak. The ridge is nearly treeless, with an occasional subalpine fir or limber pine on grass-and-sagebrush-covered slopes. The trail now heads almost directly east toward Lone Peak Cirque, traversing through open meadows and a beautiful stand of subalpine fir.

At 3.5 miles the trail traverses across broad slabs of granite for 0.5 mile. Following the route can be a bit tricky across the bare rock. Watch for cairns, or piles of rocks that other hikers have built, to point you in the right direction. Keep trending east and uphill; even if you get a little off trail, all paths lead to Lone Peak Cirque. From the granite slabs, the trail funnels into a boulder-choked gully, which leads up to the cirque.

If the cirque is your goal, keep climbing and stay to the right, which leads to a field of gigantic boulders. Boulder-hop through the maze of granite and up into the surprisingly flat, open cirque floor. This is a great place to camp if you're backpacking or if you've come to rock climb on the cirque's impeccable alpine walls. A large snowfield provides water for campers in the cirque until sometime in midsummer. But after it's melted away, there's no water source. Plan accordingly.

If summiting 11,253-foot Lone Peak is your goal, continue left at the top of the gully. Traverse north, skirting the lower rim of the cirque heading toward Lone Peak's north ridge. Look carefully for cairns along the base of the ridge marking the path of least resistance. It's easy to get sucked into a steep gully on the lower ridge and do more work than is necessary. Gain the ridge and then hike up the stunning granite spine. A trail leads to within 200 yards of the summit before giving way to a short rock scramble. The last couple hundred feet are not for the faint of heart, and definitely step into the realm of mountaineering. Take your time and move carefully across this section of exposed terrain.

Options

Lone Peak can also be climbed via the Draper Ridge Trail, which climbs the first 3.8 miles via Draper Ridge, for a 12-mile round-trip option with an elevation gain of 5,973 feet. The trailhead is one mile further down on the Corner Canyon Road, which can be an advantage when the road is snowbound or closed in winter or spring. On the downside, the Draper Ridge Trail is not maintained and is overgrown in places.

Directions

From Salt Lake City, drive south on I-15 for 14 miles to Exit 291 for 12300 South. Turn left off the exit ramp and continue on 12300 South for 1.9 miles. Turn right on 1300 East and drive for 0.2 mile to the continuous-flow traffic circle. Exit the circle heading east on Pioneer Road. Drive for 1 mile on Pioneer Road and turn right on 2000 East. Drive 0.2 mile on 2000 East to the Orson Smith trailhead on the left side of the road. Turn left into the trailhead and then turn right onto the Upper Corner Canyon Road. Drive 2.6 miles on the dirt Upper Corner Canyon Road to the Ghost Falls trailhead parking area on the right side of the road. The Jacob's Ladder Trail begins a short distance up the road from the parking area on the left.

GPS Coordinates: N 40°49.442' W 111°81.718'

Information and Contact

There is no fee. Dogs on leash are allowed. Maps are available at the Public Lands Information Center, 3285 East 3300 South (inside REI), Salt Lake City, UT 84109, 801/466-6411. For more information, contact Salt Lake City Ranger District, Uinta-Wasatch-Cache National Forest, 125 South State Street, Salt Lake City, UT 84138, 801/236-3400, www.fs.fed.us.

② GHOST FALLS
Corner Canyon Regional Park

🦌 🐾 👫

Level: Easy   **Total Distance:** 2.6 miles round-trip

Hiking Time: 1-2 hours   **Elevation Change:** 436 feet

Summary: A family-friendly hike to a sometimes impressive, other times elusive, waterfall.

Named Ghost Falls for its ability to nearly disappear during dry parts of the year, this waterfall can be a gushing torrent of water or a gurgling trickle. But during spring runoff when the water is plentiful, the falls makes for a nice destination—an added bonus to a multi-use trail exploring the foothills of Corner Canyon.

Located between Lone Peak and Traverse Mountain, Corner Canyon Regional Park is a recreation hot spot. Mountain bikers, horseback riders, and hikers share an extensive network of trails weaving through the park. Ghost Falls is one of the park's best trails for hikers. Although the interconnected trail system makes it possible to reach Ghost Falls from several trailheads, the Coyote Hollow trailhead creates a 3-mile round-trip that's perfect for families. Watch for deer along the trail, and be aware that rattlesnakes are common in the area.

Starting from the paved parking area at the Coyote Hollow trailhead, hike east down the trail. The trail quickly merges with a wide gravel road for the first 0.25 mile. At the bottom of this downhill there's a four-way trail junction. Head right, following the sign for Ghost Falls. At 0.5 mile follow the sign for Canyon Hollow Trail and leave the gravel road for a single-track trail. The dirt trail sees lots of mountain bike traffic, which makes for easy walking on its smooth surface. Mature Gambel oaks and Rocky Mountain maples shade the trail. At 0.8 mile you'll reach a trail junction with options to take the Ghost Falls North Loop or the South Loop. Head to the right for the South Loop. The trail continues to climb gently uphill, and then at 1.2 miles it crosses a small wooden footbridge and reaches another junction. Turn left and cross a second bridge leading down a short hill to a metal bridge. During high water flows you'll hear it before you see it, but at other times you'll be surprised to see Ghost Falls pouring down a granite slab just above the bridge.

Continue down the trail to the right from the falls to complete the Ghost Falls Loop. This is the north side of the loop. The trail opens up here to reveal views down to the Draper Utah Temple and across the valley to the Oquirrh Mountains. At 1.6 miles, you'll reach another junction, turn left, and descend across the ravine on a bridge to link back up with the main trunk of the Ghost Falls Trail. Having completed the little loop portion of the trail, retrace your steps to the Coyote Hollow trailhead.

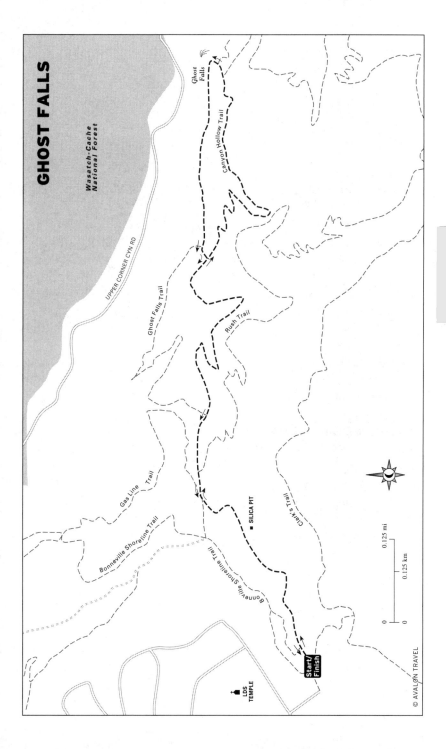

GHOST FALLS

Wasatch-Cache National Forest

UPPER CORNER CYN RD

Ghost Falls

Canyon Hollow Trail

Ghost Falls Trail

Rush Trail

Gas Line Trail

Bonneville Shoreline Trail

Bonneville Shoreline Trail

■ SILICA PIT

Clark's Trail

0   0.125 mi

0   0.125 km

Start/Finish

LDS TEMPLE

© AVALON TRAVEL

Options

There are many variations and possible route options leading to Ghost Falls within the Corner Canyon Trail system. Free trail maps are available at the trailheads.

Directions

From Salt Lake City drive south on I-15 for 16 miles to Exit 288 for Bluffdale. From the exit ramp turn left onto Highland Drive and continue for 2.6 miles to Rambling Road. Turn right on Rambling Road and drive for 0.8 mile to the traffic circle. Take the second exit from the circle onto Sage Hollow Drive. Continue on Sage Hollow for 0.6 mile to Coyote Hollow Court. Turn left on Coyote Hollow Court and continue for one block to the Coyote Hollow trailhead.

GPS Coordinates: N 40°29.391' W 111°50.211'

the view down Corner Canyon, from the Ghost Falls Trail to the Draper Utah Temple

© MIKE MATSON

Information and Contact

There is no fee. Dogs are allowed but must be on leash at all times, and their waste must be collected because the park is a watershed. Free maps of the Corner Canyon trail system are available at all the designated trailheads, including Coyote Hollow. For more information contact the City of Draper at Ghost Falls, City of Draper Parks & Trails, 72 East Sivogah Court (14525 South), Draper, UT 84020, 801/576-6557, www.cornercanyontrails.com.

3 DRY CREEK CANYON TO HORSETAIL FALLS
Uinta National Forest

🚶 ✈ 🐾 🐎

Level: Moderate

Total Distance: 4.0 miles round-trip

Hiking Time: 2-3 hours

Elevation Change: 1,965 feet

Summary: A wide, gently rising trail leads to Horsetail Falls, a braided waterfall cascading down a granite slab.

Dry Creek Canyon is between two of the Wasatch Mountain's highest, most prominent peaks: 11,253-foot Lone Peak to the north and 11,101-foot Box Elder to the south. The Dry Creek Canyon Trail to Horsetail Falls is a nice walk up a forested canyon, with a view of a lovely waterfall as its reward. Dry Creek Canyon is also a good spot to find birds; look for winter wrens, warbling vireos, and MacGillivray's warblers along the trail.

From a gravel parking lot, wide Dry Creek Canyon Trail follows an old gravel roadbed up the canyon through Gambel oak, box elder, and Rocky Mountain maple trees. After 0.3 mile the trail enters the shelter of an evergreen forest. At 0.35 mile, the Phelps Canyon Trail branches off to the right from the main trail; stay on the main trail and continue up the canyon. The trail enters the Lone Peak Wilderness Area at 0.7 mile. You'll reach the first of several deceiving splits in the trail at 1 mile. (These side trails parallel the main trail for a short distance before rejoining.) At 1.3 miles the trail opens up into the first of several grassy meadows. At 1.5 mile, cross one of several tributaries to Dry Creek flowing down off the northern slopes of Box Elder Peak. A side trail at 1.6 miles branches off to the left of the main trail, leading a few steps to a huge rocky overlook of Dry Canyon. Looking up-canyon, you'll see the braided strands of Horsetail Falls pouring down a granite slab. Return to the main trail and you'll reach a junction with a sign pointing right for both the Deer Creek/Dry Creek Trail and for the North Mountain Trail. Head left here instead for a closer view of Horsetail Falls.

DRY CREEK CANYON TO HORSETAIL FALLS

7,600ft

East Hamongog 6,673ft

7,243ft

6,491ft

Chipman Canyon

Dry Creek

6,000ft

Phelps Canyon

Phelps Canyon Trail

Start/ Finish

GROVE DR

0   500 yds

0   500 m

© AVALON TRAVEL

Box Elder Canyon

Note that this trail is popular with both hikers and horseback riders. Hikers should be aware that the trail gets heavy horse traffic, and it shows. The wide trail gets churned up by horses, and there's plenty of horse droppings, too, as well as the black flies that go along with it.

Options

For hikers seeking a longer adventure, Dry Creek Canyon Trail can be the start of a route to the summit of Box Elder Peak, offering an alternative to climbing Box Elder from the Granite Flat Campground on the south side of the mountain. Follow Dry Creek Canyon Trail for 2 miles to a junction with the Deer Creek Trail. Beautiful high-elevation meadows reward hikers at the pass where Dry Creek Canyon Trail and the Deer Creek Trail meet. From the junction, an unmaintained trail leads south to the summit of Box Elder Peak. The total hiking distance is 12 miles round-trip.

Horsetail Falls pours down a granite slab along the Dry Creek Canyon Trail

Directions

From I-15 in Salt Lake City, take Exit 287 and head east for 5.4 miles. Turn north onto 5300 West Street and drive 2 miles through Alpine. Turn right at 600 North and continue 0.3 mile. Turn left at the intersection and continue for 1.4 miles. Take the right fork onto Oak Ridge Drive and then turn left onto Grove Drive. Follow the road for 0.2 mile to a dirt road; drive another 0.2 mile on the dirt road and then park.

GPS Coordinates: N 40°48.285' W 111°75.043'

Information and Contact

There is no fee. Dogs on leash are allowed. For more information, contact the Pleasant Grove Ranger District, Uinta-Wasatch-Cache National Forest, 390 North 100 East, Pleasant Grove, UT 84062, 801/785-3563, www.fs.fed.us.

4 BOX ELDER
Uinta National Forest

🏕 🦌 ✈ 🌿 🐕

Level: Butt-kicker

Hiking Time: 7-8 hours

Total Distance: 9.4 miles round-trip

Elevation Change: 4,704 feet

Summary: A wild, rewarding hike to the summit of little-visited Box Elder.

At 11,101 feet, Box Elder is one of the highest mountains in the southern portion of the Wasatch Range. Located directly between the popular summits of Pfeifferhorn to the north and Mount Timpanogos to the south, it's surprising that Box Elder's summit doesn't see more traffic. From a wilderness lover's perspective, however, it's a blessing. Climbing Box Elder is a much wilder experience than you'll have on those more popular peaks, with opportunities to view wildlife and a solitude not often found in much of the Wasatch Range. Mountain goats, mule deer, and golden eagles can all be seen on the steep slopes of the peak.

There are a several possible routes to the summit of Box Elder Peak. This route starts on the east side of the mountain at the Granite Flat Campground. The peak can also be climbed from the west via the Dry Creek Canyon Trail. Regardless of which approach you use, the summit ridge portion of the route up Box Elder is not listed as a maintained trail on maps. However, the trail is no more difficult to follow than other Wasatch summit trails.

© MIKE MATSON

Box Elder

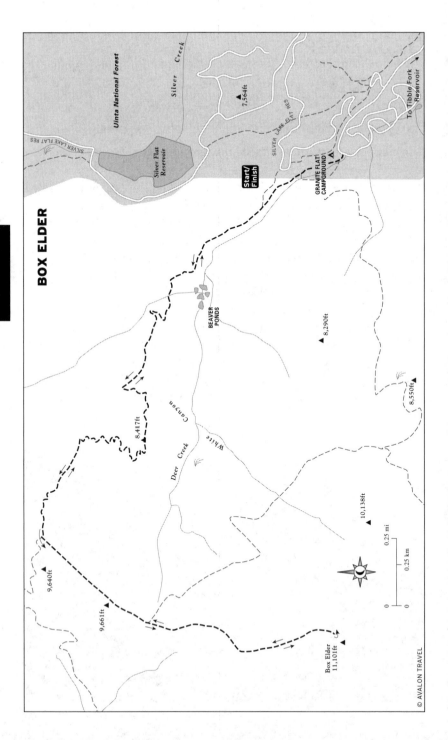

BOX ELDER

Uinta National Forest

Silver Creek

SILVER LAKE FLAT RES

Silver Flat Reservoir

7,564ft

SILVER LAKE FLAT RES

To Tibble Fork Reservoir

Start/Finish

GRANITE FLAT CAMPGROUND

BEAVER PONDS

8,290ft

8,550ft

8,417ft

Deer Creek

White Canyon

10,138ft

9,640ft

9,661ft

Box Elder 11,101ft

0.25 mi
0.25 km
0

© AVALON TRAVEL

Leaving the parking strip at Granite Flat Campground, the trail starts out wide and rocky as it climbs gently up the forested canyon. The trail is called the Dry Creek/Deer Creek Canyon Trail at the trailhead, but after 0.2 mile you'll take the left fork at a trail junction onto Box Elder Trail. After the junction, the trail quickly enters the Mount Timpanogos Wilderness area, a mixed forest of Rocky Mountain maple, quaking aspen, and Douglas fir. At 1 mile, views open up across a wetland dotted with beaver ponds and stands of subalpine fir and spruce.

The trail leaves the valley floor at 1.4 miles and starts to climb through squatty Gambel oak shrubs and clumps of arrowleaf balsamroot wildflowers. By 2.3 miles, you've reached the lower part of White Canyon, marked by a massive white talus field on its north slope. To the southwest, Box Elder Peak's triangular summit ridge rises over the valley. Moving through White Canyon, the trail switchbacks through stands of ancient limber pine. Lupine become more plentiful as the elevation increases, and Silver Flat and Tibble Fork Reservoirs both come into view to the east at about 2.5 miles.

For the next 0.5 mile the trail switchbacks through the boulder-strewn north slope of White Canyon. At 3 miles, the path gains a broad ridge-top meadow marked by a trail junction sign. Continue straight here, following the arrow for the White Canyon Trail/Box Elder Trail.

As you follow the ridgeline southwest, this section of trail heads directly toward Box Elder Peak's north ridge. The views are already impressive and include Pfeifferhorn to the north and the Mount Timpanogos massif to the south. The trail actually loses elevation as it drops down to a small saddle before starting up the ridge to the summit. There's a fork in the trail at 3.8 miles; take the right fork and stay high. Ascend steeply through the trees, following the sometimes faint but always visible path.

The final mile along the ridge is above tree line. Simply follow the west side of the ridge to the summit, enjoying the breathtaking scenery every step of the way. Utah Valley stretches out to the west, Lone Peak is visible to the northwest, and the Twin Peaks of American Fork can be spotted directly to the north. A pile of brown limestone rocks marks Box Elder's summit. Once you've soaked in the views, return down the ridge and follow the trail back the way you came.

Options

Box Elder Peak can be hiked from the west side as well, using the Dry Creek Canyon Trail. However, the Dry Creek Canyon route is both longer and gains more elevation than approaching the mountain from Granite Flats. The Dry Creek route is 12 miles round-trip and gains 5,301 feet in elevation.

Directions

From Salt Lake City drive south on I-15 for 25 miles to Exit 284 for Alpine/ Highland and then drive east on Highway 92 for 8 miles to the base of American Fork Canyon. Continue 4.7 miles into the canyon and turn left on State Route 144. Drive 2.4 miles to the Tibble Fork Reservoir. Turn left onto the paved road to Granite Flat. From the lake it's another 0.75 mile to the Granite Flat Campground. Trailhead parking will be at the first small parking area on the right side of the road after you enter the campground. The trail sign is for Deer Creek/ Dry Creek Trail.

GPS Coordinates: N 40°49.120' W 111°65.572'

Information and Contact

There is no fee. Dogs on leash are allowed. For more information, contact the Pleasant Grove Ranger District, Uinta-Wasatch-Cache National Forest, 390 North 100 East, Pleasant Grove, UT 84062, 801/785-3563, www.fs.fed.us.

5 SILVER LAKE FROM
SILVER FLAT RESERVOIR

American Fork Canyon and Lone Peak Wilderness Area,
Uinta National Forest

Level: Moderate   **Total Distance:** 4.1 miles round-trip

Hiking Time: 2-3 hours   **Elevation Change:** 1,522 feet

Summary: Enjoy this lightly used alpine lake trail in the Wasatch Mountains.

Looking for Little Cottonwood Canyon–style scenery without the crowds? Check out Silver Lake, reached through American Fork Canyon. Although Silver Lake is just a few miles as the crow flies from the mega-popular White Pine Lake, it has only a fraction of the visitors. Silver Lake is on the south side of 11,321-foot White Baldy, the same mountain that towers over the south end of White Pine Lake. But because the trailhead is accessed from American Fork Canyon, and requires a 3-mile drive on a rocky dirt road, the Silver Lake Trail has a completely different feel from White Pine.

With the crowds left far behind, there are plenty of chances to sight wildlife. Moose are often seen below the lake in a wetland area, or even near the trailhead in the valley meadows above Silver Flat Lake. Deer also frequent the meadows along this trail. If you're interested in birds, keep an eye out for McGrillivray's warbler, green-tailed towhee, and fox sparrow.

The Silver Lake Trail starts from a reservoir called Silver Lake Flat. Leave the dirt parking lot and head north along the gently rising trail through an aspen forest. The trail is wide at first, with large granite boulders scattered on the forest floor. At 0.5 mile the trail enters the Lone Peak Wilderness Area. By 0.75 mile the trail is heading west and climbing steadily up a wide, avalanche debris–filled canyon. The aspen trees have given away to scrub Gambel oak, with spruce trees and subalpine firs clinging to the limestone walls above.

Mine tailings are visible on the right side of the trail—which should be expected, given that the hike leads from Silver Flat Lake to Silver Lake. The first mine was called the Silver Creek South Mine, and the higher tailing is from the Silver Creek North Mine. At 0.9 mile the trail crosses Silver Creek—the stream that links Silver Lake and Silver Flat Lake. The best views of Mount Timpanogos found along this trail start at 1.4 miles. Continue climbing through long, steady switchbacks toward the cirque at the top of the canyon. Look for wildlife feeding in the wetland below the trail at 1.75 miles. Here you might spot deer or even moose enjoying the lush vegetation.

Silver Lake fills a punch bowl–shaped alpine cirque. Limestone cliffs rise above

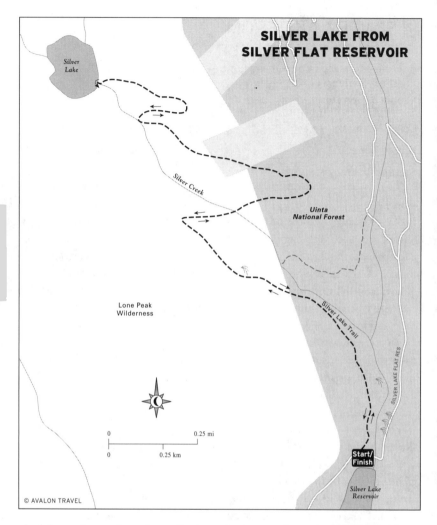

the lake to the south, and granite slopes lead up to the peak of White Baldy to the northwest. Like many lakes in the Wasatch, Silver Lake is a reservoir with a dam; later in the season the water can be drawn down, detracting from the lake's beauty. If the water level is low, take in the surrounding beauty and look for wildlife in the thick underbrush around the lake.

To return, follow the trail down the way you came.

Options

If reaching Silver Lake leaves you wanting more and you're up for an adventure, consider hiking up to Silver Glance Lake, a little-visited natural alpine lake. There's no official trail to Silver Glance Lake, so bring a map or GPS for this side trip. At Silver Lake, locate the stream of Silver Creek as it enters the lake on the north side. Follow the ridge just to the right (east) of the stream uphill for 1 mile to Silver Glance Lake. This option adds 2 miles round-trip to the hike for a total hiking distance of 6.1 miles and 960 feet in elevation gain (2,482 feet total elevation gain).

White Baldy reflected in the calm waters of Silver Lake.

Directions

From Salt Lake City drive south on I-15 for 25 miles to Exit 284 for Alpine/Highland and then drive east on Highway 92 for 8 miles to the base of American Fork Canyon. Continue 4.7 miles into the canyon and turn left on State Route 144. Drive 2.4 miles to the Tibble Fork Reservoir. Continue on the paved road toward Granite Flat campground for 0.7 mile and turn right on the gravel road signed for Silver Lake Flat. Continue 2.4 miles across a very bumpy and heavily potholed dirt road to the trailhead at the far end (north side) of Silver Lake Flat.

GPS Coordinates: N 40°50.694' W 111°65.627'

Information and Contact

There is an American Fork Canyon fee of $6 for a three-day pass, $12 for a seven-day pass, or $45 for an annual pass. The America the Beautiful pass is accepted here. Dogs on leash are allowed. For more information, contact the Pleasant Grove Ranger District, Uinta-Wasatch-Cache National Forest, 390 North 100 East, Pleasant Grove, UT 84062, 801/785-3563, www.fs.fed.us.

6 PITTSBURG LAKE
American Fork Canyon, Wasatch-Cache National Forest

🦌 🚲 🐕

Level: Moderate

Total Distance: 3.0 miles round-trip

Hiking Time: 2-2.5 hours

Elevation Change: 1,512 feet

Summary: A short, steep hike to one of the quietest mountain lakes in the Wasatch Range.

Looking for solitude at an alpine lake in the heart of the Wasatch? Then Pittsburg Lake might be the perfect spot for you. Reaching the trailhead requires navigating six miles of very rough dirt road, but if you have a high-clearance vehicle, then you can leave the crowds behind only a few miles from the boundaries of Alta and Snowbird Ski Resorts. Located near the top of American Fork Canyon, under the steep black limestone of the Devil's Castle, Pittsburg Lake is one of the Wasatch Range's least-visited lakes. Although its mileage is relatively short, the challenging drive and the lake's remote character make this trail feel like a very adventurous outing.

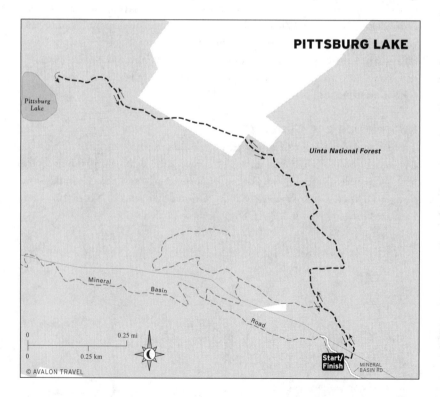

PITTSBURG LAKE

Pittsburg Lake

Uinta National Forest

Mineral

Basin

Road

0   0.25 mi

0   0.25 km

Start/Finish

MINERAL BASIN RD.

© AVALON TRAVEL

quaking aspens in front of the Devil's Castle on the Pittsburg Lake Trail

The Pittsburg Lake Trail leaves a rocky parking lot and heads gently up an old, overgrown mining road. A series of aspens have fallen across the trail in the first 0.2 mile, but after that it is well maintained and easy to follow. The trail parallels the right side of American Fork Creek for the first 0.3 mile before starting up a set of steep switchbacks. It ascends quickly for 0.5 mile up an old road that is badly eroded in places. You're just as likely to see deer prints as human footprints along this section of the trail. This is prime moose habitat as well; look for them eating the willows along American Fork Creek and around the shoreline of Pittsburg Lake.

At 1 mile the trail starts to level off, entering an open meadow on the lower flanks of the Devil's Castle. In autumn, the aspens ringing the meadow turn a vibrant orange, adding a beautiful contrast to the charcoal-gray limestone rock on the peak. The trail becomes a narrow ribbon through the meadow for the last 0.5 mile to the lake. An old miner's cabin and scattered pieces of old, rusting mining machinery add a little historical flair to this otherwise pristine setting. Anglers can expect to find brook trout in the lake.

Options

Pittsburg Lake is an excellent trail for a short backpacking trip. The remote location and light trail traffic offer a unique opportunity to camp in solitude in the heart of the Wasatch Range. There are good campsites in the meadow to the east of the lake, on the right side of the trail, and just to the south of the lake under clumps of evergreen trees.

Directions

From Salt Lake City drive south on I-15 for 25 miles to Exit 284 for Alpine/ Highland and then drive east on Highway 92 for 12.4 miles to the entrance of American Fork Canyon. Continue 5.2 miles up the canyon to Tibble Fork Reservoir and turn right onto American Fork Canyon Road. From Tibble Fork Reservoir drive 6.1 bumpy miles to the Pittsburg Lake trailhead. At 6.1 miles a short spur road will lead across the creek; the trailhead is on the right side of the creek. Note: This road is very rough and shouldn't be driven without a high-clearance vehicle, ATV, or motorbike.

GPS Coordinates: N 40°54.922' W 111°60.188'

Information and Contact

There is an American Fork Canyon fee of $6 for a three-day pass, $12 for a seven-day pass, or $45 for an annual pass. The America the Beautiful pass is accepted here. Dogs on leash are allowed. For more information, contact the Pleasant Grove Ranger District, Uinta-Wasatch-Cache National Forest, 390 North 100 East, Pleasant Grove, UT 84062, 801/785-3563, www.fs.fed.us.

7 TIMPANOGOS CAVE NATIONAL MONUMENT

American Fork Canyon, Uinta National Forest

Level: Moderate

Total Distance: 2.5 miles round-trip

Hiking Time: 3-3.5 hours

Elevation Change: 1,197 feet

Summary: Timpanogos Cave is a narrow, twisting, underground passageway filled with unique geology, including "soda pop straws."

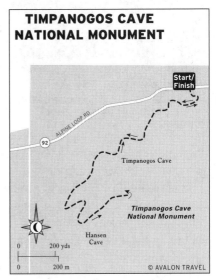

TIMPANOGOS CAVE NATIONAL MONUMENT

Timpanogos Cave is 1,100 feet above the valley floor on the steep southern slope of American Fork Canyon. Hiking to the cave is worth the experience itself and can be done without the National Park Service tour. The paved walkway is a trail-building marvel, and the surrounding American Fork Canyon scenery is stunning; nearly vertical brown, gray, and black limestone cliffs climb thousands of feet above the canyon floor.

The hike up to Timpanogos Cave starts with a safety talk from a National Park Service ranger. Once versed on the potential hazards of this dizzying trail, you'll head steeply up an asphalt ribbon winding its way through steep rock walls, gullies, and rocky talus slopes. Interpretive signs along the trail explain the often-complex geology of American Fork Canyon; you'll hike past seven different types of rock along this single mile of trail: three different kinds of limestone, two kinds of quartzite, shale, and dolomite. All of these rock types were formed on what was once an ocean floor and have been lifted to their current heights by earthquakes along the Wasatch Fault. The trail leads through several rock arches, where the park service has placed iron gates. Every 0.25 mile a distance-marker sign reminds you how far you've come.

It's hard to imagine pioneer Martin Hansen following mountain lion tracks through the snow up these steep rocky slopes. But in 1887, while logging timber in American Fork Canyon, Hansen noticed the cat's prints and followed them to the mouth of this cave, where the cougar had a den. The cougar's

the steep limestone walls of American Fork Canyon, from the Timpanogos Cave National Monument Trail

den is now the entrance to Timpanogos Cave, where the National Park Service tour begins.

Timpanogos Cave is characterized by small rooms and narrow passageways. You'll find yourself ducking under stalactites and resisting the urge to reach out and touch the geology of this fragile underworld. This is as close as you'll ever get to spelunking, or cave exploration, on a guided National Park Service tour. The 1.5-mile trail through the cave is considered strenuous. The tour takes about an hour, but with the hike to the cave, plan on about 3–3.5 hours. Though this hike is appropriate for children, strollers and wheeled carriers are not permitted on the trail.

Options

Avid spelunkers should check out the Introduction to Caving Tour offered by the National Park Service. For this tour, visitors don a helmet and headlamp to crawl off the paved trail, returning to Hansen Cave Lake, the site of Martin Hansen's original cave tours in the 1800s. This is a strenuous tour that lasts 1.5 hours and is limited to five people (must be at least 14 years old). Tours are offered Memorial Day–Labor Day and cost $15 per person. Tickets can be purchased by calling 801/756-5238, or in person at the visitors center.

Directions

From Salt Lake City drive south on I-15 for 25 miles to Exit 284 for Alpine/

Highland and then drive east on Highway 92 for 8 miles to the base of American Fork Canyon. Enter American Fork Canyon and continue 2 miles to the parking area for the Timpanogos Cave National Monument on the right side of the road. **GPS Coordinates:** N 40°44.342' W 111°70.480'

Information and Contact

From May 12 through October 14, the National Park Service offers daily guided tours of the cave 7:20 A.M.–4 P.M.; from September 4 through October 14, tour hours are 8 A.M.–3:30 P.M. Mid-October through May, the cave is locked and the trail is closed. Tours are limited to 16 people and cost $7 for adults, $3–5 for children and youth; call 801/756-5238 (8 A.M.–5 P.M., $0.50 fee) to purchase tour tickets in advance.

8 TIMPOONEKE TRAIL

BEST ☾

Pleasant Grove Ranger District, Uinta National Forest

Level: Butt-kicker

Total Distance: 12.7 miles round-trip

Hiking Time: 9-10 hours

Elevation Change: 4,937 feet

Summary: Climb Mount Timpanogos through the Giant Staircase and the unparalleled beauty of Timpanogos Basin.

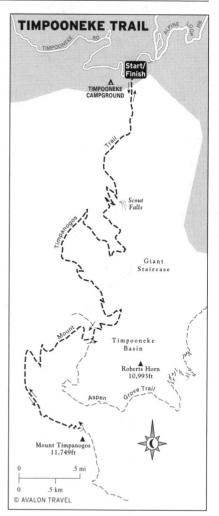

Many people think Mount Timpanogos is the most visually appealing peak in the state. This, combined with the peak's high altitude—it's the second-highest summit in the Wasatch Range—make it a must-do on many locals' bucket list. Regardless of why hikers come to climb Timpanogos, the mountain rarely disappoints. The Timpooneke Trail gains 4,900 feet over six inspiring miles. Views from the top stretch to the horizon in all directions. To the west are the Utah Valley, the green waters of Utah Lake, and the city of Provo. To the north are all of the prominent peaks in the Central Wasatch, including the Twin Peaks and the Pfeifferhorn.

The lower part of the Timpooneke Trail climbs a massive stepped glacier-carved valley called the Giant Staircase. The trail visits the lovely Scout Falls before climbing through the alpine wonderland called Timpanogos Basin—a treeless high-elevation cirque where wildflowers and mountain goats fight for hikers' attention. Steep layered limestone walls ring the basin, and permanent snowfields linger throughout the summer months. Backpackers often stay the night in the basin, and it's a spectacular place for a lunch break before heading on to the summit.

The Timpooneke Trail leaves the Timpooneke Campground trailhead and heads into the thick forest. Engelmann spruce and other evergreens shade the trail for the first 0.5 mile as it starts climbing along a gentle grade. The trail opens up above a wide meadow on the valley floor and traverses above the west side for 0.4 mile. At 1 mile you'll cross the first in a series of small streams trickling across the trail. Then at 1.4 miles, there's a signed junction for Scout Falls. Go left, and walk less than 100 yards to check out the moss-lined falls cascading over a limestone ledge. Turn right to continue up the trail.

Indian paintbrush blooming on the Timpooneke Trail

The trail climbs up the first major step in the Giant Staircase at 2 miles. Willows and thick vegetation cover the valley floor. By 3 miles the trail is crossing a giant, sweeping talus field. The trail continues on a steady incline, weaving through stunted subalpine fir trees and Indian paintbrush. At the 4-mile mark, views start to open up to the north of Box Elder Peak and Lone Peak.

Enter Timpanogos Basin at 4.4 miles. A trail leading to Emerald Lake and the Aspen Grove Trail breaks off on the left as you enter the basin. Indian paintbrush, asters, bluebells, fireweed, and lupine bloom in a stunning display during the midsummer months. Look along the steep cliff bands for the Timpanogos herd of mountain goats. This herd of at least 40 goats can usually be spotted somewhere along this upper half of the trail.

At 5.5 miles the trail reaches an 11,000-foot pass. Step through this rocky gap onto the west side of the ridge and continue climbing toward the rocky summit. The route traverses broken limestone slopes to the south before climbing along the ridge to the peak's apex. On the summit, an old metal hut with a red triangular roof welcomes hikers.

Enjoy the all-encompassing summit views. To the east you'll see Emerald Lake directly below, the 10,993-foot Roberts Horn, and Deer Creek Reservoir in the distance. To the north are the major summits of the central Wasatch. In the west, the towns of Pleasant Grove and Provo stretch across the Utah Valley floor to

Utah Lake. And in the distance to the south is Mount Nebo, the only summit higher than Mount Timpanogos in the Wasatch Range.

Options

Consider leaving a car at the Aspen Grove trailhead and hiking up Timpooneke Trail and down the Aspen Grove Trail for a one-way adventure. It helps keep this long trail interesting the whole way!

Directions

From Salt Lake City drive south on I-15 for 25 miles to Exit 284 for Alpine/ Highland and then drive east on Highway 92 for 16 miles. Turn right onto the Timpooneke Road for the Timpooneke Campground. Drive past the entrance to the campground loop and turn left into the trailhead parking lot.

GPS Coordinates: N 40°43.149' W 111°63.911'

Information and Contact

There is an American Fork Canyon fee of $6 for a three-day pass, $12 for a seven-day pass, or $45 for an annual pass. The America the Beautiful pass is accepted here. Dogs on leash are allowed. For more information, contact the Pleasant Grove Ranger District, Uinta-Wasatch-Cache National Forest, 390 North 100 East, Pleasant Grove, UT 84062, 801/785-3563, www.fs.fed.us.

9 ASPEN GROVE TRAIL   BEST ◖

Uinta National Forest

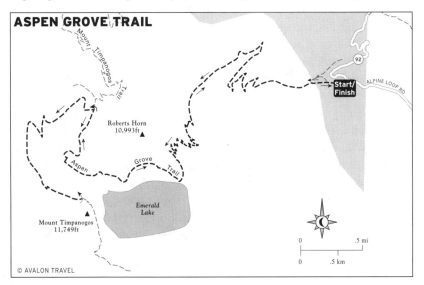

Level: Butt-kicker   **Total Distance:** 12.0 miles round-trip

Hiking Time: 8-10 hours   **Elevation Change:** 4,900 feet

Summary: The Aspen Grove Trail takes hikers past the lovely Timpanogos Falls and by Emerald Lake on the way to sweeping views from the summit hut.

Aspen Grove Trail on Mount Timpanogos is one of the most popular mountain hikes in Utah and one of the most heavily used trails in the entire Rocky Mountains. The mountain's visual appeal, it's high altitude and stunning views, and it's challenging trails make it one of the best hiking options in the region.

The Aspen Grove Trail starts on the east side of the mountain at the bottom of the glacier-carved gorge, called Primrose Cirque. The trail begins gently enough for the first 0.75 mile, following a creek up the avalanche debris–littered canyon. After crossing the intermittently wet streambed, the path becomes paved and works its way up toward lower and upper Timpanogos Falls at 1 mile. This lovely waterfall could be a destination hike in itself. Lush vegetation fed by the fall's mist grows on limestone ledges around the cascade.

After the falls, the pavement ends and the trail becomes noticeably steeper, making long switchbacks up the amphitheater-shaped canyon below the prominent

ASPEN GROVE TRAIL

Mount Timpanogos Trail

Roberts Horn
10,993ft ▲

Aspen   Grove   Trail

Emerald
Lake

▲
Mount Timpanogos
11,749ft

Start/
Finish

92

ALPINE LOOP RD

0   .5 mi

0   .5 km

© AVALON TRAVEL

the view south from the summit of Mount Timpanogos

peak, Robert's Horn. The switchbacks get shorter and more focused as the trail climbs higher before opening up into the dramatic upper bowl, 3.5 miles from the trailhead. This sweeping cirque holds a waning permanent snowfield, the remains of the Timpanogos Glacier. The glacier is all but extinct; its last ice has receded beneath the rocks of the talus field. However, the snowfield has completely melted away in 1994 and 2003, leaving the glacier clinging to existence—a tangible reminder of climate change in Utah. Notice as you hike up how huge piles of rock have fallen on top of the permanent snowfields, and it's easy to imagine there might be significant ice fields hiding beneath the rocky surface. Also listen closely to running water beneath the trail.

The snowfields feed the icy, picturesque Emerald Lake. From here hikers also get a good look at the mountain's summit ridge and the tiny hut on the summit marking their goal.

The trail continues through copious lupine and Indian paintbrush as it progresses up the cirque. Watch for the herd of mountain goats living on this part of the mountain as well. This herd of around 100 animals was introduced to the area in 1981 from Washington state's Olympic National Park. Though somewhat controversial, the non-native goats have since become one of the favorite parts of many a hiker's experience on the mountain. From here the trail passes a large metal-and-rock shelter built in 1959, Emerald Hut. The hut was constructed to accommodate hikers on the historic Timp Hike that was held every year from 1911 to 1972.

The trail climbs through the upper part of Timpanogos Basin for 1 mile across giant talus fields spilling down from the vertical cliffs of Timpanogos summit ridge. Crossing through a rocky notch, the final 0.8 mile of the trail follows the west side of an exposed, but safe, ridgeline to the summit. Drink in the view from the summit hut and enjoy your accomplishment!

Options

The Aspen Grove Trail is one of two trails leading to the summit of Mount Timpanogos. The other is the Timpooneke Trail (see listing in this chapter). These trails share many similar characteristics, but both have unique advantages and disadvantages. One fun way to see both trails in the same day is to park a car at each trailhead and make the hike a one-way trip. The Timpooneke Trail, starting from Timpooneke Campground in American Fork Canyon, is nearly identical in length and elevation gain to the Aspen Grove Trail. The trails join at the saddle above Timpanogos Basin and become a single trail to the summit. Many hikers choose to climb one trail and descend the other, thereby making it a one-way hike. This requires a car shuttle, though, adding to an already long day.

Directions

From Salt Lake City, drive south on I-15 for 33 miles and take Exit 272. Drive east along Highway 52 (800 North) in Orem for 3.7 miles to the junction with Highway 189/Provo Canyon Road. Drive east on Highway 189 for 7 miles and turn left on Highway 92/Alpine Scenic Byway. Continue 4.8 miles and turn left into the Aspen Grove trailhead parking lot.

GPS Coordinates: N 40°38.460' W 111°63.600'

Information and Contact

There is an American Fork Canyon fee of $6 for a three-day pass, $12 for a seven-day pass, or $45 for an annual pass. The America the Beautiful pass is accepted here. Dogs on leash are allowed. For more information, contact the Pleasant Grove Ranger District, Uinta-Wasatch-Cache National Forest, 390 North 100 East, Pleasant Grove, UT 84062, 801/785-3563, www.fs.fed.us.

10 STEWART FALLS
Uinta National Forest

Level: Easy

Total Distance: 3.8 miles round-trip

Hiking Time: 2 hours

Elevation Change: 342 feet

Summary: A mostly level walk leads to a picturesque falls cascading off the Mount Timpanogos massif.

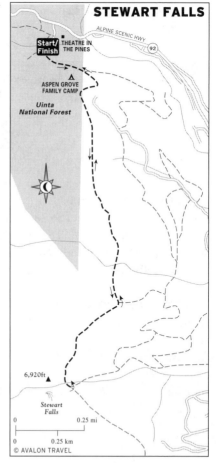

Mount Timpanogos is made up of gray and brown limestone bands that look distinctly like layers of an oversized tiramisu. Where streams tumble down these cliffs, they make for dramatic waterfalls, with curtains of water often falling long distances before splashing down to the ground. These many waterfalls add to the mountain's beauty and charm. Perhaps the best of these falls is Stewart Falls, near the Sundance Ski Resort on the mountain's eastern slopes. Stewart Falls is a double falls, dropping over two limestone shelves before reaching the canyon floor. Ribbons of green moss and vegetation grow on either side of the water, adding contrast to steep rock walls. In autumn when the maple and aspen trees have turned red and yellow, the color palate found at the falls and along the trail is a feast for the eyes.

The Stewart Falls Trail starts on the far left side of the Aspen Grove Trail parking lot near the Theatre in the Pines. The trail starts off steeply, but quickly levels off to the nearly flat grade it maintains all the way to the falls. The path leads through a forest of evergreens and aspens, punctuated by Rocky Mountain maples.

© MIKE MATSON

Stewart Falls on Mount Timpanogos

At 0.3 mile a trail joins the Stewart Falls Trail from the left, leading up from the Aspen Grove Family Camp and Conference Center. At 0.6 mile the forest has become almost entirely aspen trees, with a blanket of bracken ferns cloaking the forest floor. The trees open up at 1.2 miles to reveal views down to Sundance Ski Resort to the left of the trail and the gray cliff bands of Mount Timpanogos to the right. You'll starting getting glimpses of Stewart Falls at 1.6 miles as the trail drops gently into a large natural amphitheater. The trail reaches an overlook of the falls and a trail junction at 1.9 miles. Follow this trail down a short hill to get close to the base of the falls, or enjoy the view from the overlook before returning to the car.

Options
Stewart Falls can be reached by hiking up from the Sundance Ski Resort. The trail from Sundance is 1.5 miles long for a 3.0-mile round-trip.

Directions
From Salt Lake City, drive south on I-15 for 33 miles and take Exit 272. Drive east along Highway 52 (800 North) in Orem for 3.7 miles to the junction with Highway 189/Provo Canyon Road. Drive east on 189 for 7 miles and turn left on Highway 92/Alpine Scenic Byway. Continue 4.8 miles and turn left into the Aspen Grove trailhead parking lot.
GPS Coordinates: N 40°38.460' W 111°63.600'

Information and Contact

There is an American Fork Canyon fee of $6 for a three-day pass, $12 for a seven-day pass, or $45 for an annual pass. The America the Beautiful pass is accepted here. Dogs on leash are allowed. For more information, contact the Pleasant Grove Ranger District, Uinta-Wasatch-Cache National Forest, 390 North 100 East, Pleasant Grove, UT 84062, 801/785-3563, www.fs.fed.us.

11 GROVE CREEK
Uinta National Forest

🏠 ✈️ 🗺️ 🐕

Level: Moderate   **Total Distance:** 4.0 miles round-trip

Hiking Time: 2.5-3 hours   **Elevation Change:** 3,132 feet

Summary: A moderate hike up the steep-walled Grove Creek Canyon leads to a series of cascading waterfalls.

Grove Creek Canyon is one of several steep-walled canyons cut into the lower flanks of the Mount Timpanogos massif. Its dark limestone rock, lush vegetation, and tumbling waterfalls make the canyon an attractive destination during any season. Autumn is particularly beautiful when the maple and oak leaves turn color. A double waterfall near the head of the canyon makes an appealing destination, and views from the falls stretch down the canyon all the way west to the Utah Valley. Peregrine falcons nest in the canyon's vertical limestone cliffs, and golden eagles can be seen hunting the rocky slopes near the trail.

The Grove Creek Trail begins on a gravel road leading up the canyon from the paved parking area. Steep limestone walls rise on the right side of the trail and Gambel oak and cottonwood trees line the creek, also on the right side. A trail branches off the left side of the gravel road at 0.3 mile and heads up the steep rocky slope. Take this trail to the left. In fall, Rocky Mountain maples contrast the dark-colored canyon slopes with splotches of bright red.

At 0.5 mile the trail leaves the creek, switchbacking up the slope on the north side of the canyon. The trail gains elevation quickly, offering views up the steep-walled canyon and out to the west over Pleasant Grove and the Utah Valley at 0.6 mile.

At 1.3 miles the trail traverses through a pair of limestone cliffs. The cliffs drop off precipitously on the right side of the trail. With no guardrails, this is a spot to use care, especially with children.

By 1.7 miles you'll see a two-tiered waterfall splashing down the cliffs at the back of the canyon. Continue up to the top of the falls, where a bridge crosses Grove Creek. A picturesque cascade of water flows down a steep slope before passing under the bridge. There's a bench next to the bridge and a unique memorial plaque with a miniature tandem bicycle. The bridge is a good place to turn around for the out-and-back version of this trail.

Options

The Grove Creek Trail can be linked up with the Battle Creek Falls Trail, one canyon to the south. From the bridge at the waterfall, the trail continues

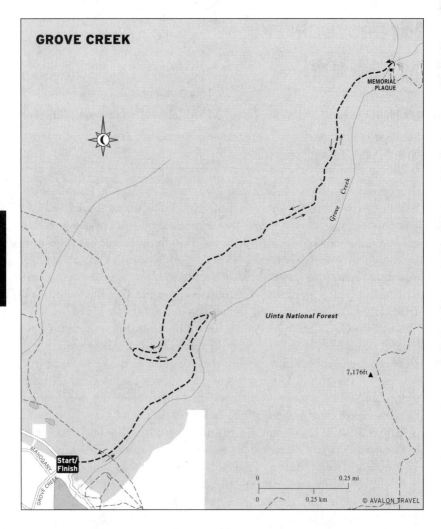

for 0.3 mile before meeting up with the Great Western Trail, which leads south to Battle Creek Canyon. By running a car shuttle to the Battle Creek Falls trailhead it's possible to make this a one-way hike. This trail link-up is 5.7 miles one-way.

Directions

From Salt Lake City, drive south on I-15 for 30 miles and take Exit 275 for Pleasant Grove. From the exit ramp turn left onto Pleasant Grove Boulevard and drive 1.6 miles and continue onto Center Street. Drive 0.6 mile on Center Street and turn left on 100 East. Drive 0.4 mile and turn right on 500 North/Grove Creek

Grove Creek Canyon

Drive. Follow Grove Creek Drive for 1.6 miles to the large paved parking lot at the trailhead.

GPS Coordinates: N 40°37.483' W 111°71.226'

Information and Contact

There is no fee. Dogs on leash are allowed. For more information, contact the Pleasant Grove Ranger District, Uinta-Wasatch-Cache National Forest, 390 North 100 East, Pleasant Grove, UT 84062, 801/785-3563, www.fs.fed.us.

12 BATTLE CREEK FALLS

BEST C

Uinta National Forest

🛩️ 🏔️ 🐕 👫

Level: Easy

Total Distance: 1.1 miles round-trip

Hiking Time: 30 minutes–1 hour

Elevation Change: 465

Summary: An easy stroll leads to a refreshing double waterfall.

Located at the western base of the mighty Mount Timpanogos, Battle Creek Falls is an appealing waterfall at the base of a limestone cliff. It's the type of falls you want to stand underneath on a hot summer afternoon. This peaceful setting is a great spot to enjoy lunch or hang out for a whole day. The trail is a perfect hike for young kids and families. Battle Creek Canyon is particularly spectacular during fall, when the leaves on the deciduous trees along the creek are turning color.

Battle Creek is named after the first battle between Mormon settlers and the Native American Ute tribe. A small group of Timpanogots Indians were attacked by a Mormon militia in the predawn hours of March 5, 1849.

BATTLE CREEK FALLS

8,320ft

Creek

Battle

Kiwanis Park

6,809ft

Start/Finish

BATTLE CREEK DR

0   500 yds

0   500 m

The wide Battle Creek Canyon Trail starts off paralleling the right side of the creek bed at the base of the canyon. Gambel oak trees line the trail, and limestone cliffs rise on the north side of the canyon. At 0.3 mile the trail reaches a culvert where Battle Creek drops underground. Then, at 0.5 mile, the trail crosses Battle Creek on a wooden footbridge to the north side of the canyon. A short, steep uphill section of trail leads to the falls pouring over a limestone ledge in a natural amphitheater.

Battle Creek Canyon is also a good spot for birding. According to Utah Birds, there's good birding near the mouth of the canyon in the riparian habitat near the stream. Expect to find some of these species there: black-headed grosbeak, Lazuli bunting, Blue-gray gnatcatcher, spotted towhee, warbling and plumbeous vireo, brown creeper, western screech-owl, common poorwill, golden-crowned kinglet, and the hermit thrush.

hikers enjoying Battle Creek Falls

Options

The Battle Creek Canyon Trail continues beyond the falls. It's two miles from the trailhead to a junction with the Great Western Trail. From there the trail can be taken north and then west to make a loop hike down the Grove Creek Trail.

Directions

From Salt Lake City drive south on I-15 for 35 miles to Exit 275 and exit the freeway. From the exit ramp drive northeast on Pleasant Grove Boulevard toward 2000 West for 1.5 miles and turn right onto West State Road. Drive 0.9 mile on West State Road and turn left on South 100 East. Continue for 0.2 mile and take the second right onto East 200 South/East Battle Creek Drive. Drive to the trailhead for Battle Creek Canyon at the end of the road.

GPS Coordinates: N 40°26.490' W 111°63.026'

Information and Contact

There is no fee. Dogs on leash are allowed. For more information, contact the Pleasant Grove Ranger District, Uinta-Wasatch-Cache National Forest, 390 North 100 East, Pleasant Grove, UT 84062, 801/785-3563, www.fs.fed.us.

13 BUFFALO PEAK
Uinta National Forest

Level: Easy

Hiking Time: 30 minutes–1 hour

Total Distance: 1.0 mile round-trip

Elevation Change: 278 feet

Summary: An easy summit hike to a stunning lookout over the Utah Valley.

Sometimes it's rewarding to get a great workout by hiking many miles and gaining thousands of feet of elevation. And sometimes, it's fun to let your car do most of the work for you! Like on Buffalo Peak, for example.

Buffalo Peak is one of the Southern Wasatch's least-visited summits. In a range of high summits and long challenging trails, Buffalo Peak is a welcomed anomaly. It isn't Buffalo Peak's height at 8,029 feet that makes it spectacular, but its position. Located just

west of Cascade Mountain and north of Squaw Peak, Buffalo Peak is perched between big mountains and the wide-open expanse of the Utah Valley. From its summit, hikers can see everything from the dramatically twisted limestone of Rock Canyon to the turquoise waters of Utah Lake.

The Buffalo Peak Trail starts from an unmarked trailhead on Squaw Peak Road. Step through the walk-through in the log fence and continue up the dirt path. There's a good chance of seeing wild turkeys and blue grouse along the trail. Buffalo Peak is visible 0.5 mile west of the trailhead. The wide trail leads across open slopes, dotted with stands of Rocky Mountain maple and Gambel oak trees. In autumn, the maples flame red and add a whole new beauty to an already stunning landscape. Aspen and lodgepole pines grow along the ridge as well. In spring and early summer, arrowleaf balsamroot wildflowers bloom yellow along the first 0.25 mile of the trail.

At 0.2 mile a spur trail branches off to the right. Take the left fork, staying on the main trail headed up the ridgeline. Views from the ridgeline look down to the south to Squaw Peak and the wild, steep limestone walls of Rock Canyon. To the west Utah Lake and the city of Provo spread across the Utah Valley. The trail climbs gently up the ridge, growing gradually steeper near the summit.

You'll quickly reach the summit, a gently sloping mound surrounded by maple and curl-leaf mountain mahogany trees.

After taking in the sights, follow the trail down the ridge the way you came.

Options

If you'd like a more challenging trail to the summit of Buffalo Peak, consider starting the hike at the Squaw Peak Overlook, which offers a five-mile, round-trip hike with 1,242 feet in elevation gain. To reach the trailhead, drive 2.1 miles on Squaw Peak Road and turn left to stay on Squaw Peak Road/Forest Service Road 027. Continue one mile on Squaw Peak Road/Forest Service Road 027 and turn left. Drive another mile and turn right, then continue 0.3 mile to Squaw Peak Overlook.

hiking towards Buffalo Peak

© MIKE MATSON

Directions

From Salt Lake City drive south on I-15 for 33 miles to Exit 272 for 800 North in Orem. Turn left and continue east from the exit ramp on 800 North for 3.7 miles to Provo Canyon. Take the left ramp onto East Provo Canyon Road/U.S. Highway 189. Continue for 1.9 miles and turn right on Squaw Peak Road. Drive 4 miles on Squaw Peak Road and turn left to stay on Squaw Peak Road/Forest Service Road 027. Continue 3.3 miles on Squaw Peak Road/Forest Service Road 027 to the trailhead. The trail starts on the right side of the road at a walk-through in the log fence. Park along the side of the road or 0.1 mile down the road in a gravel parking lot on the east side.

GPS Coordinates: N 40°28.257' W 111°60.526'

Information and Contact

There is no fee. Dogs are allowed on leash. Maps are available at the Public Lands Information Center, 3285 East 3300 South (inside REI), Salt Lake City, UT 84109, 801/466-6411. For more information, contact the Pleasant Grove Ranger District, Uinta-Wasatch-Cache National Forest, 390 North 100 East, Pleasant Grove, UT 84062, 801/785-3563, www.fs.fed.us.

14 SQUAW MOUNTAIN   BEST C
Uinta National Forest

Level: Moderate   **Total Distance:** 7.0 miles round-trip

Hiking Time: 3.5-4 hours   **Elevation Change:** 1,965 feet

Summary: This trail leads to a thrilling overlook of Rock Canyon and one of the best panoramic views of Provo.

Who would guess that Squaw Peak has some of the most dramatic views in the entire Wasatch Range? Well, it does. It's not the highest peak around, nor the most challenging, but the views from the top are hard to beat, and the trail is enjoyable to hike. You can see a little bit of everything from Squaw Peak's summit. From Mount Nebo, the highest peak in the Wasatch Range to the south, to Utah Lake to the west, to the stratified geology of the Mount Timpanogos massif to the north, this is one perfectly positioned perch. Located on the east side of Provo, the mountain is one of the most popular hikes in Utah County.

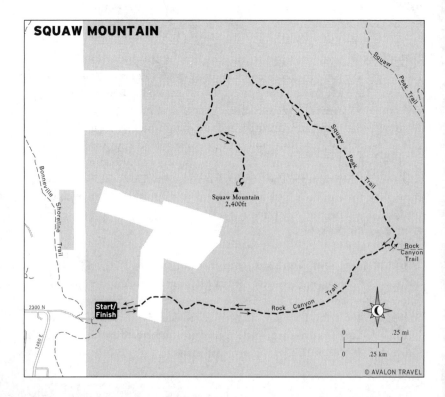

the view south from the summit of Squaw Peak

Squaw Mountain, often referred to as Squaw Peak, is the north wall of the steep-sided Rock Canyon. In 1850, there was a battle between a group of Piute Indians and a militia of Mormon men from Fort Utah. About 70 Ute warriors were led by a chief named Big Elk, and fought for several days. After many of the Native American fighters were wounded, they split up and a small group headed up Rock Canyon. Big Elk died in the canyon, and his "squaw" reportedly fell from the steep rocks on the mountain and died as well. Squaw Mountain was named after her and the battle.

The route to the summit of Squaw Peak begins at the mouth of Rock Canyon. The trail starts up an old paved road. Rock Canyon's steep brown quartzite and gray limestone walls are popular with rock climbers, and dozens of routes can be found on about 15 different walls along the canyon corridor. The trail follows an old roadbed first established in 1855; the road was later improved by the Civilian Conservation Corps. After passing by a green metal gate, the wide roadbed continues up the canyon. The trail crosses Rock Canyon Creek five times on wooden bridges before reaching a turnoff for the Squaw Peak Trail at 1.7 miles. The trail to Squaw Peak is marked by a brown flexi-pole Forest Service sign: Trail 060. Turn left at the trail marker and you quickly see a boulder with the words *Squaw Peak Trail* scrawled across it.

The Squaw Peak Trail has quite a different feeling from the wide, rocky trail in the base of Rock Canyon. A narrow dirt path climbs at a steeper grade through a mixed forest of box elder, Rocky Mountain maple, and aspen trees. At 2.4 miles from the trailhead, the forest begins to open up into a series of alpine meadows. At first the meadows are small, with tall grass growing beneath the forest canopy. But they spread out as the elevation increases.

Keep your eyes open for wildlife in these meadows. Mule deer frequent grassy meadows to feed in the early morning and evening. There's also a chance of spotting bighorn sheep higher up along the trail. Look for these elusive animals traversing the steep upper slopes of Rock Canyon. Birders may spot the following birds along the trail: American kestrel, golden eagle, peregrine falcon, canyon wren, blue grouse, great horned owl, magpie, chickadee, mountain bluebird, northern flicker, ruffed grouse, western scrub jay, and prairie falcons.

From 2.75 to 2.9 miles the trail breaks out of the forest and above the meadows, offering a look at the surrounding mountains that have been hidden from view. By 3.1 miles you'll be rewarded with the first views west to Utah Lake. The objective of Squaw Mountain summit is less than 0.5 mile to the south from here. The rocky outcrop that marks the top of Squaw Peak is a dramatic place. Looking south into Rock Canyon, there's nothing but air. This is not a spot you'd want to fall from. To the east is the imposing west face of Cascade Mountain, and to the north is Mount Timpanogos. Provo and the Brigham Young University campus stretch out below the peak to the west.

Options
If you're looking for more after visiting the summit of Squaw Peak, you can continue up Rock Canyon on the Rock Canyon Trail. The trail is 3.4 miles in total length.

Directions
From Salt Lake City, drive south on I-15 for 35 miles to Exit 269 for University Parkway in Provo. Follow University Parkway for 4.7 miles and onto 900 East. Continue 0.2 mile on 900 East and turn right on Temple View Drive. Follow Temple View for 0.5 mile and turn right on 2300 North. Drive 0.3 mile on 2300 North to the Rock Canyon trailhead at the end of the road.
GPS Coordinates: N 40°26.448' W 111°62.867'

Information and Contact
There is no fee. Dogs on leash are allowed. For more information, contact the Pleasant Grove Ranger District, Uinta-Wasatch-Cache National Forest, 390 North 100 East, Pleasant Grove, UT 84062, 801/785-3563, www.fs.fed.us.

15 Y MOUNTAIN   BEST [
Uinta National Forest

🏠 🐴 👪

Level: Easy   **Total Distance:** 1.6 miles round-trip

Hiking Time: 1 hour   **Elevation Change:** 1,115 feet

Summary: Hike to Brigham Young University's giant hillside emblem – one of the first, and largest, of its kind.

The Y Mountain/Slide Canyon Trail leads to the top of Brigham Young University's (BYU) white hillside Y. Whitewashed high school and college letters are painted on mountain slopes above small towns across the mountain West. The Y is BYU's version, on steroids. It's 380-feet high and 130-feet wide and can be seen from miles away. It was the third hillside letter of its kind, following only the C in Berkeley, California, and the University of Utah's U in Salt Lake City.

The Y was actually the brainchild of Brigham Young High School's (BYHS) junior class of 1906. Their original idea was to paint 07 on the hillside above the school. When the seniors found out about the juniors' plans, they were beside themselves. To settle the dispute, BYHS's principal and BYU's president suggested they paint BYU on the hillside instead. Plans were made, and a team of volunteers was

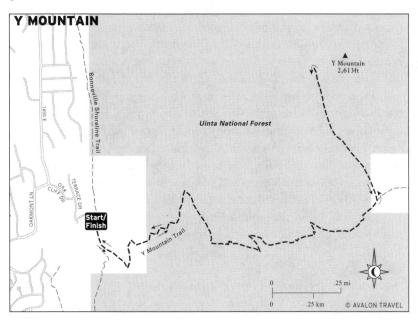

view from Y Mountain above BYU's campus in Provo

assembled. They started with the Y, which took six hours of continuous work. It must have taken a lot of effort, because they never returned to finish the B and U.

The Y has become one of the most popular hikes in Provo. At times the trail looks like an anthill, with BYU students and families from all walks of life moving up and down the series of switchbacks. The trail is wide, however, and can handle the traffic. The crowds don't take away from the experience, but add to the trail's fun character.

Start up the switchback ladder—the Y Mountain Trail is a series of 11 switchbacks, with each turn marked by a trail sign—by passing through an iron Y-shaped gate. Gambel oaks grow along the trail, which feels like a wide, super-steep gravel road. The sections between the turns are short, falling anywhere from 0.1 to 0.2 mile in length, and many of the switchbacks offer benches to rest.

Views from the trail stretch out west across BYU's campus, Provo, and the Utah Valley. They improve with each turn. Limestone boulders appear occasionally on the side of the trail, having fallen from the cliffs high above on Y Mountain.

The trail is only a mile long, so take your time and rest often. During summer, the west-facing slope bakes in the sun during the afternoon, so consider starting your hike early, before temperatures heat up. Stay off the letter itself to keep it from breaking up and eroding.

Options

The trail continues past the Y and on to the summit of Y Mountain. This trip is 6 miles round-trip with 3,346 feet in elevation gain.

Directions

From Salt Lake City, drive south on I-15 for 40 miles to Exit 265. Take Exit 265 and turn left onto West Center Street. Drive 2.1 miles. At the roundabout continue straight onto East Center Street. Continue 0.2 mile and turn left on 900 East. Drive 0.8 mile and turn right onto 820 North. Drive 0.6 miles on 820 North as it curves north and turns into Oakmont Lane. Drive 0.2 mile and turn right onto Oak Cliff Drive. At the top of Oak Cliff Drive turn right onto Terrace Drive and continue one block to the Y Mountain parking lot.

GPS Coordinates: N 40°24.456' W 111°62.670'

Information and Contact

There is no fee. Dogs on leash are allowed. For more information, contact the Pleasant Grove Ranger District, Uinta-Wasatch-Cache National Forest, 390 North 100 East, Pleasant Grove, UT 84062, 801/785-3563, www.fs.fed.us.

16 MOUNT NEBO VIA THE NORTH PEAK TRAIL

Uinta National Forest

🗂️🦌✈️🌿🐕

Level: Butt-kicker **Total Distance:** 9.3 miles round-trip

Hiking Time: 6-8 hours **Elevation Change:** 3,530 feet

Summary: Reach the summit of the highest peak in the Wasatch Range!

Mount Nebo is the tallest and southernmost peak in the Wasatch Range. The mountain is better described as a long, broad ridge, with three distinct summits. The north summit is the highest, reaching 11,928 feet. That's 179 feet higher than Mount Timpanogos, its better-known cousin to the north.

Mount Nebo is one of the spots in Utah's mountains where the state's Department of Natural Resources is trying to establish a herd of bighorn sheep. Bighorn sheep are native to the area but were wiped out by diseases contracted from domesticated sheep and from predators. In 2005, 18 sheep were reintroduced at the mouth of Willow Creek Canyon.

The North Peak Trail leads to Wolf Pass, and from the pass a ridge trail leads to Mount Nebo's north summit, the peak's highest point. Like most big Wasatch summit hikes, this is a long, challenging route with lots of elevation gain. It doesn't

looking south toward Mount Nebo's summit ridge

© MIKE MATSON

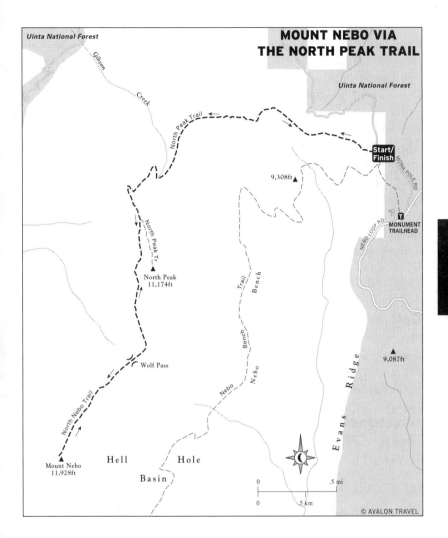

require any technical rock climbing or scrambling, just steep hiking across rocky terrain. A pair of trekking poles is nice to have on the mountain's upper ridges, where the footing is sometimes tricky. There's not a drop of water to be found, so bring enough for a long day on the trail.

The red dirt trail climbs away from the parking lot following a barbed-wire fence up a gently rising ridge. You'll notice as the hike progresses that this trail is following one ridge or another for almost its entire length. Look for hawks circling overhead in the morning hours on the first mile. Quaking aspen and limber pine trees dot the ridge at first, but the trail is mostly open and exposed to the elements.

Occasionally, bunches of Engelmann spruce and subalpine fir provide shelter from the sun. At 1.7 miles the trail crosses through a meadow filled with lupine and yellow ragweed wildflowers. The trail climbs up through a steep gully before gaining the ridge, where you'll have your first views out to the west of Mona Reservoir at 2.2 miles.

The route appears to be heading for the summit of the 11,174-foot North Peak, but then traverses across the west face of the mountain's treeless western slope. The trail drops down Wolf Pass between North Peak and Mount Nebo at 2.75 miles. This is where the real climb begins. The route plods steeply up the tree-lined ridge on loose limestone gravel, slowly making its way to the northernmost of Mount Nebo's three summits. The trail can be faint in spots, so watch closely as you ascend the summit pyramid. If you find yourself using your hands to scramble through the rocks, you're probably a little off trail.

From the summit, views look across the Mount Nebo Basin to the east, Bald Mountain to the north, Mona Reservoir to the west, and Salt Creek Peak to the south.

Options

Mount Nebo can also be climbed from the south on the Andrews Ridge Trail. The trail is 16 miles round-trip with 5,400 feet in elevation gain. The Andrews Ridge Trail leads to Mount Nebo's south summit, which was believed to be the peak's high point until the mountain was resurveyed in the 1970s.

Directions

From Salt Lake City, drive south on I-15 for 40 miles to Exit 250 for Payson. Drive south through Payson and turn left at the light onto 100 North. Continue 0.2 mile and turn right, and then continue 23.6 miles on the Mount Nebo Scenic Byway/South Canyon Road. Turn right at the sign for Monument trailhead. Then turn right again onto the dirt Mona Pole Road and follow it for 0.3 mile to the trailhead. Watch for deer and cows along the scenic byway; they both seem to think they own the road!

GPS Coordinates: N 39°84.848' W 111°72.285'

Information and Contact

There is no fee. Dogs on leash are allowed. For more information, contact the Spanish Fork Ranger District, Uinta-Wasatch-Cache National Forest, 44 West 400 North, Spanish Fork, UT 84660, 801/798-3571, www.fs.fed.us.

17 FIFTH WATER HOT SPRINGS

Uinta-Wasatch-Cache National Forest

Level: Moderate

Total Distance: 4.6 miles round-trip

Hiking Time: 2.5-3 hours

Elevation Change: 984 feet

Summary: An enjoyable walk leads to a rare find – a multipooled hot spring in a beautiful backcountry setting.

Fifth Water Hot Springs, sometimes called Diamond Fork Hot Springs, is as picturesque a hot spring as you'll find in Utah. A turquoise-colored waterfall pours over a rock ledge into the highest of a series of natural pools and built-up soaking tubs. The array of different soaking options allows for the springs to accommodate a surprising number of visitors, which is good because the hike is quite popular, especially on weekends. Spring and fall are the busiest seasons, but winter can be the best time of year to visit the pools, when freshly fallen snow offsets the dark-colored rock and aquamarine-hued waters. The springs are popular with families, so bring a swimsuit. Please treat this unique resource with respect and carry out any garbage that you bring in or see at the springs.

The trail to Fifth Water Hot Springs is a gently rolling creekside jaunt that's suitable for the whole family. Log fences have been built where the trail drops away down steep slopes, making it safe for children.

The trail is gated at the entrance to fence in the open-range cattle that graze along the river bottoms. Enter through the gate and continue straight ahead down the trail as it parallels the left side of Sixth Water Creek. (Don't cross the creek on the gated bridge.) You'll follow Sixth Water Creek up a deep-cut canyon as the trail rises and falls along the stream bank. High conglomerate rock cliffs rise

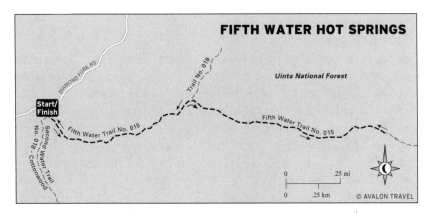

FIFTH WATER HOT SPRINGS

Uinta National Forest

DIAMOND FORK RD.

Trail No. 016

Start/ Finish

Fifth Water Trail No. 015

Fifth Water Trail No. 015

No. 018 - Second Water Trail

No. 018 - Cottonwood

0   .25 mi

0   .25 km   © AVALON TRAVEL

the sulphur hot springs of Fifth Water Creek

above the trail. In autumn, the cottonwood and Rocky Mountain maple trees along the creek brighten the scenery with beautiful yellow and red leaves. The clear creek tumbles down and pours through boulders as it makes its way through the peaceful canyon setting.

At 1.1 miles a metal bridge crosses Sixth Water Creek. Continue straight up Fifth Water Creek, where you'll start to smell the sulfur from the hot springs at about 1.5 miles. As you progress farther up the drainage, you'll notice the water starting to look milky from the dissolved minerals flowing up through the springs. At 2.1 miles, climb a short, steep hill and cross a small seep running across the trail from the left. You are now at the beginning of the hot springs; there are at least six unique soaking pools below the small waterfall.

Options

There are two good campsites 0.25-mile down the trail from the hot springs, making Fifth Water Hot Springs an excellent short backpacking trip. For hot spring enthusiasts, these campsites offer an opportunity for a longer stay and extended soaking. Consider planning backpacking trips midweek if possible to avoid weekend crowds. Also pack water for the duration of the trip, as the water in Fifth Water Creek contains sulfur and other minerals.

Directions

From Salt Lake City drive south on I-15 for 50 miles to Exit 258 for U.S. Highway

6 for Manti/Price. Merge onto U.S. Highway 6 and continue southeast for 11 miles. Turn left onto Diamond Fork Road and drive 10.2 miles to the Diamond Fork trailhead on the right side of the road.

GPS Coordinates: N 40°08.287' W 111°35.472'

Information and Contact

There is no fee. Dogs are allowed on leash. For more information, contact the Spanish Fork Ranger District, Uinta-Wasatch-Cache National Forest, 44 West 400 North, Spanish Fork, UT 84660, 801/798-3571, www.fs.fed.us.

WESTERN MOUNTAINS

© NATALIA BRATSLAVSKY/123RF

BEST HIKES

◖ Historic Sites
Sentry Trail, **page 240.**

◖ Wildlife-Viewing
Frary Peak, **page 236.**

The geography west of Salt Lake City is dramatically

different from the Wasatch Mountains flanking the city's eastern border. West of Salt Lake City is a landscape characterized by a series of north-to-south-oriented mountain ranges rising from the desert floor. Between these ranges flat, wide valleys stretch endlessly toward the horizon. An evaporated remnant of an ancient inland sea, the Great Salt Lake fills the bottom of this vast basin. The Great Salt Lake has an average water-level altitude of 4,200 feet and is about 75 miles long and 28 miles wide. With no outlet, water levels and salinity content fluctuate greatly during wet periods and times of drought. The expansive desert in western Utah, known as the Great Salt Lake Desert, is the dried-out lake bed of Lake Bonneville, once a great freshwater inland sea that was as much as 1,000-feet deep. This massive body of water covered much of northern Utah and stretched into parts of Idaho and western Nevada. The evaporated desert floor is remarkably flat, stretching for miles to the horizon without any elevation change. The Great Salt Lake Desert floor is not a particularly pleasant place to hike. But the lake islands and mountain ranges rising above the desert floor do offer high-quality hiking, with far fewer visitors than you'll find on the trails immediately surrounding the city. The Desert Peak Wilderness in the Stansbury Mountains stands out as one of the most appealing destinations here. In the Great Salt Lake itself, Stansbury and Antelope Islands offer refreshingly unique trails. During spring, fall, and winter, when temperatures are less than 75 degrees, these islands offer rewarding hikes when many of the other Salt Lake City–area trails are blanketed in snow. These desert trails travel through open grasslands and rocky, rolling terrain. On Antelope Island, wildlife sightings such as American bison, bighorn sheep, and pronghorn antelope are possible. Views include reflections in the vast Great Salt Lake and a distant perspective of the majestic Wasatch Mountains. In fact, when it comes to expansive views, it's hard to beat Antelope Island and Stansbury Island. Although their summits are not as high as those found in Utah's bigger mountains, their unique geographic locations make for awe-inspiring vistas.

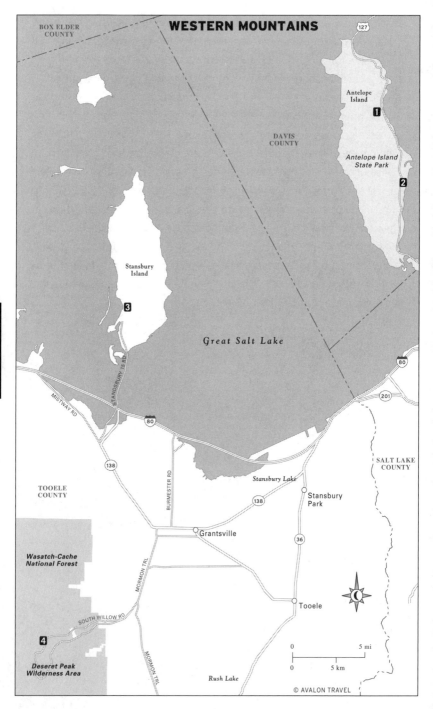

TRAIL NAME	LEVEL	DISTANCE	TIME	ELEVATION	FEATURES	PAGE
1 Frary Peak	Strenuous	6.5 mi rt	4-5 hr	2,690 ft	🔲🔲🔲🔲	236
2 Sentry Trail	Moderate	6.5 mi rt	3-4 hr	1,050 ft	🔲🔲🔲🔲	240
3 Stansbury Island Interpretive Trail	Moderate	9.5-10.5 mi rt	5-6 hr	853 ft	🔲🔲	244
4 Deseret Peak	Strenuous	7.2 mi rt	6-7.5 hr	3,599 ft	🔲🔲🔲🔲	248

1 FRARY PEAK   BEST ◖
Antelope Island State Park

🏠 🦌 ➹ 🌿

Level: Strenuous   **Total Distance:** 6.5 miles round-trip

Hiking Time: 4-5 hours   **Elevation Change:** 2,690 feet

Summary: Frary Peak Trail is a challenging desert hike to the highest mountain summit on Antelope Island, the largest island in the Great Salt Lake.

Fifteen-mile-long Antelope Island is the largest island in the Great Salt Lake and is perhaps northern Utah's most unique wildlife sanctuary. The island is home to a herd of approximately 600 American bison. The grassland habitat covering the island also supports a herd of bighorn sheep and the pronghorn antelope. Antelope Island is also an important stopover for millions of migrating birds that pause to feast on tiny brine shrimp living in the Great Salt Lake.

Hiking the Frary Peak Trail is one of the best ways to experience all Antelope Island has to offer. At 6,596 feet, Frary Peak is the island's high point, with 360-degree views of the Great Salt Lake and the surrounding mountain ranges. This exposed, arid hike is at its best when many of the other trails around Salt Lake City are snowbound. The trail can be very hot in the summer months, and is most enjoyable in spring, fall, or on warm winter days. These times also coincide with the highest concentrations of migrating shorebirds.

Frary Peak is named after homesteader George Frary, who settled on Antelope Island in 1890 and lived there through 1897—the longest of any of the island's homesteaders. In 1893, Frary helped John Dooly bring 12 American bison to Antelope Island on sailboats. Without natural predators, the herd has grown over the years and is maintained at around 600 animals, making it one of the largest publicly owned bison herds in the United States.

The Antelope Island Trail starts steeply up a sweeping switchback, climbing quickly above the gravel parking area and setting the tone for an inspiring aerobic adventure. For the first 0.5 mile the gravel path maintains this ambitious grade, ascending toward Dooly Knob, a prominent black rock marking the ridge crest. At 0.5 mile the trail gains the ridge saddle and a signed trail branches off to the south, leading a short distance to Dooly Knob. From the junction, the main trail heads west of the ridge, where views open up of the Great Salt Lake, stretching to the western and northern horizons. Big sagebrush and Indian paintbrush dot the arid landscape, and sagebrush lizards scurry between the rocks. The trail levels off and traverses the west side of the ridge for the next 0.5 mile. To the northwest are views of Buffalo Point at the tip of the island and the salt-rimmed, gray sand beach of White Rock Bay, and to the west is the 5,126-foot Elephant Head. North of the island the Promontory Mountains reach down to the lake's northern edge. The trail ducks through a keyhole slot between boulders before climbing a short series of switchbacks back up to the ridgeline. Purple patches of lupine accent the grassy slopes in spring, and birds are abundant in this exposed landscape, though not the shorebirds you'd expect to spot on the island. Listen for the guttural, clucking call of chukars, and watch the skies for circling hawks and ravens riding thermal lift near the crest of the ridge.

At 2 miles the trail reaches another saddle in the ridge before starting a steady climb toward Stringham and Frary Peaks. The rounded grassy slopes of Stringham Peak appear first. Notice the buffalo wallows, or depressions, in the hillside where the bison have rubbed away the grass. The bison roll in the dirt in these areas to protect themselves from biting insects. A radio tower crowns the top of 6,374-foot Stringham Peak and marks the 3.0-mile point on the trail. To the southwest the brown-colored Stansbury Island is visible in the Great Salt Lake. From the radio tower, the rocky summit of Frary Peak beckons. The trail drops down on the west side of the ridgeline for a short section of exposed hiking through steep terrain on somewhat slippery gravel and

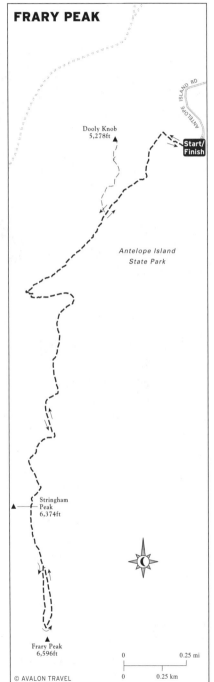

FRARY PEAK

Dooly Knob
5,278ft

Antelope Island
State Park

Start/
Finish

ANTELOPE ISLAND RD

Stringham
Peak
6,374ft

Frary Peak
6,596ft

0   0.25 mi

0   0.25 km

© AVALON TRAVEL

view looking south from the summit of Frary Peak

© MIKE MATSON

crushed shale. For this section it's nice to have a pair of trekking poles, as the hillside falls away quickly on the west side of the trail.

Follow wooden steps up through juniper trees to the summit of Frary Peak. A United States Geological Survey marker and small pile of stones mark the pleasant summit. Panoramic views extend in all directions. The Northern Wasatch Range rises directly to the east, with Salt Lake City and the Central Wasatch Mountains to the distant southeast. The Oquirrh Mountains are the range directly south of Antelope Island, with Stansbury Island backed by the Stansbury Mountain Range to the southwest. The summit of Frary Peak is frequented by the island's herd of bighorn sheep; look closely for these animals here too, especially if it's early or late in the day. From the summit retrace your steps back down. A short 0.25-mile variation is possible by scrambling back along the rocky summit ridge. This route is a rock scramble, with exposed sections where a wrong step could mean serious injury or death. It is not a route for children or anyone who is weary of heights or exposure. The scramble should not be considered if the rock is wet or covered in snow. With that said, it's an exhilarating little traverse—and it gets lots of use.

Options

A short side trail breaks off the main Frary Peak Trail after the 0.5-mile point and leads to Dooly Knob at 5,278 feet. The brown rock outcrop is named after John

Dooly, a pioneer-era entrepreneur who bought the island from the federal government and led the effort to bring the original dozen buffalo to Antelope Island.

Directions

From I-15 in Salt Lake City, take Exit 332, and then turn left on Antelope Drive and drive 6.7 miles to the park entrance gate. Continue 6.5 miles across the causeway. Take the left fork at the gate, continue 0.6 mile, and turn left, following signs to the Fielding Garr Ranch. Drive 5.1 miles, turn right, and continue 0.6 mile up a steep hill to the trailhead parking lot.

GPS Coordinates: N 40°99.468' W 112°20.242' N

Information and Contact

There is a $9 day use fee (includes a $2 causeway fee). The Utah State Parks Annual Pass is available for $75 (does not include the $2 causeway fee). Dogs are not allowed. Maps are available at the entrance station or at the visitors center. For more information contact Antelope Island State Park, 4528 West 1700 South, Syracuse, UT 84075, 801/773-2941, http://stateparks.utah.gov.

2 SENTRY TRAIL   BEST
Antelope Island State Park

🏕 🚴 🎯 👫

Level: Moderate   **Total Distance:** 6.5 miles round-trip

Hiking time: 3-4 hours   **Elevation Change:** 1,050 feet

Summary: The Sentry Trail climbs to an overlook with expansive views of the Great Salt Lake on the quiet south end of Antelope Island.

The Fielding Garr Ranch was started in 1848 by Fielding Garr, who was assigned by the Mormon Church to establish and manage herds of sheep and cattle on Antelope Island. Though the ranch changed ownership several times, it was continually inhabited until 1981, when Antelope Island became a state park. The ranch has been restored and is now maintained as equal parts museum and park, offering a wonderful place for families and children to picnic or spend an afternoon. The original adobe farmhouse build by Garr is the oldest Anglo-built structure in its original location in Utah.

The Sentry Trail starts from the parking lot for the Fielding Garr Ranch at the end of the paved road. A gate blocks the road from vehicle traffic, but hikers, mountain bikers, and equestrians with a permit are allowed to use the trail. From the gate, follow the level dirt road south through open grasslands for 0.75 mile. At the brown sign, turn right (west) on the road and continue up the gently rising trail. After 0.6 mile the trail turns south and starts curving up a steeper grade through a series of mini switchbacks. As the trail climbs up the open hillside, a gulch opens up to the south. At the top of the gulch look for the buffalo wallows, or shallow depressions in the ground, where the bison roll in the dirt in search of relief from the biting flies. Of course it's common to see bison here as well, watching you hike up the trail.

After another 0.5 mile the trail levels off onto a bench and heads north. Look carefully for pronghorn antelope grazing the hillside above the trail. These fleet-footed animals are difficult to spot because their coloring blends in perfectly with the landscape on the island. Another short, steep climb brings you to a trail junction, beginning the loop portion of the trail. Choose either direction and continue uphill for another 0.75 mile to gain the ridge and expansive views to the west. Regardless of whether you've picked the north or south side of the loop, a sun-bleached picnic table and metal hitching post will signal the beginning of a 1.0-mile section of single track that is the highlight of this trail. This narrow ribbon of trail loops around the west side of Sentry Peak, offering unobstructed views west over the Great Salt Lake. Stansbury Island is visible to the west, with the Stansbury Mountains rising behind it.

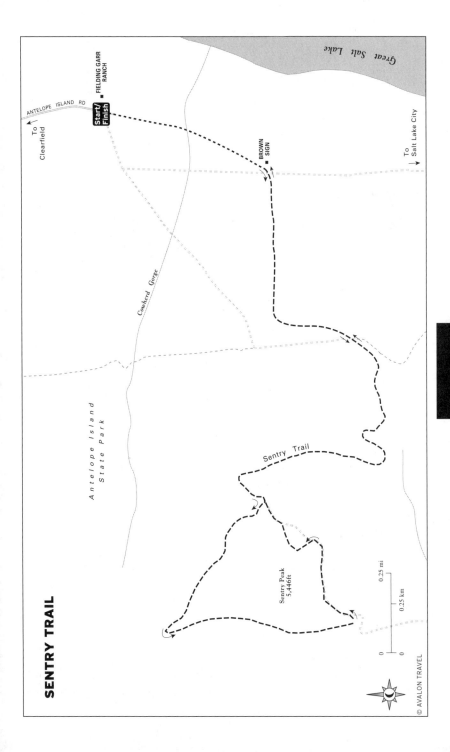

© MIKE MATSON

the Great Salt Lake from the Sentry Trail on Antelope Island

The summit of Sentry Peak is not reached via this route, and hikers are urged repeatedly to stay on the trail. Too quickly this serene section of the single track will end and you'll be greeted by a matching combination of hitching post and picnic table. Rejoin the dirt road, and follow it back down to Fielding Garr Ranch.

Options

Starting at the same trailhead at Fielding Garr Ranch, the South Island Trail offers a flat, 8.0-mile round-trip, out-and-back hike to the southern tip of the island.

Directions

From I-15 in Salt Lake City, take Exit 332, then turn left on Antelope Drive and drive 6.7 miles to the park entrance gate. Continue 6.5 miles across the causeway. Take the left fork at the gate, continue 0.6 mile, and turn left, following signs to the Fielding Garr Ranch. Drive 10.3 miles and park in the paved lot for Fielding Garr Ranch.

GPS Coordinates: N 40°92.641' W 112°16.839' N

Information and Contact

A permit ($1) is required and may be obtained from the ranch office; the ranch office is in the first building on the left as you approach the complex from the parking lot. Permits must be turned in by 5 P.M.

There is a $9 day-use fee (includes a $2 causeway fee), and an additional $1 permit fee is charged for hiking Sentry Trail. The Utah State Parks Annual Pass is available for $75 (does not include the $2 causeway fee). Dogs are not allowed. Maps are available at the entrance station or at the visitors center. For more information, contact Antelope Island State Park, 4528 West 1700 South, Syracuse, UT 84075, 801/773-2941, http://stateparks.utah.gov.

❸ STANSBURY ISLAND INTERPRETIVE TRAIL
Stansbury Island

🚹 🐎

Level: Moderate   **Total Distance:** 9.5-10.5 miles round-trip

Hiking Time: 5-6 hours   **Elevation Change:** 853 feet

Summary: Stansbury Island offers a unique desert hiking experience on the southern end of the second-largest island in the Great Salt Lake.

Stansbury Island is a geographic oddity. Officially it's the second-largest island of the seven named islands in the Great Salt Lake, but no bridges are crossed to reach it. Located at the southern end of the lake, the island has been joined to land by a dirt causeway and a peninsula of land exposed by low-water levels in the Great Salt Lake. Geographically, the island looks and feels more like a mountain range than a typical island—steep, rocky canyons dominate the island's landscape. Castle Rock, the island's highest peak, stands 6,647 feet or about 2,400 feet above the surface of the lake. The desert island receives about six inches of rain each year, and has almost no fresh water, except for a few springs on the eastern side. As a result, the vegetation is sparse and the island is uninhabited.

The Stansbury Island Interpretive Trail reflects the unique character of the island, and is a bit odd itself. Although the trail winds in and out of canyons and through steep, mountainous terrain, it is, aside from two short sections, almost completely flat. The trail follows a bench on the mountainside formed by the shoreline of the ancient Lake Bonneville. Lake Bonneville covered much of northern Utah and parts of Idaho and Nevada between 14,000 and 32,000 years ago. At its largest, the lake was 325 miles long, 135 miles wide, and more than 1,000 feet deep. When the lake level dropped, it left distinct shoreline benches, cut by wave and water erosion, on many of the mountains and foothills along the Wasatch Front. The Stansbury Island Interpretive Trail follows the contour of this bench as it traverses the canyons of southern Stansbury Island. On a map, the trail looks like a highlighted contour line, it so closely follows the historic shoreline's elevation.

As if to defy its own flat nature, the Stansbury Island Trail starts out by climbing aggressively up a steep alluvial fan. Head south out of the gravel parking loop on a section of smooth single track. The path quickly joins an old jeep road, becomes much rockier, and charges up the hillside toward the Lake Bonneville shoreline. Following the south side of a dry gully, the trail gains 640 feet of elevation in just over a mile to reach a small saddle just above the ancient shoreline bench. Along the bench notice the conglomerate rock—smooth, rounded boulders encased in

STANSBURY ISLAND INTERPRETIVE TRAIL

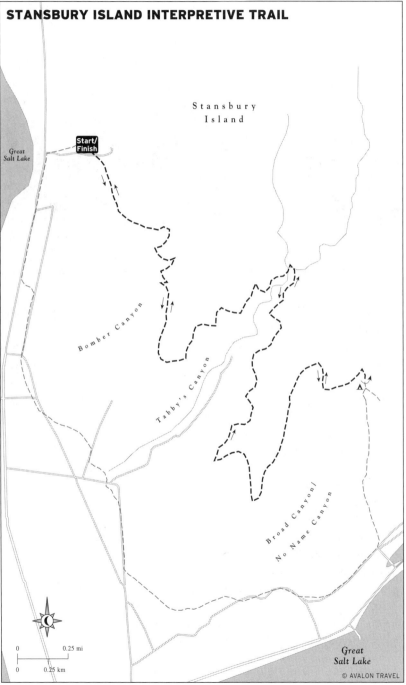

Stansbury Island

Start/Finish

Great Salt Lake

Bomber Canyon

Tabby's Canyon

Broad Canyon/ No Name Canyon

Great Salt Lake

0   0.25 mi

0   0.25 km

© AVALON TRAVEL

© MIKE MATSON

the Stansbury Island Interpretive Trail with views of the Great Salt Lake and Stansbury Mountain Range

hardened sand—that formed along the Bonneville lakeshore. From here you've earned views to the south of the Stansbury Mountain Range, crowned by the 11,031-foot Deseret Peak. Views sweep down to the west as well, over the southern end of the Great Salt Lake and to the distant Lakeside Mountain Range west of the lake.

Dropping down the south side of the saddle the trail actually loses about 100 feet in elevation as it switchbacks across a steep jeep road before settling in on the shoreline bench. As you hike south out of Bomber Canyon, notice the white salt evaporation ponds used to extract salt from the lake by five different commercial enterprises. Just before reaching the 2-mile mark, the trail bends around a rocky gray limestone ridge and enters Tabby's Canyon. Looking across the yawning chasm of Tabby's Canyon and back toward Salt Lake City, the craggy mountains of Stansbury Island have a distinctly Mediterranean feel, sharing many physical characteristics with the Greek islands in the Aegean Sea. The gently rolling trail contours deep into Tabby's Canyon, the tread alternating between sharp rocky patches and smooth gravel. Swaying grass blankets the hillsides, and occasional groups of juniper trees break the monotony of the steep topography.

At 5.2 miles the trail reaches a junction. Turn around here and retrace your steps along the single track the way you came. (This adds one mile to the hike, but avoids four miles of walking on dirt roads.)

Options

If you'd like to extend the hike, at the 5.2-mile junction follow the trail to the right (south) down Broad Canyon/No Name Canyon for 0.5 mile. A very steep, loose dirt road descends from here to meet up with the road network at the base. Brown trail signs mark the 4-mile route back to the car as it bends gently to the northwest around the base of the mountains. This part of the trail is on dirt roads that are often hot and dusty, and it doesn't compare aesthetically with the first half of this loop.

Directions

From Salt Lake City, drive west on I-80 and take Exit 84 for Grantsville. Stay on the main dirt road for 6 miles. On the right side of the road there will be a sign marking the Stansbury Island Interpretive Trail. Turn right and continue 0.3 mile to the gravel trailhead parking lot.

GPS Coordinates: N 40°80.642' W 112°52.033' N

Information and Contact

There is no fee. Dogs are allowed. For more information, contact the BLM Salt Lake Field Office, 2370 South 2300 West, Salt Lake City, UT 84119, 801/977-4300, www.blm.gov.

■ DESERET PEAK
Wasatch-Cache National Forest

🏔 🚴 🦌 🐾

Level: Strenuous	**Total Distance:** 7.2 miles round-trip
Hiking Time: 6-7.5 hours	**Elevation Change:** 3,599 feet

Summary: The center of its own federally protected wilderness area, Deseret Peak is the showcase of Utah's western mountain ranges.

Located in the heart of the Stansbury Mountain Range, Deseret Peak is the most celebrated mountain in Utah's desert mountains. Northwestern Utah is characterized by the Great Salt Lake Desert, a salty barren landscape, punctuated by a series of north-to-south-oriented mountain ranges. The Stansbury Mountains are the closest of these ranges to Salt Lake City, and Deseret Peak is their crowning summit. At 11,031 feet, the summit would be impressive in Utah's bigger ranges as well, but in the Stansbury Range, it's the center of attention. The peak inspired wilderness-area designation as part of the Utah Wilderness Act in 1984.

Starting from the gravel parking area at the western end of Loop Campground, the trail to the summit of Deseret Peak begins at the Mill Fork trailhead. The dirt path begins in a mixed forest of aspen, pine, and fir trees. Climbing gently through the trees, the trail crosses the Lake Fork of South Willow Creek at 0.6 mile. Immediately after crossing the creek bed, you'll reach a signed trail junction. Take the left fork for Deseret Peak. Look for mule deer quietly blending into the forest. The trail leaves the forest and breaks out onto an open hillside at 1 mile, offering views to the north of 9,000-foot gray limestone ridges. At 1.25 miles the trail begins climbing up the Mill Fork drainage. The trail switchbacks to the south through open meadows and subalpine fir trees as it ascends this ever-steepening drainage. In midsummer this valley is colored with lupine, Utah sweet pea, and columbine wildflowers. In fall, clumps of aspen accent the gray rock slopes to the north with yellow.

Views begin to open up to the east at 2.1 miles, including Stansbury Island in the Great Salt Lake and the salt evaporation ponds between the island and the lake's southern shore. In the upper reaches of the drainage you'll see lots of evidence of winter avalanches, with many large trees knocked down and the branches stripped off the uphill side of the remaining trees.

The trail emerges from the top of the Mill Fork drainage at a four-way intersection. Turn right to continue up the ridgeline toward Deseret Peak's summit. Lonely limber pine trees cling to this windswept ridge. Follow the broad switchbacks

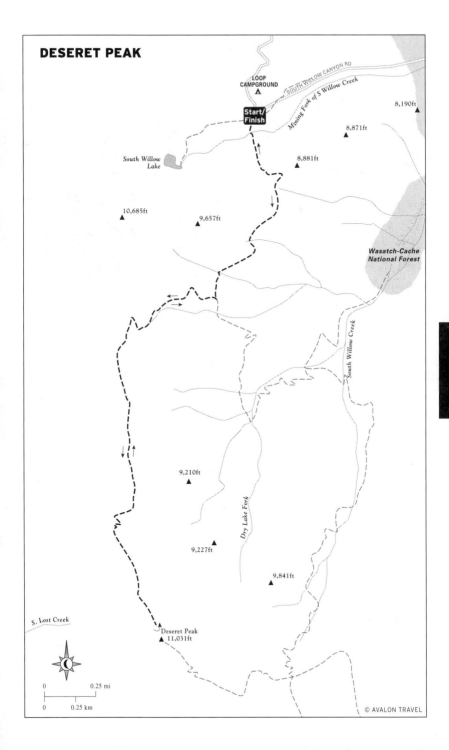

DESERET PEAK

LOOP
CAMPGROUND

SOUTH WILLOW CANYON RD

Mining Fork of S Willow Creek

8,190ft

Start/
Finish

8,871ft

8,881ft

South Willow
Lake

10,685ft

9,657ft

Wasatch-Cache
National Forest

South Willow Creek

9,210ft

Dry Lake Fork

9,227ft

9,841ft

S. Lost Creek

Deseret Peak
11,031ft

0   0.25 mi

0   0.25 km

© AVALON TRAVEL

© MIKE MATSON

the summit of Deseret Peak in the Stansbury Mountain Range

west toward what appears to be Deseret Peak's summit. This first ridge turns out to be a false summit, as the trail traverses just to its southwest. Views open up to the western desert from here, where small, north-to-south-oriented mountain ranges rise in the distance. The last 0.25 mile of the summit ridge is both beautiful and exposed as you walk to the top of Deseret Peak and the entire Stansbury Mountain Range. The mountain's summit feels like the top of the world, or at least the top of northern Utah's desert. Views take in everything from the Bonneville Salt Flats near the Utah-Nevada border to the Great Salt Lake to the Wasatch Mountains above Salt Lake City. Enjoy the lofty views before returning down the way you came.

Options

Consider making your climb a loop trail by descending Deseret Peak to the north and following a trail down Pockets Fork before rejoining the trail at the first stream crossing. This loop trip is 8.5-miles long.

Directions

From Salt Lake City drive west on I-80 for 20.6 miles to Exit 99 and merge onto State Route 36 toward Stansbury and Tooele. Drive 3.7 miles on State Route 36 and turn right on State Route 138. Drive 10.9 miles and turn left onto West Street.

Continue 5.2 miles and turn right onto South Willow Canyon Road. Drive 7.3 miles to the end of the road at the back of Loop Campground.
GPS Coordinates: N 40°49.206' W 112°61.837'

Information and Contact

There is no fee. Dogs on leash are allowed. Maps are available at the Public Lands Information Center, 3285 East 3300 South (inside REI), Salt Lake City, UT 84109, 801/466-6411. For more information, contact Salt Lake City Ranger District, Uinta-Wasatch-Cache National Forest, 125 South State Street, Salt Lake City, UT 84138, 801/236-3400, www.fs.fed.us.

UINTA MOUNTAINS

© TOM GRUNDY/123RF

BEST HIKES

For hikers looking for high-elevation walks, alpine

lakes, and cool summer temperatures, the Uintas present a mountain experience different from the busy trails close to home. When the Wasatch
Mountains are sweltering under summer heat, the Uintas are at their best.
Ranging in elevation between 9,000 and 12,000 feet, the Uinta hikes can
be as much as 20-25 degrees cooler than hikes in the Wasatch Mountains
on the same day. That's a welcome relief when temperatures in Salt Lake
City are topping out above 100°F.

The Uinta Mountains are very different in character and appearance
from the Wasatch Mountains, making them a compelling destination
for Salt Lake hikers looking to add variety to their hiking experiences.
Broad, bald-topped peaks, broken by wide glacier-cut valleys charac-

terize the Uinta Range. Long-since-retreated glaciers have left more than 1,000 mountain lakes in the scoured landscape. These lakes draw interest from anglers for the solitude they offer and the array of trout species living in them. This unusual range runs west to east, rather than north to south like most of the subranges in the Rocky Mountains. It is also home to the highest peaks in Utah. The High Uinta Wilderness Area contains a collection of peaks exceeding 13,000 feet, including Utah's tallest mountain, Kings Peak, reaching 13,528 feet.

The Mirror Lake Scenic Byway winds through the northwest quadrant of the range. The trailheads along this road are within a 90-minute drive of Salt Lake City. The road accesses hikes that lead to the top of wind-buffeted peaks, and trails that connect mountain lakes in bunches.

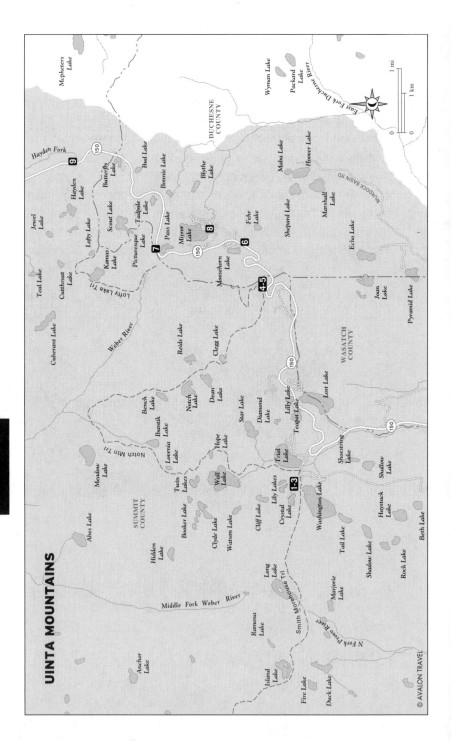

UINTA MOUNTAINS

© AVALON TRAVEL

TRAIL NAME	LEVEL	DISTANCE	TIME	ELEVATION	FEATURES	PAGE
1 Lakes Country Trail	Moderate	8.1 mi rt	4-5 hr	2,315 ft	🥾🏕	258
2 Divide Lakes	Moderate	3.5 mi rt	2-3 hr	866 ft	🥾🏕🐾🏕	262
3 Haystack Lake Trail	Moderate	4.9 mi rt	2.5-3 hr	115 ft	🥾🔭🐾🏕	265
4 Bald Mountain	Easy/Moderate	2.7 mi rt	1.5-2 hr	1,227 ft	🥾🏕🏕	268
5 Notch Mountain	Strenuous	9.8 mi rt one-way	6-7 hr	2,233 ft	🥾🏕🏕	271
6 Fehr Lake	Easy/Moderate	3.4 mi rt	2.5 hr	402 ft	🔭🥾🏕🏕	274
7 Mirror Lake Shoreline Trail	Easy	1.4 mi rt	1 hr	288 ft	🔭🥾🏕🐾	277
8 Lofty Lake Loop	Moderate	3.9 mi rt	2-3 hr	1,332 ft	🥾🏕	280
9 Ruth Lake	Easy	1.5 mi rt	1 hr	518 ft	🏕🥾🏕	283

1 LAKES COUNTRY TRAIL
Wasatch-Cache National Forest

🐕 👫

Level: Moderate   **Total Distance:** 8.1 miles round-trip

Hiking Time: 4-5 hours   **Elevation Change:** 2,315 feet

Summary: A high-country romp through open meadows leading to a dozen alpine lakes.

The Lakes Country Trail is accurately named. In fact, at no point on this trail do you ever feel more than a few steps from the next small body of water. Lakes, ponds, wetlands, glorified puddles—this trail reaches all of those and more. This is backcountry fishing heaven, and many of the lakes are stocked with trout. It's also an ideal trail for a first backpacking trip for youngsters. On weekends you'll see tents pitched near many of the lakes.

The Lakes Country Trail leaves the Crystal Lake trailhead at the north end of the busy parking lot. Three different trails start at this parking area, so be sure you're on the right trail. The Lakes Country Trail does have a small, brown trail sign at the beginning of the trail listing a few of the larger lakes it leads to, ideally clearing up any confusion.

The trail leads gently downhill from the trailhead through clumps of lodgepole pine, spruce, and subalpine fir trees. The narrow but easy-to-follow trail is a pleasure to walk. Quartzite rock, ranging from red to brown to pink in color, breaks up the dirt trail, sometimes in the form of small boulders and other times as rock outcrops.

Crystal Lake is the first major lake this trail passes by, sitting to the left of the trail at a mere 0.25 mile from the trailhead. The long ridge of Haystack Mountain rises to the south of the trail on the left in the first mile. Turn left at a trail junction at 1 mile for the widest possible loop.

At the second trail junction make sure to turn right and follow the rusty metal trail signs for Duck Lake and Weir Lake. The meadows between the second junction and Weir Lake are notable for their beautiful, slow-moving streams. Backpackers take note: Weir Lake has excellent established campsites on its northeast shoreline. Traverse around the lake and take the right fork at the trail junction on the lake's northwest edge, following the sign for Duck Lake.

The trail passes by small Pot Lake before reaching another junction for Duck Lake. Turn left and follow a short spur trail down to Duck Lake. Duck Lake has established campsites in a lovely setting below low-slung cliffs. Return to the main trail and head northeast to continue the loop.

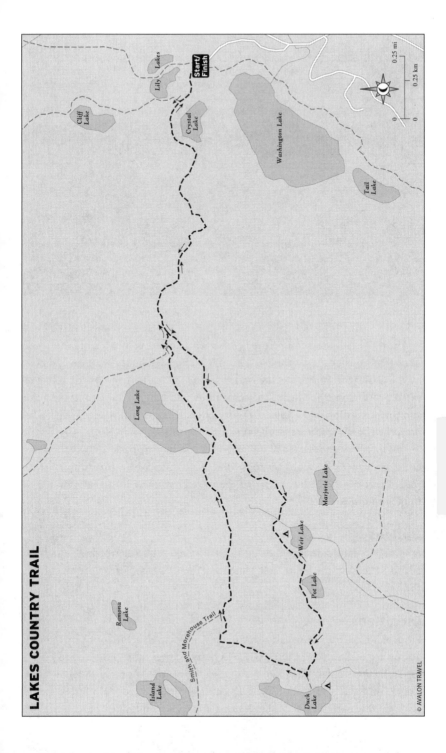

LAKES COUNTRY TRAIL

Lily Lakes

Start/Finish

Cliff Lake

Crystal Lake

Washington Lake

Tail Lake

Long Lake

Marjorie Lake

Ramona Lake

Smith and Morehouse Trail

Weir Lake

Pot Lake

Island Lake

Duck Lake

0.25 mi

0.25 km

0

© AVALON TRAVEL

© MIKE MATSON

Long Lake with Mount Watson behind

The trail heads northeast here to connect with the longer Smith and Morehouse Trail that leads to the northwest. The Smith and Morehouse Trail isn't marked by the trail signs, but this is the trail that leads to Island Lake. If you'd like to extend your loop trip a little farther, consider climbing 0.5 mile to Island Lake and then returning to the Lakes Country Loop. If you've had your fill of lakes by now, then head right (east) at the junction.

You'll pass by another small unnamed lake on the way back. Long Lake is the last of the larger lakes along the route, and you'll reach it before reaching the first trail junction—the turn that started the loop. From there it's an easy walk back to the trailhead.

Options

A short, 0.5-mile side trip leads up to Island Lake, another worthy Uinta lake. Island Lake is on the Smith and Morehouse Trail, which heads northwest from the Lakes Country Loop.

Directions

From Salt Lake City drive east on I-80 for 25 miles to Exit 146 for U.S. Highway 40 toward Heber. Merge onto U.S. Highway 40 and drive 3.8 miles to Exit 4 for Park City/Kamas. Take Exit 4 and turn left off the exit ramp to follow State Route 248 for 11.4 miles to Kamas. From the intersection of Main Street (Route 32) and 200 South (Route 248) in Kamas, drive north on Route 32 and turn right (east) after one block on Mirror Lake Scenic Byway (Route 150). Continue east on Route 150 for 25.4 miles and turn left, following signs to the Crystal Lake trailhead. Drive 0.6 mile and turn right. Continue for 0.4 mile to the Crystal Lake trailhead. The Lakes Country Trail is marked by a brown sign at the parking lot. **GPS Coordinates:** N 40°68.148' W 110°96.321'

Information and Contact

There's a fee of $6 for a three-day pass, $12 for a seven-day pass, and $45 for an annual pass. America the Beautiful passes are accepted. Dogs on leash are allowed. For more information, contact the Heber-Kamas Ranger District, Uinta-Wasatch-Cache National Forest, 50 East Center Street, Kamas, UT 84036, 435/783-4338, www.fs.fed.us.

2 DIVIDE LAKES   BEST ◖
Wasatch-Cache National Forest

🏕 🦌 🌸 🐴 👥

Level: Moderate   **Total Distance:** 3.5 miles round-trip

Hiking Time: 2-3 hours   **Elevation Change:** 866 feet

Summary: A Uinta masterpiece leading to three high-elevation lakes near tree line.

Sitting in a slight depression between 11,521-foot Mount Watson and 11,206-foot Notch Mountain, the Three Divide Lakes look down over an alpine landscape freckled with lovely, high-country lakes. With so many appealing little bodies of water along the way, it's difficult to distinguish the journey from the destination on this hike. The whole route is a pleasure to hike, but the last mile is the highlight, as the trail climbs up onto the shoulder of Mount Watson, providing generous views across the glacier-carved landscape. Sighting a moose is possible along this trail, with its many lakes providing them with lots of food and good habitat. In the midsummer months, wildflowers, including Indian paintbrush and blue flax, fill the meadows with color.

Leaving the Crystal Lake trailhead, the Divide Lakes Trail branches off the Lakes Country Trail to the right after just 0.2 mile. A rusted metal sign for Cliff Lake marks the trail. Immediately upon leaving the Lakes Country Trail, the trail will pass by the Lily Lakes, which are easily identified by the blanket of lily pads on their surface. Not to be confused with Lilly Lake, about a mile farther up the Mirror Lake Highway, these Lily Lakes look like a deer-hoof print on the map. Lodgepole pine, subalpine fir, and Engelmann spruce trees make up the patchy forests that grow around the lakes.

The trail climbs up a short, rocky slope just to the west of the upper Lily Lake and continues on to Cliff Lake at 0.6 mile and Petit Lake at 0.8 mile. Anglers will find cutthroat trout in Cliff Lake and brook trout in Petit Lake. Mount Watson is visible from Cliff Lake, rising over the lake's western shore.

Watson Lake is the next named lake, at 1.2 miles from the trailhead. Fittingly, the bald-topped Mount Watson rises to the west of Watson Lake. Watch closely for where the trail leaves the northern tip of Watson Lake. At the end of a small rocky talus field, the trail climbs quickly up a short hill. The trail is marked by a rock cairn and is easy to miss.

Now climbing at a moderate grade, the trail works its way north toward Clyde Lake. Clyde Lake provides the best fishing of the lakes on this trail, perhaps because it's the largest at 16 acres.

The trail accesses the western tip of Clyde Lake. Continue 0.2 mile northwest from Clyde Lake to reach the easternmost of the Three Divide Lakes. These three, small, shallow lakes are notable more for their inspiring surroundings than for their fishing. Perched right between Mount Watson and Notch Mountain, the lakes define the beauty of the high Uintas. Clumps of low-slung trees grow in the thin alpine soil around the lakes. Huge expanses of exposed rock rise in gently sloped yet massively imposing mountains. The scale of the landscape is hard to quantify, as views of the immense Uinta Range stretch for miles to the south. Seemingly countless lakes stretch away from the divide, their wind-riffled surfaces glistening in the sun.

Try to take it all in before returning down from this out-and-back adventure the way you came.

Options

From the Three Divide Lakes it's possible to walk cross-country to the notch in Notch Mountain and join the Notch Mountain Trail for a loop trip rather than an out-and-back trip. A map and the skills to navigate successfully in the backcountry are essential for this variation. This option adds a mile to the total length of the trail.

Directions

From Salt Lake City, drive east on I-80 for 25 miles to Exit 146 for U.S.

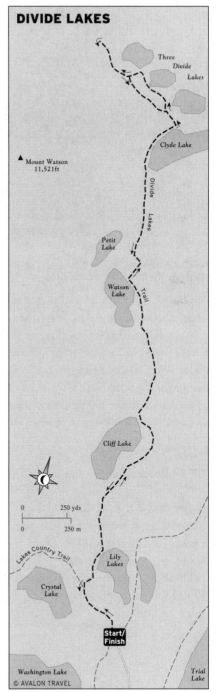

DIVIDE LAKES

Three Divide Lakes

Clyde Lake

▲ Mount Watson 11,521ft

Divide Lakes

Petit Lake

Watson Lake

Trail

Cliff Lake

0 — 250 yds
0 — 250 m

Lakes Country Trail

Lily Lakes

Crystal Lake

Start/ Finish

Washington Lake

Trial Lake

© AVALON TRAVEL

Wall Lake from the Divide Lakes Trail

Highway 40 toward Heber. Merge onto U.S. Highway 40 and drive 3.8 miles to Exit 4 for Park City/Kamas. Take Exit 4 and turn left off the exit ramp to follow State Route 248 for 11.4 miles to Kamas. From the intersection of Main Street (Route 32) and 200 South (Route 248) in Kamas, drive north on Route 32 and turn right (east) after one block on Mirror Lake Scenic Byway (Route 150). Continue east on Route 150 for 26 miles and turn left, following signs to the Crystal Lake trailhead. Drive 0.6 mile and turn right. Continue for 0.4 mile to the Crystal Lake trailhead. The Divide Lakes Trail uses the same trailhead for the Lakes Country Trail, which is marked by a brown sign at the parking lot.
GPS Coordinates: N 40°68.148' W 110°96.321'

Information and Contact

There's a fee of $6 for a three-day pass, $12 for a seven-day pass, and $45 for an annual pass. America the Beautiful passes are accepted. Dogs on leash are allowed. For more information, contact the Heber-Kamas Ranger District, Uinta-Wasatch-Cache National Forest, 50 East Center Street, Kamas, UT 84036, 435/783-4338, www.fs.fed.us.

3 HAYSTACK LAKE TRAIL
Wasatch-Cache National Forest

Level: Moderate

Total Distance: 4.9 miles round-trip

Hiking Time: 2.5–3 hours

Elevation Change: 115 feet

Summary: The Haystack Lake Trail links six mountain lakes, all within the shadow of the broad, bald-topped Haystack Mountain.

The Haystack Lake Trail leads to three midsized lakes: Washington Lake, Tail Lake, and Haystack Lake. As a bonus, the trail also comes close to three smaller lakes: Shadow Lake, Rock Lake, and Azure Lake. The 10,982-foot Haystack Mountain runs from north to south the entire length of the six lakes. The trail is mostly flat, descending very gradually about 50 feet total over 2.5 miles.

The Haystack Lake Trail starts at the south end of the Crystal Lake trailhead. It skirts the Washington Lake Campground as it circles the east side of Washington Lake, following the lake's earthen dam. The water level in this reservoir can vary considerably through the course of a summer and be very low by autumn. For this reason, this might be a good Uinta hike to do in early to midsummer, despite the fact that the mosquitoes will be worse. The lake varies in size from 100 acres when it's full to only 60 acres when it's drawn down.

Surprisingly, Washington Lake is a good place to spot bald eagles, who fish

Haystack Lake from the eastern shore with Haystack Mountain behind

the lake's waters. Eagles and anglers catch cutthroat, brook, and rainbow trout in Washington Lake. At 0.4 mile the trail leaves the top of the dam and there's a fork in the trail. Follow the sign for Haystack Lake and go right. You'll reach the first of several raised boardwalks leading through boggy spots in the meadows at 0.6 mile. The pine-needle-blanketed trail moves through small pockets of meadows, but mostly stays in the open stands of subalpine fir, Engelmann spruce, and lodgepole pine. At 1 mile the trail reaches Tail Lake, extending like a beaver-tail from Washington Lake's southwestern shore. Tail Lake is 9.8 acres in size and 13 feet deep. Anglers can expect to catch brook and rainbow trout. The path crosses a small inlet stream at 1.3 miles at the south end of Tail Lake. Leaving the lake, the trail descends gently toward Haystack Lake. At 2.26 miles a trail sign points right at a junction for Haystack Lake. Follow the rock-lined trail the last 0.2 mile down to Haystack Lake.

Haystack Lake is the largest of the natural lakes along the trail, and the most aesthetically appealing. The lake is 17 acres in size, and has brook and cutthroat trout for fishing. Haystack Mountain is visible from its eastern shore and the lake has a quiet, secluded feel compared with Washington and Tail Lakes. There are several good campsites in the forest on the eastern side of the lake, making it a

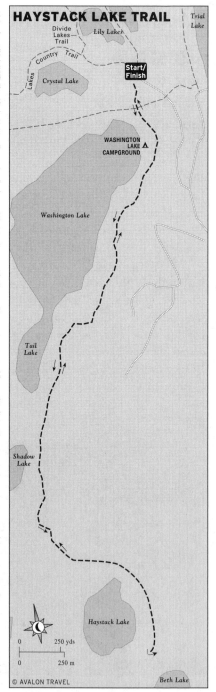

HAYSTACK LAKE TRAIL

great backpacking destination for families looking for a short, first backpacking adventure for their kids.

Enjoy the lake before heading back to the Crystal Lake trailhead the way you came.

Options
Both the Lakes Country Trail and Divide Lakes Trail start from the same Crystal Lake trailhead.

Directions
From Salt Lake City drive east on I-80 for 25 miles to Exit 146 for U.S. Highway 40 toward Heber. Merge onto U.S. Highway 40 and drive 3.8 miles to Exit 4 for Park City/Kamas. Take Exit 4 and turn left off the exit ramp to follow State Route 248 for 11.4 miles to Kamas. From the intersection of Main Street (Route 32) and 200 South (Route 248) in Kamas drive north on Route 32 and turn right (east) after one block on Mirror Lake Scenic Byway (Route 150). Continue east on Route 150 for 26 miles and turn left, following signs to the Crystal Lake trailhead. Drive 0.6 mile and turn right. Continue for 0.4 mile to the Crystal Lake trailhead.
GPS Coordinates: N 40°68.148' W 110°96.321'

Information and Contact
There's a fee of $6 for a three-day pass, $12 for a seven-day pass, and $45 for an annual pass. America the Beautiful passes are accepted. Dogs on leash are allowed. For more information, contact the Heber-Kamas Ranger District, Uinta-Wasatch-Cache National Forest, 50 East Center Street, Kamas, UT 84036, 435/783-4338, www.fs.fed.us.

4 BALD MOUNTAIN

BEST 〖

Wasatch-Cache National Forest

🏕 🐎 👫

Level: Easy/Moderate

Total Distance: 2.7 miles round-trip

Hiking Time: 1.5-2 hours

Elevation Change: 1,227 feet

Summary: This is the best short day hike to a commanding overlook on the Mirror Lake Scenic Byway.

Looking for an alpine experience that's truly above tree line? The exposed, wind-swept, rock ridge of Bald Mountain will not disappoint. The tiny fluorescent-green lichen that cling to red quartzite rock are about the only signs of life you'll find on the upper slopes of Bald Mountain.

During summer, the summit of Bald Mountain offers a pleasantly cool escape from the heat of Salt Lake City. There's almost always a breeze on the upper ridge, and temperatures promise to be 30 degrees cooler at 12,000 feet. The weather always seems to be different in the Uintas than it is in Salt Lake City, so plan accordingly. Thunderstorms often build in the afternoon, making Bald Mountain a better morning destination. Also remember to throw in a rain jacket and some warm clothes, even if it feels crazy when you leave home.

The Bald Mountain Trail heads northwest from the gravel parking lot. The red dirt trail climbs gently for the first 0.5 mile, following a series of long mellow switchbacks through boulders and stands of subalpine fir trees. Right from the start of the trail, the views on Bald Mountain are sweeping, and they grow more spectacular with each passing switchback. The Mirror Lake Scenic Byway is visible below, looping up and over Bald Mountain Pass.

The wide, well-traveled trail is easy to follow as it climbs through a series of rock ledges on the mountain's southwest ridge. By 1 mile, the patches of evergreen

BALD MOUNTAIN

Bald Mountain 11,943ft

Start/Finish

Notch Mountain Trail

150

MIRROR LAKE SCENIC BYWAY

0   200 yds

0   200 m

© AVALON TRAVEL

the view from Bald Mountain to Mirror Lake

trees have completely disappeared and the landscape is dominated by expansive slopes of rock talus. Bald Mountain is one large exfoliating mound of rock. Frost wedging causes much erosion of the peak. Melted snow trickles down into the surface rocks and freezes, expanding and breaking the top layers of rock into smaller pieces. After millions of years of repetition, this process has turned this ridge into one giant talus field of small boulders. This trail sees enough traffic that many of the boulders have been tossed aside, leaving a smooth path to walk on.

At 1.2 miles the trail reaches the edge of the dramatic cliffs marking the top of the east wall of Bald Mountain. The view down to Mirror Lake, almost 2,000 feet below, is astounding. Beyond the lake, 12,479-foot Hayden Peak dominates the skyline.

The last 0.5-mile walk along the ridge is what spending time in the mountains is all about. Bounding across the lichen-blanketed rocks, it's hard not to be struck by the sheer open expanse of space and beauty that stretches out around you in every direction. Lakes dot the wide, glacial-scoured valleys below, reflecting the light from the sky. Treeless ridges rise like backbones from the valley floor, which is covered by a carpet of green forest. By 1.4 miles you'll have reached the summit. Soak up the beauty a little longer before heading back down the way you came.

Options

If you're looking for an extension to the Bald Mountain Trail, you can add as many miles as you'd like by continuing on down from the parking lot on the

Notch Mountain Trail. The Notch Mountain Trail leads 10 miles to the Crystal Lake trailhead.

Directions

From Salt Lake City drive east on I-80 for 25 miles to Exit 146 for U.S. Highway 40 toward Heber. Merge onto U.S. Highway 40 and drive 3.8 miles to Exit 4 for Park City/Kamas. Take Exit 4 and turn left off the exit ramp to follow State Route 248 for 11.4 miles to Kamas. From the intersection of Main Street (Route 32) and 200 South (Route 248) in Kamas drive north on Route 32 and turn right (east) after one block on Mirror Lake Scenic Byway (Route 150). Continue east on Route 150 for 29.1 miles to the Bald Mountain trailhead on the left side of the road. **GPS Coordinates:** N 40°68.880' W 110°90.388'

Information and Contact

There's a fee of $6 for a three-day pass, $12 for a seven-day pass, and $45 for an annual pass. America the Beautiful passes are accepted. Dogs on leash are allowed. For more information, contact the Heber-Kamas Ranger District, Uinta-Wasatch-Cache National Forest, 50 East Center Street, Kamas, UT 84036, 435/783-4338, www.fs.fed.us.

5 NOTCH MOUNTAIN
Wasatch-Cache National Forest

🏠 🌿 🐾

Level: Strenuous

Hiking Time: 6-7 hours

Total Distance: 9.8 miles one-way

Elevation Change: 2,233 feet

Summary: A long, mostly downhill jaunt leads around the broad Notch Mountain, past approximately 15 mountain lakes.

If you like visiting beautiful, high-elevation lakes—and don't mind a long walk—then Notch Mountain is the trail for you. This trail passes by at least 15 different mountain lakes or ponds in almost 10 enjoyable miles. Although the trail is long for a day hike, its mostly downhill grade makes it feel shorter than it actually is. By running a car shuttle, and making the trail a one-way adventure, you'll be able to maximize your miles and minimize your effort. And by starting at the Bald Mountain trailhead at 10,931 feet and ending at the Crystal Lake Trailhead at 10,206 feet, much of the trail is a downhill cruise.

The Notch Mountain trail descends to the west through open meadows from the Bald Mountain trailhead. The imposing Bald Mountain is on the right of the trail and the cone-shaped Reid's Peak comes into view as you move out from Bald Mountain's shadow.

The dirt trail is exposed to the elements for the first few miles. It passes through groups of subalpine fir trees, and lodgepole pines sprout up individually in the open grassland. In July, Indian paintbrush and blue flax wildflowers dot these short-grass meadows. At 1.5 miles you'll reach Clegg Lake, the first named lake along the route. Clegg Lake offers a great photo opportunity, with both Reid's Peak and Bald Mountain reflecting on its surface. The lakes are tightly spaced along the next 2 miles of trail, but the large Notch Lake makes a good point of reference at 2.6 miles from the trailhead.

From Notch Lake the trail begins a long traverse around the north arm of Notch Mountain. At 4.4 miles there's a trail junction with a trail leading off to the right. This trail leads to the Weber Canyon Trail. Stay left on the main Notch Mountain Trail. The junction also marks the lowest point along this traverse. The trail stops descending and starts slowly climbing back up toward the pass at Notch Mountain. At 4.6 miles a second trail branches off to the right; this leads to Meadow Lake, offering a 1.0-mile round-trip side trip.

Climbing steadily now toward Notch Mountain, you'll reach Ibantik Lake at 5.4 miles. The lake is flanked on the south shore by the steep walls of Notch

Mountain. At 6 miles you'll pass Lovenia Lake and several small, unnamed lakes. Climb from these lakes through the only steep section of switchbacks on the trail to pass at Notch Mountain. The notch provides the trail's best views, looking back down the valley to the north, and over the densely clustered lakes to the south.

The trail drops quickly down from the notch through a series of switchbacks. At 7 miles there will be a junction in the trail and you'll want to take the left fork. At 8.1 miles you'll reach Wall Lake, a large reservoir. Take the right option at the trail junction at the southeast corner of Wall Lake. The trail reaches Lily Lakes at 9.6 miles and finishes at the Crystal Lakes Trailhead on the south side of these shallow lakes.

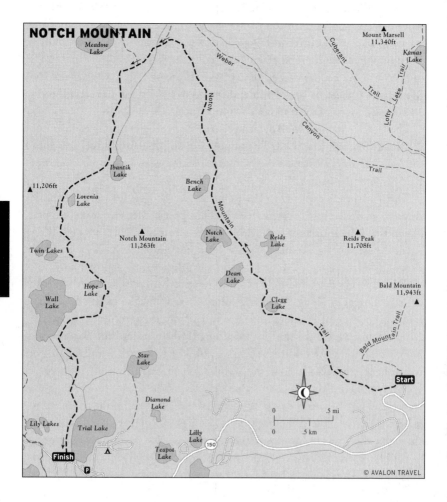

© MIKE MATSON

Lovenia Lake on the Notch Mountain Trail

Options

A short, 0.5-mile side trail leads to Meadow Lake; look for the unsigned trail junction at 4.6 miles from the Bald Mountain trailhead.

Directions

From Salt Lake City drive east on I-80 for 25 miles to Exit 146 for U.S. Highway 40 toward Heber. Merge onto U.S. Highway 40 and drive 3.8 miles to Exit 4 for Park City/Kamas. Take Exit 4 and turn left off the exit ramp to follow State Route 248 for 11.4 miles to Kamas. From the intersection of Main Street (Route 32) and 200 South (Route 248) in Kamas, drive north on Route 32 and turn right (east) after one block on Mirror Lake Scenic Byway (Route 150). Continue east on Route 150 for 29.1 miles to the Bald Mountain trailhead on the left side of the road. The Bald Mountain and Notch Mountain Trails share a trailhead.
GPS Coordinates: N 40°68.880' W 110°90.388'

Information and Contact

There's a fee of $6 for a three-day pass, $12 for a seven-day pass, and $45 for an annual pass. America the Beautiful passes are accepted. Dogs on leash are allowed. For more information, contact the Heber-Kamas Ranger District, Uinta-Wasatch-Cache National Forest, 50 East Center Street, Kamas, UT 84036, 435/783-4338, www.fs.fed.us.

6 FEHR LAKE

BEST ◖

Wasatch-Cache National Forest

Level: Easy/Moderate

Total Distance: 3.4 miles round-trip

Hiking Time: 2.5 hours

Elevation Change: 402 feet

Summary: A short, kid-friendly walk to three mountain lakes.

The short Fehr Lake Trail leads to three midsized alpine lakes: Fehr Lake, Shepard Lake, and Hoover Lake. The trail is an easy walk with frequent board-walk sections leading through open, sometimes soggy meadows. In midsummer, wildflowers, including elephant's head and shooting stars, adorn the meadows with highlights of color. It's a great trail for families with children and a desti-nation for anglers looking for some backcountry angling. Fehr Lake, Shepard Lake, and Hoover Lake are all stocked with trout. Fish species found in the Uinta lakes include rainbow trout, brown trout, cutthroat trout, golden trout, brook trout, and arctic grayling.

The Fehr Lake Trail departs from the trailhead, crossing a meadow on one of the many raised boardwalks found along the trail. In the early-summer months these meadows act as mosquito breeding grounds, so plan your trip later in the season or come prepared to deal with the bugs. Leaving the boardwalk, the dirt and rock trail slopes gently downhill as it passes through pockets of

a hiker passes by Fehr Lake

© MIKE MATSON

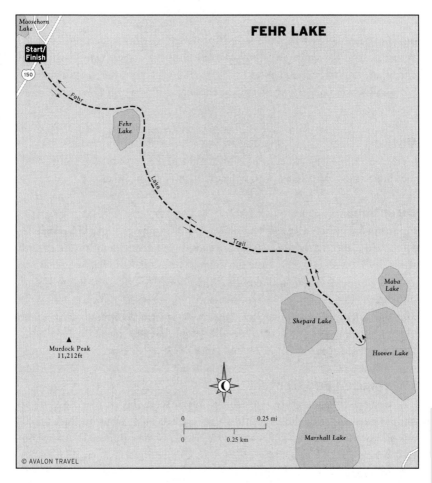

subalpine fir and Engelmann spruce trees. Bird-watchers can expect to spot red crossbills and pine siskins near the tops of these conifers picking seeds out of the tree's cones.

You'll reach Fehr Lake, the smallest of the three lakes on this trail, at 0.4 mile. The lake is about six acres in size and 30 feet deep. There are a few short rock-climbing routes on the shore. Anglers can expect to catch brook trout.

Continuing slightly downhill to the southeast, the second lake you'll encounter is Shepard Lake, 1.4 miles from the trailhead. The lake is 14 acres in size and 30 feet deep, and is home to cutthroat and brook trout. Murdock Peak rises to 11,212 feet to the west of Shepard Lake.

The trail drops a short distance from Shepard Lake to Hoover Lake. Hoover Lake, the last lake on the Fehr Lake Trail, is 1.7 miles from the trailhead. Hoover is the largest of the three lakes on the trail, covering 19 acres. It can be accessed on its eastern shore by an ATV trail, so although it's the lake farthest from the Fehr Lake trailhead, it is not always the quietest. Anglers will find grayling and cutthroat trout in Hoover Lake.

From Hoover Lake simply follow the trail back the way you came to the parking lot.

Options
Consider walking the shoreline of Hoover Lake to the north to see another small mountain lake, Maba Lake. This will add 0.5 mile to the hike.

Directions
From Salt Lake City drive east on I-80 for 25 miles to Exit 146 for U.S. Highway 40 toward Heber. Merge onto U.S. Highway 40 and drive 3.8 miles to Exit 4 for Park City/Kamas. Take Exit 4 and turn left off the exit ramp to follow State Route 248 for 11.4 miles to Kamas. From the intersection of Main Street (Route 32) and 200 South (Route 248) in Kamas drive north on Route 32 and turn right (east) after one block on Mirror Lake Scenic Byway (Route 150). Continue east on Route 150 for 30.5 miles to the Fehr Lake trailhead on the right side of the highway.
GPS Coordinates: N 40°69.291' W 110°89.197'

Information and Contact
There's a fee of $6 for a three-day pass, $12 for a seven-day pass, and $45 for an annual pass. America the Beautiful passes are accepted. Dogs on leash are allowed. For more information, contact the Heber-Kamas Ranger District, Uinta-Wasatch-Cache National Forest, 50 East Center Street, Kamas, UT 84036, 435/783-4338, www.fs.fed.us.

7 MIRROR LAKE SHORELINE TRAIL
Wasatch-Cache National Forest

Level: Easy

Hiking Time: 1 hour

Total Distance: 1.4 miles round-trip

Elevation Change: 288 feet

Summary: Reflect on life as you walk the easy interpretive trail around Mirror Lake.

On warm summer afternoons, puffy white clouds often build over the Uinta Mountains, reflecting perfectly in the calm waters of Mirror Lake. This picture-perfect scene is repeated often, attracting campers, anglers, and hikers to the shores of Mirror Lake.

The short, level trail ringing Mirror Lake is equal parts interpretive trail and angler-access path. Signs with fossil-like animal tracks add a fun element to the first 0.5 mile of the trail. This, combined with the flat, smooth surface of the trail, makes it an obvious choice for young children and families. Fly fishers cast from the shoreline and from nonmotorized boats for rainbow and brook trout. For those interested in birds, gray jays, Clark's nutcracker, pine grosbeaks, and three-toed woodpeckers can be spotted in the trees around the lake.

Head to the right from the parking lot to see animal-track interpretive signs

Mirror Lake from the Mirror Lake Shoreline Trail

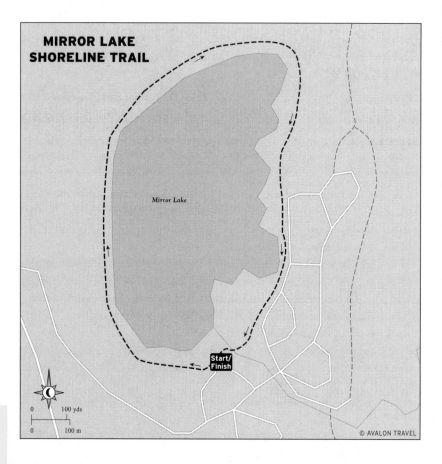

MIRROR LAKE SHORELINE TRAIL

Mirror Lake

Start/Finish

0   100 yds
0   100 m

© AVALON TRAVEL

on the first section of the trail. The path begins as a wide gravel trail as it bends along the lake's eastern shore. A boardwalk begins at 0.2 mile and continues for 250 yards across delicate shoreline habitat. Across the lake to the west, 11,943-foot Bald Mountain dominates the skyline.

The trail rises and falls gently as it circles the far end of the lake, accessing many shoreline fishing spots. Spruce, subalpine fir, and lodgepole pine trees surround the lake. The shoreline is mostly rocky, but aquatic grasses grow in the shallows, and fallen logs create hiding places for fish.

Options

If you'd like a little more challenge than the Mirror Lake Shoreline Trail offers, consider extending the hike on the Mirror Lake Trail, which links up with the Highline Trail. The Highline Trail is the Uinta's premier backpacking trail and is 70 miles in length.

Directions

From Salt Lake City drive east on I-80 for 25 miles to Exit 146 for U.S. Highway 40 toward Heber. Merge onto U.S. Highway 40 and drive 3.8 miles to Exit 4 for Park City/Kamas. Take Exit 4 and turn left off the exit ramp to follow State Route 248 for 11.4 miles to Kamas. From the intersection of Main Street (Route 32) and 200 South (Route 248) in Kamas, drive north on Route 32 and turn right (east) after one block on Mirror Lake Scenic Byway (Route 150). Continue east on Route 150 for 32.1 miles and turn right. Drive 1 mile down to the parking lot for the Mirror Lake Shoreline Trail.

GPS Coordinates: N 40°70.109' W 110°88.789'

Information and Contact

There's a fee of $6 for a three-day pass, $12 for a seven-day pass, and $45 for an annual pass. America the Beautiful passes are accepted. Dogs on leash are allowed. For more information, contact the Heber-Kamas Ranger District, Uinta-Wasatch-Cache National Forest, 50 East Center Street, Kamas, UT 84036, 435/783-4338, www.fs.fed.us.

8 LOFTY LAKE LOOP   BEST ◖
Wasatch-Cache National Forest

🏕 🐴

Level: Moderate   **Total Distance:** 3.9 miles round-trip

Hiking Time: 2-3 hours   **Elevation Change:** 1,332 feet

Summary: A high-elevation trail links a chain of alpine lakes and sweeping vistas for the quintessential Uinta day-hiking experience.

Lofty Lake is the highest-elevation lake in the western Uinta Mountains, and the trail that leads to it is one of the most popular day hikes in the range. The loop winds through pristine alpine meadows, across exposed ridges, and past trout-stocked lakes. The combination of high vistas with so many lakes gives this trail broad appeal.

Starting out from the Pass Lake trailhead, hike northeast toward Scout Lake. The sand and dirt trail climbs gently through scattered boulders and bunches of conifer trees. You'll notice that many lodgepole pine and Engelmann spruce trees along the trail have died but are still standing. As much as 50 percent of the trees in some parts of the Uinta Mountains have been killed by bark beetles. The beetles lay their larvae in the tree's bark while at the same time introducing a fungus called the blue stain fungus to the tree's wood. The fungus blocks water and nutrient transport within the tree. The combined effects of the fungus and the beetle larvae eating the bark kills the infested trees. The beetle infestation has decimated forests across the western United States and Canada, and forest ecologists believe it may be the worst, most widespread beetle infestation to date. Intensely cold winters have historically kept beetle populations in check, and it is thought that a long pattern of warmer winters over the last decade is to blame for the dying forests.

At 0.4 mile you'll reach Picturesque Lake on the right side of the trail. Scout Lake is the larger lake just past Picturesque at 0.6 mile. The trail crosses a dirt road at Scout Lake, named after the Boy Scouts of America Camp Steiner, on the lake's eastern shore.

From Scout Lake the trail climbs west up a ridge through red and gray boulders to 10,780-foot-high Lofty Lake, 1.4 miles from the trailhead. Lofty Lake sits in an alpine bowl surrounded by Mount Marsell, Scout Peak, and Lofty Peak. Now heading south, the loop trail drops through a notch and down to the larger Kamas Lake. Then at 3 miles the trail enters a large, tree-lined meadow. This is also where the Cuberant Trail branches off from the Lofty Lake Loop Trail. The headwaters of the Heber River meander slowly through the meadow. Crossing the meadow, the Lofty trail bends back to the east to complete the 3.9-mile loop.

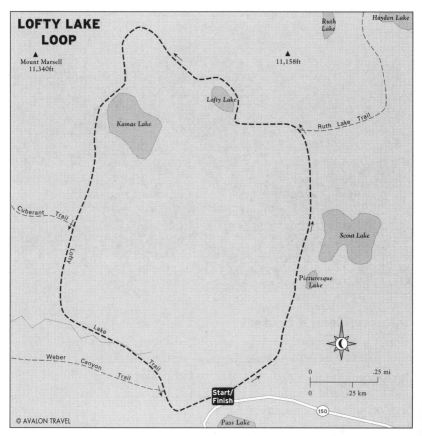

Options

If you're looking to extend the Lofty Lake Loop, the Cuberant Trail adds a 3.0-mile round-trip extension leading to Cuberant Lake on the northwest side of 11,340-Mount Marsell. The Cuberant Trail junction branches off to the right (west) of the Lofty Lake Loop 0.3 mile (3 miles from the trailhead) past Kamas Lake.

Directions

From Salt Lake City, drive east on I-80 for 25 miles to Exit 146 for U.S. Highway 40 toward Heber. Merge onto U.S. Highway 40 and drive 3.8 miles to Exit 4 for Park City/Kamas. Take Exit 4 and turn left off the exit ramp to follow State Route 248 for 11.4 miles to Kamas. From the intersection of Main Street (Route 32) and 200 South(Route 248) in Kamas drive north on Route 32 and turn right (east) after one block on Mirror Lake Scenic Byway (Route 150). Continue east on Route 150 for 32.1 miles to the Pass Lake trailhead on the left side of the road.
GPS Coordinates: N 40°71.396' W 110°89.340'

Kamas Lake on the Lofty Lake Loop Trail

Information and Contact

There's a fee of $6 for a three-day pass, $12 for a seven-day pass, and $45 for an annual pass. America the Beautiful passes are accepted. Dogs on leash are allowed. For more information, contact the Heber-Kamas Ranger District, Uinta-Wasatch-Cache National Forest, 50 East Center Street, Kamas, UT 84036, 435/783-4338, www.fs.fed.us.

9 RUTH LAKE

Wasatch-Cache National Forest

BEST

Level: Easy

Hiking Time: 1 hour

Total Distance: 1.5 miles round-trip

Elevation Change: 518 feet

Summary: A short interpretive trail leads to a sparkling mountain lake.

The Ruth Lake Trail is an excellent easy hike for children and families near the crest of the Mirror Lake Highway. Although the trailhead sits above 10,000 feet, less than 300 feet of elevation is gained on the hike itself, allowing hikers a glimpse of the Uinta high country without an arduous hike in. Wildflower-accented meadows and exposed glacier-polished bedrock make for interesting eye candy along the trail. Ruth Lake is one of many small lakes in this immediate area.

The Ruth Lake Trail starts from a small parking lot on the Mirror Lake Scenic Byway and meanders up a gently sloped grade toward the lake. A stand of Engelmann spruce and subalpine fir shades the trail at first, but quickly opens into rocky terrain. Kid-friendly interpretive trails line the path, explaining the natural history of the surrounding environment. About halfway to the lake the trail crosses through several small marshy areas fed by Ruth Lake's outlet stream. From here, rock climbers are often visible clinging to the short cliffs left of the trail. Continue less than half a mile uphill to a small pond-sized lake and then a few steps farther to the eastern shoreline of Ruth Lake. Enjoy the view of the barren Lofty Peak rising across the west side of the lake.

Because of its high elevation, this trail is snowbound until at least mid-July. Small lakes and ponds are everywhere in the Uinta high country. This means

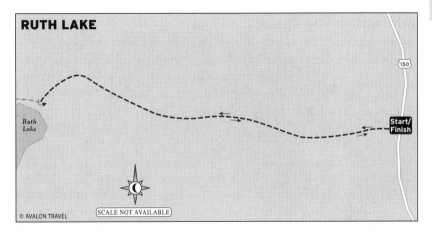

RUTH LAKE

Ruth
Lake

Start/
Finish

150

SCALE NOT AVAILABLE

© AVALON TRAVEL

the mosquitoes can be thick at times. Plan accordingly—bring bug repellent, or wait until late summer to visit.

Options

Ruth Lake can also be connected with the more ambitious Lofty Lake Loop Trail. This 5-mile loop (or one-way if desired) starts at the Pass Lake trailhead and visits Kamas, Lofty, and Scout Lakes along its route. A car shuttle between the Pass Lake trailhead and Ruth Lake trailhead can make this a one-way hike.

Directions

From Salt Lake City drive east on I-80 for 25 miles to Exit 146 for U.S. Highway 40 toward Heber. Merge onto U.S.

Hayden Peak reflected in Ruth Lake

Highway 40 and drive 3.8 miles to Exit 4 for Park City/Kamas. Take Exit 4 and turn left off the exit ramp to follow State Route 248 for 11.4 miles to Kamas. From the intersection of Main Street (Route 32) and 200 South (Route 248) in Kamas, drive north on Route 32 and turn right (east) after one block on Mirror Lake Scenic Byway (Route 150). Continue east on Route 150 for 35 miles to the Ruth Lake trailhead on the left side of the road. Parking spots are on the side of the highway.

GPS Coordinates: N 40°73.325' W 110°86.781'

Information and Contact

There's a fee of $6 for a three-day pass, $12 for a seven-day pass, and $45 for an annual pass. America the Beautiful passes are accepted. Dogs on leash are allowed. For more information, contact the Evanston-Mountain View Ranger District, Uinta-Wasatch-Cache National Forest, 1565 Highway 150 South, Suite A, Evanston, WY 82930, 307/789-3194, www.fs.fed.us.

RESOURCES

NATIONAL PARKS AND FEDERAL RECREATIONAL LANDS PASS

The National Park Service sells an annual recreation pass (www.nps.gov/fees_passes.htm) granting access to most federally owned lands. The Interagency Pass Program gives holders access to National Park Service, U.S. Department of Agriculture, Forest Service, Fish and Wildlife Service, Bureau of Land Management, and Bureau of Reclamation lands and parks.

An annual pass is also available online (www.stateparks.utah.gov/parkspass) that allows entrance into all the Utah State Parks.

Day passes or annual passes are available for purchase upon leaving Mill Creek Canyon.

U.S. FOREST SERVICE

The United States Department of Agriculture Forest Service administers land in seven different National Forests in Utah. Each National Forest is broken down further into Ranger Districts. Detailed Forest Service maps are also available by mail or online.

1400 Independence Ave., SW
Washington, DC 20250-0003
800/832-1355
www.fs.fed.us

Heber-Kamas Ranger District

50 East Center Street
P.O. Box 68
Kamas, UT 84036
435/783-4338

Intermountain Region

Federal Building
324 25th Street
Ogden, UT 84401
801/625-5306
www.fs.fed.us/r4

Ogden Ranger District

Union Station Visitor Center
2501 Wall Avenue
Ogden, UT 84401
801/625-5306

District Office
507 25th Street
Ogden, UT 84401
801/625-5112

Pleasant Grove Ranger District

390 North 100 East
Pleasant Grove, UT 84062
801/785-3563

Salt Lake Ranger District

Public Lands Information Center
3285 East 3300 South (inside REI)
Salt Lake City, UT 84109
801/466-6411

Spanish Fork Ranger District

44 West 400 North
Spanish Fork, UT 84660
801/798-3571

**Uinta-Wasatch-Cache
National Forest**
Supervisor's Office
857 West South Jordan Parkway
South Jordan, UT 84095
801/999-2103
www.fs.fed.us/uwcnf

NATIONAL MONUMENTS

Timpanogos Cave National Monument is the only National Park Service–administered hike in this guide.

**Timpanogos Cave
National Monument**
R.R. 3 Box 200
American Fork, UT 84003
801/756-5238 (summer only)
or 801/756-5239
fax 801/756-5661
www.nps.gov/tica

STATE PARKS

Two hikes in this guide are found on Antelope Island, which is a Utah State Park.

**Utah State Department of
Natural Resources**
P.O. Box 145610
1594 W. North Temple
Salt Lake City, UT 84114-5610
801/538-7200
http://naturalresources.utah.gov

Utah State Parks and Recreation
1594 West North Temple, Suite 116
P.O. Box 146001
Salt Lake City, UT 84114

801/538-7220
or 877/887-2757
www.stateparks.utah.gov

OTHER RESOURCES
Maps
High Uintas Wilderness
National Geographic Maps
P.O. Box 4357
Evergreen, CO 80437-4357
800/962-1643

**Wasatch Front Panoramic
Hiking Map**
published by Fern/Horn Endeavors,
dba Trail Tracks. Revised May 2009
Available online ($11)

Wasatch Hiking Trails
cartography by Daniel Smith, Artistic
Printing, 2011
Available at REI, the USG bookstore,
Kirkhams, Wasatch Touring, and the
Utah Travel Council ($10)

Flora and Fauna
**National Audubon Society Field
Guide to the Southwestern States.**
by Peter Alden and Peter Friederici;
published by Alfred A. Knopf: New
York, 1999
Available online ($12)

**National Forest Service
Fall Colors Hotline**
800/354-4595
August–November

**National Forest Service
Wildflowers Hotline**
800/354-4595
April–August

**Utah Division of
Wildlife Resources**
1594 West North Temple, Suite 2110
Salt Lake City, UT 84114
801/538-4700
fax 801/538-4745
http://wildlife.utah.gov/index.php

TRANSPORTATION
**Utah Department
of Transportation**
4501 South 2700 West
Salt Lake City, UT 84114
866/511-8824
www.dot.state.ut.us

Index

Acknowledgements

Writing a guidebook is truly a collaborative process. From inception to publication, it takes the input of a whole team of talented individuals to produce an informed guide. I'd like to thank the editoral team at Avalon Travel–Sabrina Young, Leah Gordon, Albert Angulo, Domini Dragoone, and Grace Fujimoto–for all their hard work and guidance on this project.

Without these trails, this book would have no reason for being. I'd like to include a note of appreciation for those who pioneered these paths and walked them before us, and for those who continue to maintain and manage them: the employees of the Forest Service, National Park Service, Utah State Parks, as well as the many volunteers who love and care for their local trails. Without your efforts, hiking in Salt Lake City, Utah wouldn't be the enjoyable experience it is today.

Finally, I'd like to thank the people in my life who helped with this project in many ways, whether it was offering their camaraderie on the trail, providing a local's opinion, or supporting my efforts in other ways. Jeff and Barbara Duenwald, Paul Corrigan, Michelle White, Adam Grudzien, Eric Duenwald, Dheven Duenwald, Kamran Duenwald, John Matson, and Shannon Matson all played a part in making this such an enjoyable endeavor.

To my most frequent hiking companions, my wife Sonja and my son Harvey: Thank you for all your love and support, and for helping me along every step of the way. I look forward to the many hikes in our future!

Notes

Notes

Notes

Notes

Notes

Notes

Notes

Notes

Notes

Notes

www.moon.com

DESTINATIONS | ACTIVITIES | BLOGS | MAPS | BOOKS

MOON.COM is ready to help plan your next trip! Filled with fresh trip ideas and strategies, author interviews, informative travel blogs, a detailed map library, and descriptions of all the Moon guidebooks, Moon.com is all you need to get out and explore the world—or even places in your own backyard. While at Moon.com, sign up for our monthly e-newsletter for updates on new releases, travel tips, and expert advice from our on-the-go Moon authors. As always, when you travel with Moon, expect an experience that is uncommon and truly unique.

MOON OUTDOORS

YOUR ADVENTURE STARTS HERE

MOON TAKE A HIKE SALT LAKE CITY

Avalon Travel
a member of the Perseus Books Group
1700 Fourth Street
Berkeley, CA 94710, USA
www.moon.com

Editors: Leah Gordon, Sabrina Young
Series Manager: Sabrina Young
Copy Editor: Laurel Robinson
Graphics Coordinator: Kathryn Osgood
Production Coordinators: Christine DeLorenzo,
    Domini Dragoone
Cover Designer: Domini Dragoone
Interior Designer: Darren Alessi
Map Editor: Albert Angulo
Cartographers: Chris Henrick, Andy Butkovic,
    Heather Sparks, and Kaitlin Jaffe

ISBN-13: 978-1-61238-532-7
ISSN: 2325-5188

Printing History
1st Edition — June 2013
5 4 3 2 1

Text © 2013 by Mike Matson.
Maps © 2013 by Avalon Travel.
All rights reserved.

Some photos and illustrations are used by permission and are the property of the original copyright owners.

Front cover photo: Trail to Sundial peak, Big Cottonwood Canyon, © Utah-based Photographer Ryan Houston/Flickr/Getty Images
Title page photo: Hidden Glen in the Wasatch Mountains, © Bonnie Avonrude/123RF
Back cover photo: © Peter Cade/Getty Images

Printed in Canada by Friesens

Keeping Current

We are committed to making this book the most accurate and enjoyable hiking guide to the region. You can rest assured that every trail in this book has been carefully reviewed in an effort to keep this book as up-to-date as possible. However, by the time you read this book, some of the fees listed herein may have changed and trails may have closed unexpectedly.

If you have a favorite gem you'd like to see included in the next edition, or see anything that needs updating, clarification, or correction, please drop us a line. Send your comments via email to feedback@moon.com, or use the address above.